GENOCIDE

SPONSORING THE DESTRUCTION OF PALESTINE

FINTAN DRURY

MERRION PRESS

First published in 2026 by
Merrion Press
10 George's Street
Newbridge
Co. Kildare
Ireland
www.merrionpress.ie

978 1 78537 595 8 (Paper)
978 1 78537 598 9 (eBook)

A CIP catalogue record for this book is
available from the British Library.

Text typeset in Minion Pro 11/17 pt

Cover design by Fiachra McCarthy

Front cover image: © Anadolou/Getty Images

Merrion Press is a member of Publishing Ireland.

FSC
www.fsc.org
MIX
Paper | Supporting responsible forestry
FSC® C021394

PRAISE FOR *GENOCIDE*

'With clarity, force and deep moral seriousness, *Genocide* lays bare the structures of power behind the destruction of Palestine. Bold, incendiary and meticulously argued, it demands that readers look not only at what was done to Palestine, but at who enabled it.'

Brian Conaghan, author of *The Weight of a Thousand Feathers*

'In his latest book, Fintan Drury makes it clear that, when it comes to genocide, there can be no shirking of the truth. With eloquence and razor-sharp clarity, he catalogues the lies, treachery and the unprecedented scale of Israel's slaughter of Palestinians and is unequivocal about the fact that Israel could not conduct the genocide in Gaza without the unconditional support and impunity it enjoys from its main sponsors in the West. From the pen of a rigorous, humane journalist, *Genocide* is urgent, unapologetic, and breathtaking in its knowledge and reach. I am full of admiration for Fintan Drury.'

Mary Costello, author of *Academy Street* and *A Beautiful Loan*

'Drury's work makes clear how nothing that has happened to the Palestinian people in recent years has been accidental, but is instead the result of a deliberate strategy. *Catastrophe: Nakba II* was a vital read for all those wishing to understand the history of the conflict in Palestine. In *Genocide: Sponsoring the Destruction of Palestine* he explains who is profiting from the on-going suffering of a people and the attempted destruction of a nation. An important book that demands our attention.'

Donal Fallon, historian and author

'*Genocide* is a searing indictment of "white colonial fraternity" and its role in the systematic erasure of Palestine and its people. In this forensic, transparent account of the continued destruction of Palestine, Drury exposes the West's deep-seated complicity, as he navigates and exposes the chilling dissonance of global powers through decades of immense Palestinian suffering. This is a devastating, yet clear-sighted exposé of nations that have weaponised influence to remain steadfast in their support of Israel's genocidal Zionist campaign. Hugely informative, courageous and intelligent, *Genocide* is a definitive and vitally important work on the damning legacy of the Western world's complicity in the destruction of Palestine.'

Elaine Feeney, author of *How to Build a Boat* and *Let me Go Mad in My Own Time*

'Fintan Drury is calling out facts that cannot be ignored.'

Hugo Hamilton, author of *Conversation with the Sea*

'Drury is merciless in his savage account of events on October 13, 2025, the day when Donald Trump jetted to the Middle East, collecting unctuous accolades and even a sycophant's Nobel Peace Prize nomination. Ordinary Gazans' horrific testimony weaves into Drury's own knowledge of history, and his astonishing new book not only reveals the true nature of Gaza's present so-called ceasefire but also marks a high point in the practice of flash history, *histoire événementielle* – an account of one day that illuminates an entire world. Drury's revelations make this book required reading.'

Harold Aram Veeser, Professor of Post Colonial Literature, City College of New York and author of *Edward Said: The Charisma of Criticism*

This book is dedicated to my four little grandchildren, Bahia, Ruan, Liham and Féile, in the hope of a gentler world for them, the children of Palestine and children everywhere. It's to be hoped that their generation, unlike mine, will prioritise kindness, respect and tolerance above all else.

CONTENTS

In April 1946, the director of the American Friends of the Fighters for the Freedom of Israel in America wrote to Albert Einstein. He was seeking a meeting. Einstein's reply was short and terse. It read:

Dear Sir:

When a real and final catastrophe should befall us in Palestine the first responsible for it would be the British and the second responsible for it the Terrorist organisations built up from our own ranks. I am not willing to see anybody associated with those misled and criminal people.

Sincerely yours,
Albert Einstein

A NOTE TO READERS

This book's title has been given careful consideration. Sadly, it accurately reflects the story. The International Court has not yet definitively ruled that Israel's conduct is genocide, but most independent experts and some prominent Jewish scholars believe that it is. Separately, Israel's prime minister, Benjamin Netanyahu, and one of his ministers have been charged with committing war crimes. Hamas leaders faced the same charge for the attack on Israel on 7 October 2023.

What is remarkable and should be alarming is that this genocide has been conducted in full public view. Western powers have facilitated it. Some have gone further, actively participating in it, and, at the very least, they are open to the charge of dispensing with the mores they claim to uphold while insisting on them from others. That is what this book is about. There is no room for ambiguity. There should be no basis on which some of the West's most powerful nations can escape the same charge as that facing Israel – of direct involvement in and sponsorship of a genocide.

In October 2025, President of the United States of America Donald J. Trump launched a peace initiative called the 'Comprehensive Plan to End the Gaza Conflict'. On 8 October, a ceasefire was announced, and five days later, Trump went on a twenty-four-hour visit to the Middle East to stage the official signing of the plan and promote its merits. It had very few, if any. It was not a serious effort to correct the multiple wrongs done to the Palestinians over three-quarters of a century. It was a business plan, and not a very good one at that.

This book looks at Israel's genocide and the West's support of it through the lens of that one day, 13 October 2025. It highlights the West's sham diplomacy and Israel's stranglehold on its Western allies. Trump suggested that October day was one of celebration. Instead, for Palestinians, it was a day that marked their complete betrayal.[1]

INTRODUCTION

It will be some time before it's known how many Palestinians were slaughtered by Israel over the course of its genocide in Gaza and the aggressive theft of land in the West Bank during that same period. The estimates range from 100,000 to more than three times that number. However, the exact quantum is not the primary issue. What matters most is that the killing stops and that such a thing never happens again. Undoubtedly, it will stop – these things always do – but at present it seems inevitable that it will start again. When remains to be seen, but the evidence of the past seventy-eight years is that, due to its status in the West, Israel will once again be allowed to decide on how and when to inflict further suffering on the people of Palestine. The present genocide has taught us that, if nothing else. The evidence is that Israel will continue to enjoy the impunity that has been a hallmark of its status since its foundation. It is this sense of total freedom to do as it wishes, without fear of consequence, that marks Israel as a nation unlike any other.

Israel's own army says 82 per cent of those it has slaughtered were civilians. What its current epic, egregious onslaught on innocent people has demonstrated is that the most critical strand in Israel's conduct is the West's kowtowing to its every whim. Generation after generation of Western powers has allowed the integrity of their decision-making to be hopelessly compromised. Across the world, tens of millions of civilians have engaged in multiple forms of public protest over Israel's genocide throughout the conflict. Yet the commitment of the masses has, with a few honourable exceptions, been ignored by those who serve them. A blind eye had to be turned for this situation to arise, whereby the institutional West betrayed its people through its deliberate complicity in, and in some cases active sponsorship of, Israel's genocide.

The history of this symbiotic relationship between most of the West and the brutal authoritarian state of Israel is what allowed events to unfold as they did. Worse, the contemporary decision-making massively increased the West's responsibility for the resulting devastation. Western hands are stained with the blood of every one of those slaughtered, both those accounted for, as well as each and every body still to be recovered from the 60 plus million tonnes of rubble that is Gaza today. The West's institutional conscience went AWOL, and for the many millions who protested, millions more did not. Overall, public engagement on Palestine's cause was profound, but it was never so overwhelming that governments and institutions felt compelled to act. The record will show that the weight of public opinion was not sufficient to force those nations powerful enough to have done so to persuade Israel to end its onslaught. More revealing is that they never even tried.

This is about more than the grotesque levels of armaments Israel received from some of the West's major powers. It is about more than the manner in which we continued to trade, play sport and generally connect with Israel. It is about more than our retreat into silence rather than face the, generally manufactured, charge of being antisemitic. The broad support that Israel somehow largely still enjoyed as it sought to cleanse the Palestinian people from the Earth should be alarming. It reveals as much about those in the West as it does about Israel. The uncritical support of Israel by the West since before its foundation in 1948, is cultural. It is racist. For decades, the predominantly white, Judeo-Christian West has chosen to support the oppressor, not the oppressed. When Israel engaged in a genocide, institutional support remained robust.

I am a white European, and I am horrified by what we have allowed to happen to the people of Palestine. I am also Irish. We know a thing or two about being colonised, about oppression. We know a great deal about famine, just like that deliberately induced by Israel in Gaza from spring 2024. My great-grandparents lived during the catastrophe of *An Gorta Mór* (the Great Famine) in the 1840s. Over a million Irish people died, and many millions fled to America and Australia to save themselves from the same fate. In the early twentieth century in Belfast, my grandfather fought politically for the rights of the nationalist people and later took up arms against the British occupation. Most Irish families have flecks of these experiences in their DNA, allowing us to relate easily to the Palestinian struggle. Yet while many protested, however meekly, the majority did not.

Ireland is liked by the Palestinian community. We did some things well, but really only those things that carried or could carry no risk of material cost. Still, Ireland was lauded in certain quarters for its support, but, certainly institutionally, we failed Palestine. The government protested, made diplomatic noises, but stopped short of expelling the ambassador of a genocidal state. Ireland formally recognised Palestine, and the government sought to use its influence at the European Union (EU) level, but to no effect. Even the Occupied Territories Bill, an economic fig leaf designed to stop trade with Israeli businesses in the West Bank and East Jerusalem, proved a step too far for the Irish government. The deliberate prevarication marked an epic display of cowardice. In 2024, Ireland was the world's second-largest importer of Israeli goods,[1] and yet its government wouldn't even legislate to stop trading with those Israeli businesses based in the illegally occupied territories.

Ireland's economic dependence on the US makes it sovereign putty in Washington's hands. The evidence is that the US military uses Irish airspace and Shannon airport in fulfilment of the US administration's support of Israel. Any US flight that stopped in Shannon potentially contributed to the genocide, but Ireland's government accused those concerned by this of having a political agenda. It seemed reluctant to place humanitarian considerations and the rule of law above all other considerations. In denying that Shannon had been used for this purpose, the Taoiseach, Micheál Martin, said there was no way of knowing, as it was 'difficult' to intervene or to 'investigate' any possible breach. It was, therefore, an assumption-based denial; the assumption being that a US administration that renamed the Secretary of Defense as Secretary of War could be trusted to operate to whatever protocols Ireland is supposed to have in place. In fact, on 17 March 2026, St Patrick's Day, as the Taoiseach was meeting Donald Trump in Washington, the investigative online news platform *The Ditch* reported that 'a US military cargo plane had been authorised to land at Shannon on its way back to the

US after delivering munitions to Israel'.[2] Shannon Airport's marketing slogan is *We Make It Easy*.

The direct support of Israel's genocide by some Western powers amounts to complicity and must be pursued as such. As the genocide continued, seamlessly, into 2025, it was clear Israel was not alone; it never was. It could not have done what it has without the deliberate support of many in the West and the indifference of others. So, it is not only Israel that should be in the dock. Many states should be, but there are a select few that have chosen to sponsor Israel in its most wicked endeavours. The genocide is not the fault of Israel alone; other nations are culpable for sponsoring it. While Canada, the EU, Germany, Italy and France all stand accused, the worst offenders are the US and the UK.

This book looks at the scale and nature of the genocide. Western support beams have allowed Israel to pursue this without fear of repercussions, consistent with a decades-long refusal by the West to ever fully call Israel to account. This is what encouraged Israel's brutality. The scale of the challenge to change this behaviour is evidenced by how, over the course of Israel's genocide, national elections in the US and the UK saw changes in administration, from Conservative to Labour in the UK, and Democrat to Republican in the US, yet there was no change in the support of Israel. This should be alarming. Political parties that represent the great majority of the people in each country saw it as incumbent on them to directly support another nation in the conduct of a genocide. So, while the International Criminal Court (ICC) has already indicted Israel's Prime Minister Benjamin Netanyahu and former Defense Minister Yoav Gallant, its reach should include many more in Israel, as well as some notable names in the West.

The book examines how a watching world, led by the US, sponsored the destruction of Palestine, and how that was shockingly manifest in the events of just one day, Monday, 13 October 2025. On that day, Donald J. Trump chose to parade what he called his comprehensive peace plan to the world through events in Israel and Egypt. It was offensive, but also weirdly instructive on where Palestine's cause is, more than a century after the seminal events of the early twentieth century. On 13 October, Trump became the fourth US president to address Israel's parliament, the Knesset. Later, he travelled to Sharm el-Sheikh, Egypt, for the formal signing of his peace plan in front of a group of world leaders, including many of Israel's Western allies.

Trump would describe the day as 'memorable', and history will probably mark it as such, though perhaps not for the reasons America's forty-seventh president would wish. The speeches, the choreography and participants in the events, both in Israel and in Egypt, showcased the unique hold that Israel, a small settler-colonial, apartheid state in the Middle East, has on the West. In the events of that one day, we learned enough to understand how a genocide was possible and why the US the UK and others must be held to account. On that one day, some Arab nations, many Western powers and the parliament of Israel participated in what amounted to a celebration of a genocide.

Monday, 13 October 2025, was Genocide Celebration Day.

March 2026

'Israeli fighter jets bombed our house. In an instant, everything collapsed on us. We had some relatives displaced from the north and east of Gaza staying with us. Sixteen of them – my uncles and cousins – were killed and buried under the rubble ... I was in shock when I saw Hassan and Rima – they were lying on the ground screaming, with their legs cut off. I fell to the ground and couldn't get up ... We rushed them to al-Awda Hospital in Tal a-Za'tar. The place was extremely crowded, full of wounded people and without electricity, medications and surgical tools ... The operating rooms were flooded with blood. The doctors said there was nothing they could do except apply iodine and bandages.'

Muhammad Abu 'Aytah
(2 July 2025)

ONE

VICTORY PARTY

A CELEBRATION

'This is not only the end of a war, this is the end of an age of terror and death, and the beginning of the age of faith and hope and of God. It's the start of a grand concord and lasting harmony for Israel and all the nations of what will soon be a truly magnificent region. I believe that so strongly. This is the historic dawn of a new Middle East.'[1]

With these words President Donald Trump addressed the parliament of Israel, the Knesset, on 13 October 2025. Trump is not known for his eloquence or, indeed, his religious conviction. The wild overreach of his address, coupled with the choice to preview his plan with a political pageant in the parliament of one of the two parties involved, showed its intent. The US president chose to prostrate his nation before the oppressor, not the oppressed. The cataclysmic nature of what had been meted out to Palestine over the previous twenty-four months made the choreography of that morning in Jerusalem woefully inappropriate. Only Trump could have delivered this speech with any conviction. The occasion was significant. He was on his way to Egypt for a meeting of leaders, including other Western powers and some Arab nations, to formally announce the terms of the ceasefire in Gaza.

It was three days since the agreement had come into effect, at noon on 10 October. Trump's trip to the Middle East for the events in Israel and Egypt coincided with the early searches of Gaza's rubble. It was reported that at least 274 bodies had been recovered. On the weekend before Trump's trip, Hamas killed thirty-two people in what was described as a crackdown between opposing factions of the Palestinian resistance,[2] while four civilians were killed by the Israel Defense Forces (IDF). Worse was to follow in the days and weeks ahead – as Israel maintained its attacks, Palestinians continued to perish in their hundreds. The fire had not, in fact, ceased.

President Trump's day of celebration was not marked by the essentials of peacemaking. A ceasefire is generally predicated on a cessation of combat, not just a reduction in fighting. But Donald Trump, who professes to be an exceptional negotiator, wasn't concerned by such details. Any deal he could claim solved the Palestine–Israel crisis was to be celebrated, no matter its lack of substance. In actuality, the plan was no more than a collection of papers and PowerPoint presentations from a group of advisers, including outside consultants. It did not address the challenges from a Palestinian perspective and had made no effort to do so. There was, however, enough in the meeting minutes and the various documentation to pull together a plan that would please the Israelis; the rest, whatever it might involve, could follow.

Trump was on a peace-deal roll. For now, all that mattered to him was getting to Israel and reporting his tally. Weeks earlier, he'd announced that he'd 'settled six wars, and a lot of people say seven because there's one that nobody knows about'.[3] Most of these were grounded in his imagination, but in the world of Trump, this Middle East 'deal' would make it seven, maybe eight. For him, Monday 13 October would mark the day when the world saw he'd done the impossible – established peace in the Middle East.

◆◆◆

When a US president travels overseas, it is normal for the presidential party to be accompanied by a media group called the White House press pool, with one of their number assigned as the official pool reporter. Their reports are logged and available to the networks and media outlets that are not assigned places on the trip, as well as global agencies. On 13 October 2025, Dasha Burns of *Politico* logged the pool account of events right through the schedule in the Middle East.

Sent:	**Reports:**
October 12, 2025	
16:32 EDT	*WH Travel Pool note #1: JBA Arrival* Hello! I'll be your pooler for this quick swing to the Middle East. POTUS motorcade arrived at JBA at 4:31pm ET (all times stamps from the trip will be in local time) It is cold and windy with a light drizzle.[4]

The president's trip and that of his entourage began at 4.25 p.m. on 12 October, when Marine One landed at Joint Base Andrews (formerly Andrews Air Force Base) in wet, windy conditions. Fifteen minutes earlier, he'd walked from the White House to the waiting helicopter, while those travelling with him on his planned lap of honour were already boarding Air Force One. As well as a press corps of thirteen, others on board included Secretary of State Marco Rubio, Secretary of War (Defense) Pete Hegseth, Chief of Staff Susie Wiles, Trump's personal adviser Stephen Miller and Ambassador Monica Crowley.

When Trump boarded, he told the travelling press that it would be a momentous twenty-four hours. He claimed, 'They had 500,000 people yesterday and today, in Israel, and also the Muslim and Arab countries are all cheering. Everybody's cheering at one time. That's never happened before. Usually, if you have one cheering, the other isn't[;] the other is the opposite. This is the first time; everybody is amazed and they're thrilled, and it's an honor to be involved, and we're gonna have an amazing time, and it's gonna be something that's never, never happened before.'[5]

It was true that events as he described them hadn't happened before. It was also true that they had not been remotely as he had profiled them over the previous few days. Yet, little or no attention was paid to the inaccuracy of his claims. The narrative was being set. Donald Trump would travel to the Middle East to showcase his unparalleled diplomacy and deal-making skills to the world. While the Nobel Peace Prize he coveted had already been awarded to Venezuelan María Corina Machado days earlier, he intended to press the merits of his case to the world.

Middle East peace had eluded every previous US president, largely because none of them dared to address the fundamentals. Trump was no different, but his capacity to inhabit a parallel universe allowed him to claim to have achieved it. Trump's motivation is seemingly always about himself. Claiming to have shaped a lasting Middle East solution would allow him to parade his credentials as an exceptional peacemaker. In October 2025, the US State Department posted photographs of the president under the headline, 'President Trump remains the greatest dealmaker in the world.'[6] It wasn't a new claim. Well before he ran for public office, Trump posted on Twitter (now X), 'Deals are my art form. Other people paint beautifully or write poetry. I like making deals, preferably big deals.'[7]

Deals don't come much bigger than resolving the decades-long occupation of Palestine by Israel and its Zionist ambition to crush the Palestinian people. Although the continued violence meant the first forty-eight hours of the supposed ceasefire had not gone entirely to plan, this was not of concern to Trump. Monday 13 October would mark the day the forty-seventh US president would set out the longer-term transformation he envisaged for the region. Choosing to preview this plan with Israel's parliamentarians reflected its primary purpose: to protect the interests of Israel and its allies, especially the US. The primal relationship between the US and Israel is what had allowed Israel to conduct a genocide since the Hamas attack on its soil in October 2023. The two nations are bound at the sovereign hip. Without that connection, Israel's genocide would not and could not have occurred. The West, generally, is complicit, but the US, along with the UK – its standard warring partner – has sustained a pro-Israel line throughout. In their commitment to this position, these countries have betrayed an almost complete disinterest in human rights and the international rule of law. In this context it was appropriate for Trump to make Israel the centrepiece of his day of triumph.

AN ISRAELI AGENDA

The special meeting of the Knesset where Trump spoke took place almost a week after the second anniversary of the brutal Hamas attack that claimed approximately 1,200 lives. Israel's genocidal campaign had commenced within hours of the attack, which remains commonly considered to be the cause of Israel's actions. It is deviously and deliberately presented as such by Israel and its supporters.

The narrative Israel offers is that most Palestinians were living peaceful, meaningful lives on their land alongside their Israeli neighbours until the Hamas terrorist faction changed everything by attacking Israel. The evidence to the contrary has always been overwhelming, but it has taken Israel's slaughter of innocent Palestinians – at unprecedented levels and by any means over 2024 and 2025 – to grow international awareness of its decades-long malevolence. However, while international courts have tried to hold it to account, with international indictments of some of its leaders, Israel has not suffered any consequences. Most Western powers have remained allied to Israel, so it has done what it has done with impunity, live before the world. It has conducted a genocide. This lack of accountability is the single most important issue to be addressed if justice is ever to be done, yet many who are upset by Israel's actions believe it will never be held to account for its barbarity.

Today, there is a greater global awareness of Palestine's ongoing oppression at the hands of Israel. There is alarm at the number of civilians it has slaughtered and that its tactics have included an induced famine. The egregious disproportion of its response is revealed in the IDF's own figures, showing that at least 83 per cent of Palestinians killed in Gaza up to September 2025 were civilians.[8] Even Israel's renowned global propaganda machine, its hasbara, has struggled to combat the unprecedented public anger, but in the US, in particular, it remains very powerful. In the UK too. These two nations, which subscribe to the view of Western culture and values as superior, are especially bound to Israel. The UK did most to establish it, while the US has done more than any other nation to support its colonial excesses.

While polls show that public disdain for Israel in the West is at record levels,[9] use of the antisemitic trope by its allies continues to provide a strong form of defence. Globally, antisemitism has long been used to protect Israel from criticism as part of a sophisticated propaganda armoury. There are, of course, occasions when antisemites do clothe their hatred of Jews in protests against Israel. However, the great majority of those who support Palestine do so because of its long and brutal oppression at the hands of the state of Israel and its collaborators in the West. Their disgust is with Israel, not with people of the Jewish faith. They are, in fact, objecting to racism as manifest in the institutional and constitutional discrimination on which Israeli society is based.

Former Israeli Cabinet Minister Shulamit Aloni once described this use of the antisemitism trope: 'Well, it's a trick. We always use it. When from Europe somebody is criticizing Israel, then we bring up the Holocaust. When in this country [the US] people are criticizing Israel, then they are antisemitic … it's very easy to blame people who criticize certain acts of the Israeli government as antisemitic and to bring up the Holocaust and the suffering of the Jewish people. And that justify [*sic*] everything we do to the Palestinians.'[10]

The actions of Jewish institutions globally demonstrate the truth of this assertion. In 2016, the International Holocaust Remembrance Alliance (IHRA) established a very broad definition that rendered pretty much any and all criticism of Israel antisemitic. It has been adopted by most national governments in the West, even though many independent Jewish thinkers believe it fails to adequately decouple criticism of Israel, which is legitimate, from the expression of hatred of Jews, which is racist. The 2020 Jerusalem Declaration on Antisemitism, signed by 370 Jewish thought leaders, makes a clear distinction between the expression of hostility towards Jews and criticising the state of Israel. It says much of what pro-Palestinian protesters want – 'justice and the full grant of their [Palestinian's] political, national, civil and human rights, as encapsulated in international law' – is not antisemitic.[11] It also states that evidence-based criticism of Israel, opposition to Zionism and Boycott, Divestment and Sanctions (BDS) campaigns do not constitute antisemitic behaviour.

Definitions matter on something this potentially divisive. The IHRA one was used by the New York mayor Eric Adams during his term from 2022 to 2025. Adams, a big supporter of Israel, had tightly strapped New York's freedom of speech and protest to the more restrictive definition of antisemitism that included criticism of Israel. He introduced a number of executive orders, including one signed in his last month in office, that barred all of the city's agencies from any engagement with the BDS movement. In January 2026, on his first day in office, New York's newly elected mayor, Zohran Mamdani, revoked all but one of Adams's orders that supported Israel. Predictably, there was an outcry from the Zionist lobby. It made no reference to Mamdani's commitment to continue to support the work of the city's Office to Combat Antisemitism. As Phylisa Wisdom of the New York Jewish Agenda pointed out, 'not everyone thinks you need to codify IHRA to keep the Jewish people safe'.[12]

Frustration with Israel is just that; it is not a commentary on people of the Jewish faith. Dislike of Israel and its policies is not antisemitic. No government of Israel has been prepared to acknowledge that, like all states, its conduct is open to commentary, to criticism. Any and all negative analysis is profiled as racist; as antisemitic. It cannot afford to acknowledge its errant behaviour as a cause for concern; to do so would involve reform and the abandonment of the 'Greater Israel' project. Sadly, any enlightenment there was about the need to address the fundamentals, especially the rights and needs of the Palestinians, has long since all but disappeared from Israeli politics.

REPEATED FAILINGS

It was between 2006 and 2008 that Palestinian leader Mahmoud Abbas and Israeli Prime Minister Ehud Olmert made the last serious attempt to find common ground for peace. Previous attempts had all come to nothing. Three years earlier, Israel had ruled out proposals made by the Arab League that would involve its withdrawal to pre-1967 borders and the right of return for all Palestinian refugees. Bill Clinton's Camp David summit of 2000 had amounted to nothing. The assassination of Israeli Prime Minister Yitzhak Rabin by a right-wing extremist in 1995 brought the Oslo Accords to an end. Going all the way back to the Camp David Accords of 1978, the different attempts at peace over the decades were all initiated by the US and were all focused on the interests of Israel. This is the primary reason they were destined to fail.

Experienced US public servants would have known the chances of success in 2025 were equally slim, especially given the backdrop of a genocide. Team Trump, though, only thinks in terms of success. It has a mentality whereby, based exclusively on Trump's terms, it believes it will always win. No attention would have been paid to why numerous other US-led peace efforts had failed. Team Trump's modus doesn't prioritise research, learning or careful consideration. Any such process would have revealed the consistent fatal flaw in US plans: prioritising the interests of the oppressor over those of the oppressed. From Camp David to the present, Israel's interests have taken precedence over those of the Palestinians, whose land Israel has occupied for generations. It was blindingly obvious that, without addressing this flaw, failure would follow any new initiative. The plan that President Trump was bringing to Egypt for a highly choreographed official signing was every bit as defective as those that preceded it. History will undoubtedly record how this 'momentous occasion' was simply pure political theatre.

◆◆◆

With the president in his quarters, the White House press pool log registered '[c]onsider this your wheels up' as Air Force One taxied to the runway for take-off and the eleven-hour overnight flight to Israel.[13] With a team of chefs on board, it's possible Trump was offered more than his favoured burger and chips with a Diet Coke before he slept. As the flight progressed, Israel was preparing to greet the president it knew would serve up precisely what it wanted.

Trump's decision to spend over three hours in the Knesset exposed just how in hock the US political establishment is to Israel. The speeches of Israel's politicians would reveal how its government and its opposition were aligned on keeping it that way. This was a moment to be turned to Israel's advantage. Trump's own long address would show the hopelessness of Palestine's cause as long as America was helming any process. Two years into its genocide, almost six decades into the illegal occupation of Palestine and the vicious oppression of its people, the first clause of the twenty-point plan drafted by Trump's cabal of family and advisers focused on the internal security of Israel. It read, 'Gaza will be a deradicalized terror-free zone that does not pose a threat to its neighbors.'[14] Where the Trump plan differed from others was in terms of how it was geared towards long-term economic outcomes that would benefit the principal sponsor of Israel's colonialism. Its own strategic interests drive most US overseas interventions, but rarely has this been presented quite so transparently.

In his first term as president, Trump had courted Israel and certain Gulf states, ignoring almost entirely the cause of Palestine, in his determination to unlock wealth in the Middle East. Now, he was back at it. The approach he was advocating, to allow Israel and key Gulf allies to unite, would meet with general approval in America. Support for Israel in the US is cross-party; the Democrats are no less 'owned' by the Zionist lobby than the Republicans. With Trump's son-in-law, Jared Kushner, very involved, there was also every reason to believe that what was being proposed would directly benefit the president's family. In contrast, concern for Palestine's interests would not be in evidence. Potentially, just ending the genocide would be enough for them to accept this latest turn of international diplomacy's wheel of misfortune.

The terms of the deal were so unbalanced that, despite the Palestinians' extraordinary levels of suffering, the fractured nature of their leadership would mean the international community would not be forced out of its indifference. The emphasis in the published terms on how Israel and the US would determine the economic and political future of Palestine gave little hope to its people that life would improve. In the West's twisted logic on this decades-long diplomatic thrombosis, any approach that offered hope to Palestine meant upsetting Israel. Israel's two greatest supporters, the US and UK, would never countenance such an outcome. So, it made perfect sense that, before Trump's plan was signed, it would be hyped up in Israel's parliament, an objective met in full.

◆◆◆

The Knesset is an unremarkable building. Its construction was funded by Baron James de Rothschild, who died before the cornerstone was laid in 1958. His munificence was an early signal of the powerful link between this new state, founded just ten years earlier, and the Jewish people across the world. Rothschild had served as a major in the British Army in Palestine and succeeded his father as president of the Palestine Jewish Colonization Association (PJCA) in 1924. An MP for sixteen years (1929–45), he was a committed Zionist and one of the founding directors of the Hebrew University in Jerusalem. By the time of his death, he had 'renewed PJCA and eventually his assets were passed on to the young state of Israel'.[15] The robust relationship between Jewish political influence in the West, money and the state of Israel, which started in these early days, remains as robust today. That has never been more in evidence than over the course of Israel's genocide in Palestine in 2024 and 2025.

In the planning and construction of the Knesset, the attention paid to the building's entrance betrayed an early unease about Israel's security. There was no disputing that, aesthetically, an entrance from the south was the only choice due to 'the spectacular view seen from that direction, the monumentality of the front of the building, as seen by the person entering the building'.[16] Another attraction was that, by placing the entrance on the south side, a clear distinction could be established between the Knesset and the nearby government buildings.

Israel's armed forces, the IDF, had a different perspective, arguing that putting the entrance on the south side represented a military threat, as it could be 'observed from several firing positions across the Jordanian border … a fact that theoretically enables the opening of flat-trajectory fire … with a fair chance that it would hit its target'.[17] Those security considerations prevailed, and the entrance was oriented to the north. It may have been less aesthetically appealing, but the IDF argued that it made the centre of Israel's legislature considerably more secure. The decision represented an insight into a national obsession with security; Israel's origins and its own conduct since its foundation make that obsession understandable.

◆◆◆

Trumpets heralded the US president's arrival at the entrance to the Knesset chamber. The showbiz had started an hour earlier as Air Force One approached Tel Aviv. It had banked over the city's coastline, allowing the travelling press a sight of a giant 'Thank You' sign with an image of Trump and a Star of David. The sense of celebration and gratitude was evident throughout the journey to Jerusalem on the Highway One motorway. It carried through to the parliament itself, where many in attendance wore red baseball caps emblazoned with 'Trump the President of Peace'. It was, perhaps, the moment where MAGA met Middle East diplomacy.

Most of the Knesset's 120 members, the visitors' gallery of senior figures from Trump's administration and other luminaries rose to applaud and cheer him as he entered the plenum. The Knesset Speaker, Israel's prime minister and its president were alongside him. Trump was already over an hour into the four-hour schedule in Israel. With his own predilection for long, rambling speeches, there was little scope for parliamentary window-dressing, but others needed to seize the moment to extract political capital for themselves. The already happy mood was boosted by news that, as Air Force One was approaching Israel, Hamas had released the last twenty living hostages taken in 2023. The Knesset believed it was witnessing a historic moment in the generations-long trauma that is Palestine and Israel.

Knesset Speaker Amir Ohana accompanied Presidents Trump

and Herzog to the dais, as Prime Minister Netanyahu took his seat on the government benches. Trump received a prolonged standing ovation; some members chanted his name. Fifty miles away, it was also being chanted by thousands gathered in Tel Aviv's Hostage Square watching events on the giant jumbotrons. Waving Israeli flags, the crowds shouted 'Trump, Trump, Trump', as US networks and Israeli TV broadcast scenes of an IDF military convoy carrying the released hostages home.

Most of the crowd stayed to watch as Ohana opened proceedings in Jerusalem. He was to be both a busy master of ceremonies and a fawning host to the US president and his team. In his remarks, he emphasised the importance of the US president's decision to bomb Iran in June 2025. It had been a highly controversial move, even among Trump's own base. But the value of drawing Iran directly into events has never been lost on Israel's political leaders. On this day, Monday 13 October, it was notable that all the speakers in the Knesset took a similar line. One after the other they focused on Iran; on the alleged threat it uniquely represents and the purported nuclear danger. The Islamic Republic of Iran remains Israel's best means of maintaining the West's steadfast support, because Israel needs the West to think that Iran is fixated on the destruction of Western civilisation. With about as much concern for accuracy as that frequently shown by the Knesset's guest of honour, Ohana quickly focused on this much-hyped threat. 'Four months ago, when our Prime Minister started Operation Rising Lion [Israeli attacks on Iran in June 2025], you followed with Operation Midnight Hammer, which was a courageous action; there was nothing like it until you arrived at the White House. In that [decision], Mr President, you prevented a nuclear holocaust that Iran wanted to bring about to the world.'[18] This is the lie that Western powers, especially the US, need to promote to justify their unqualified support for Israel as 'protector in chief' of Western values in the Middle East.

Speaker Ohana also repeated Israel's contention that the last two years of carnage in Gaza were exclusively the fault of Hamas. 'Tomorrow it will be Simchat Tora [a Jewish holiday], and two years ago it was the most difficult day for the state of Israel since its establishment and for the Jewish people since the Holocaust … The Satan [Hamas] not only murdered and raped many of our brothers and sisters, but he also abducted the living and the dead. Since then, this has been the longest and the most just war.'[19] This exaggerated account of the events of 7 October 2023 had remained critical to Israel's defence of its actions throughout 2024 and 2025, and to those nations in the West who chose to sponsor its genocide.

There was nothing new in this; nothing different compared to how Israel has justified other acts of brutal oppression of the Palestinians. It was the actions of Hamas guerrilla fighters that forced Israel to act as it did; that was the political narrative, not just in the Knesset but from most of its allies. It has long been the case that, whatever the circumstances and the course of events, Israel wants its fight to be seen as 'just'. Those nations that align themselves with Israel have never faltered in that view, no matter the evidence to the contrary. Even in this case, as it carried out a globally live-screened genocide, Israel protested that it was conducting a 'just war' and asserted that the IDF was 'the world's most moral army'.[20]

Ohana's speech was laden with effusive praise for Donald Trump. Placing the mantle of greatness on him was a consistent theme all day, but it was the Speaker who set the tone. The hyperbole rush included a promise that thousands of years hence, the Jewish people would still remember him. Trump would be, 'a giant of Jewish history, one for whom we must look back two and a half millennia into the mists of time to find a parallel: Cyrus the Great [an odd choice as, while his edict freed the Jews from Babylon, he's an equally loved figure in Iran]. You, President Donald J. Trump, are a colossus who will be enshrined in the pantheon of history.'[21]

Ohana then turned to Benjamin Netanyahu. A member of the largest party, Likud, Ohana said that, without Netanyahu's leadership, without his ability to make the right decisions, the peace now in prospect could not have been achieved. Netanyahu received a standing ovation as he made his way from the government benches to speak. Donald Trump, whose seat was beside the lectern, proffered his trademark clumsy fist pumps, and they exchanged some whispered words before Netanyahu began his address.

Israel's traditional 'winner-takes-all' approach was in evidence in the words of, arguably, its most aggressively expansionist leader ever. Prime Minister Netanyahu said that the US had recognised Israel's sovereignty over the Golan Heights and that the proposed peace plan recognised Israel's 'rights in Judea and Samaria, the ancestral homeland of the Jewish people.'[22] He was clear on the purpose of the Trump plan, despite the absence of supporting detail. It would protect Israel's claim to Palestine – it was the stake in the colonial ground – a point which Trump made no attempt to challenge. Knowing this president's avariciousness for praise, he wrapped his interpretation of what the US and the other parties to it were doing with the plan in a series of 'thank yous', each of which was met with a standing ovation. Throughout, a bowing, nodding Donald Trump preened in the glow of the adulation.

In reference to America targeting Iran the previous June, Netanyahu recalled how, in his first term, Trump withdrew the US from the Obama Iran nuclear agreement. 'Donald Trump is the greatest friend that the state of Israel has ever had in the White House. No American president has ever done more for Israel.'[23] Given the unbroken support Israel has received from US presidents since 1948, this represented quite an accolade. Trump had pledged to undo the Obama nuclear deal late in his 2016 presidential campaign, telling an American Israel Public Affairs Committee (AIPAC) meeting that his 'No. 1 priority is to dismantle the disastrous deal with Iran.'[24] Whether that made him the most pro-Israel president is arguable. What's not in dispute is how every US president since Israel's foundation in 1948 has promoted Israel's interests ahead of those of the people of Palestine.

There's some evidence that John F. Kennedy may have been the exception to this rule had he lived, while Jimmy Carter and Ronald Reagan both later expressed regret for their support for Israel during their administrations. However, in general, America's two political parties have been equally at fault for Israel's special standing in US politics. Even over the course of this genocide or the terms of the last three presidents – of Democrats Joe Biden and Barack Obama, and of Republican Trump – it's hard to find the width of a blade of grass between the two parties' commitment to the Zionist cause. Obama proved a complete let-down for the liberals who'd expected him to challenge the Israeli lobby. In his second term as president, it amounted to nothing that his political career had significant backing from Arab friends in his early years in Chicago. Obama proved as malleable in Zionist hands as the other thirteen presidents who had gone before him since Israel's foundation. Then came Trump, whose decision to move the US embassy from Tel Aviv to Jerusalem in his first term was incendiary, although it had only diplomatic significance. Joe Biden's total support of Benjamin Netanyahu's savagery following the Hamas attack facilitated a genocide that saw Palestine reduced to rubble and littered with the bones and ashes of tens of thousands of its people. Despite the two men's antagonistic relationship, Trump showed no hesitation in following in his predecessor's footsteps in this one policy.

The events of 13 October 2025 in the Knesset showed that, despite the irrefutable evidence of a genocide, it remains hugely important for a US president to be seen as Israel's 'friend'. Netanyahu knew this about America. A 2001 recording of him talking with settlers (occupiers) in the West Bank during the Second Intifada demonstrates to the settler community just how well he understands the US mindset. 'America is a thing you can move very easily, move it in the right direction. They won't get in their way.'[25] It was this insight that allowed him to swat away Bill Clinton's Oslo Accords and later ensured any early intentions of Barack Obama would falter. More than a decade ago, the president of the Arab American Institute, James Zogby, wrote, 'President Obama tried to pressure Netanyahu during his first term, but after the Israeli prime minister played the US Congress against him, Obama relented.'[26]

All these years later, Netanyahu was still 'playing' the US establishment, even with the immediate backdrop of a genocide that had led to the slaughter of an estimated over 100,000 Palestinians, most of them civilians. But now, the toxicity of this morally bankrupt Israel–US relationship had spread. The genocide, the institutional indifference and general media equivocation extended beyond the US. The horror of the genocide, even in the long history of Israel's savagery-littered oppression of the Palestinians, showed the abandonment of Palestine by the West more generally. Israel rode that wave of indifference in pursuing its obliteration. The world knew what Israel was doing and, from early 2024, was fully aware of its intent. Still, the West's major powers supplied it with phenomenal quantities of arms and supported its genocidal campaign in a myriad of ways. There are multiple horrors occurring across our world, but the assault on the civilian population of Palestine is unique. Its barbarity is evident to all, yet that does not seem to matter. It is far more serious than simply an absence of condemnation; the West's major powers provided Israel with the support it needed to pursue its genocidal ambition.

JUDEO-CHRISTIAN BROTHERHOOD

Concurrently, in a different part of the world, the West had united to provide massive support to Ukraine following the invasion of its territory by Russia. Public support for Ukraine and opposition to Russia's belligerence was matched by nations and blocs like the EU supporting the international order. From the moment of the full-scale Russian invasion in early 2022, the US, Britain, Germany and other major powers provided arms and aid to Ukraine, the oppressed. It imposed sanctions on Russia, the oppressor. The West's powers are united in believing that for hostilities to end, Ukraine must return to its people. There can be no doubt where loyalty and sympathy will still lie if, in 2097, seventy-five years after Russia's invasion, the people of Ukraine are still trying to wrestle back control. It is inconceivable that Ukraine would be abandoned to its own devices and that the West's major powers would be providing huge levels of support to Russia. Yet with Palestine, the West has shown only disinterest. That is despite, or perhaps because of, the seeds of the genocide being planted by those who refuse to come to Palestine's aid. It is seventy-five years and counting …

Much of the illogical but entrenched support for Israel is rooted in the Judeo-Christian idea of how the world should be managed. Islam is seen as a significant threat to this ideal, one that needs to be controlled so it cannot threaten the hegemonic cultural model that most in the West believe is superior. Israel plays to this and has done for decades. It accentuates cultural differences, creating Islamic bogeymen, and promotes itself as a Western-style democracy in a part of the world the West neither understands nor allows itself to trust.

In his Knesset address, Netanyahu played on this theme, naming two Israeli citizens and linking them to biblical figures. Ari Spitz, an American-Israeli soldier, was in the public gallery. Netanyahu explained that he'd been on a mission in Gaza when he lost three limbs in an explosion; two of his colleagues were killed. The prime minister intoned, 'Ari, you are the spirit of Joshua. You are the spirit of David. You are the spirit of the Maccabees. You are the spirit of Israel.'[27] Then he addressed an Israeli who he said was watching the morning's events from the country's consulate in Los Angeles. Sabine Taasa's husband was killed on 7 October when he threw himself on a grenade to protect two of his sons. Netanyahu said Sabine now tours the world to promote

Israel's cause. Addressing her directly, he again drew on historical figures: 'Sabine ... you embody the spirit of our biblical heroines, Deborah, Ruth, and Esther. You too are the spirit of Israel, and we all salute you.'[28]

The citing of legendary biblical or historical figures by Israeli politicians serves a dual purpose. It is designed to wrap individual Israelis – be it a brave soldier or the wife and mother of victims – in the cloak of exceptionalism. We are told that Joshua brought the Israelites to the Promised Land. We are reminded of David, the diminutive Israelite who slew Goliath, while Deborah, Ruth, and Esther were all exceptional women in the Old Testament. Israeli politicians cite such figures as beacons of faith, loyalty and courage. Invoking their memory and their standing in the context of the campaign to destroy Palestine meant, by implication, that those opposed to it were evil or satanic, as the Speaker had claimed. Even to a liberal, secular West, this kind of imagery and use of biblical names can subliminally reinforce a closeness, a symmetry. It carries ideas of safety or security and hints that this could not be achieved with the Arab or Islamic world remaining intact. The choreography has always been part of how Israel has strengthened its position with the big Western powers.

Netanyahu wove the rightness of Israel's cause into the fabric of survival, not dominance. The Holocaust, the horrific annihilation of Europe's Jews, well in advance of the establishment of the state of Israel, is Israel's reference point for its right to act as it sees fit. Yet many Jews, including some who survived the Holocaust, have spoken out fearlessly against the idea that what happened in 1930s' and 1940s' Europe justifies Israel's genocide. It has mobilised a powerful movement of Jewish academics and thought leaders, with the support of many Jews around the world, to call for Israel's government to be held to account. There are groups within Israel, including outstanding non-governmental organisations (NGOs) such as Yesh Din, HaMoked, and B'Tselem, as well as the Association for Civil Rights in Israel (ACRI), that are relentless in drawing attention to ongoing human rights and civil liberties abuses by the government. Many Western nations and the EU fund their work, although given how many of these nations have conducted themselves, it's hard not to conclude that the support is more about 'conscience money' than a real commitment to driving change.

Prime Minister Netanyahu and the US president share a belief that peace can be achieved only through strength; each emphasised this in their speeches. Netanyahu was clear in his justification of this: 'The Jewish people have risen from the ashes time and again, but when we formed the state of Israel and the army of Israel, we pledged never again. Never again would we be defenseless against our enemies. And that, that resolute strength, not only assures our survival, it assures our future, it assures peace. We have paid, we have paid a high price for this war, but our enemies now understand just how powerful and just how determined Israel is. They understand that attacking Israel on October 7th was a catastrophic mistake. They understand that Israel is strong and that Israel is here to stay. And this, Mr President, is the indispensable foundation of peace. Peace through strength.'[29]

When Netanyahu referenced the 'heavy cost' Israel had paid, the estimated total number of Israeli lives lost was 2,000, most of them soldiers. By spring 2026, the official number of Palestinians killed stood at well over 70,000, the vast majority civilians, with the most conservative estimates putting the real toll at over 100,000. Israel's territory and infrastructure were largely untouched. Its unprecedented bombardment of Gaza had destroyed whatever limited infrastructure that country had and created tens of millions of tonnes of rubble.[30] The theft of land in the West Bank during that period was at unprecedented levels. Palestinian Arab citizens of Israel, representing about 20 per cent of the population, were discriminated against more than ever. In the midst of the carnage Israel had caused, its prime minister referenced, without a hint of irony, the high cost his country had to bear.

In his speech, Netanyahu attributed the failure to reach an earlier ceasefire to the weakness of many in the West. The account that followed was typically untruthful. There is overwhelming evidence that he deliberately stalled progress on many occasions. Qatar's prime minister, who was involved in negotiations from the outset, was unequivocal: 'If we look at the pattern of Netanyahu's actions … it's been in a very systematic way trying to undermine any chance of stability, any chance of peace, and any chance of retrieving his own hostages.'[31] In contrast, Netanyahu told the Knesset the failure to recover hostages was the fault of the West for not sustaining its support of Israel. That was why more hostages hadn't been released earlier. He argued that after early progress, everything stalled as 'more governments bought into Hamas's false propaganda', which contributed to a growing antisemitic narrative in the West.[32]

This claim that the West had turned on Israel was another misrepresentation. The lie, even by his standards, was off the scale. Most of the institutional West had hardly paused in its support, never mind changed tack, as Israel's savagery in Gaza gathered pace. The major powers remained steadfast in their support of the coloniser. One of the best analysts of Middle Eastern affairs, Robert Fisk, regularly argued that proportionality is rarely a consideration for Israel, as it knows that there's no risk of consequences for doing as it wishes. Genocide included, it would seem.

In contrast, from mid-2024, public opinion became more vocal in its dismay and its dislike of Israel. The longer Israel's bombardment continued, well beyond the first anniversary of the Hamas attack, the more Israel's credibility with Western public opinion became eroded as increasing evidence emerged of the scale of the horror it was unleashing.

GENOCIDE DENIAL

Western governments that shifted ground to offer Palestine diplomatic support did so because of public opinion. Support for Palestine among citizens across the West and, more gradually, many Arab nations challenged political leadership to look beyond the standard playbook. That change had nothing to do with Hamas propaganda, as Netanyahu tried to suggest. It was simply that hundreds of millions of people around the world were seeing a genocide unfold and realising that no matter how they felt about 7 October 2023, Israel's actions could not be justified. With that realisation came a need to learn more, and as the number of informed people increased, some governments came under increasing pressure to act.

Israel had not anticipated the extent to which the world would be able to follow its genocide in Gaza. Refusing global media access did not prevent people seeing the results for themselves. Israel's information wound was self-inflicted. Palestinian journalists and civilian reporters did not need to provide comment. The tech-enabled world saw the gross disproportionality of Israel's response to 7 October. Even many who were horrified by Hamas's attack were enraged by Israel's conduct.

Israel's persecution complex is well known; its current prime minister wears it with distinction. Its body politic would never accept that it is possible to oppose Hamas's action on 7 October but understand its source. It thinks that it is impossible to consider Hamas's attack a war crime and Israel's response a genocide. Israel cannot and never has accepted that these two things are not mutually exclusive.

With the passage of time and no easing in Israel's genocidal intent, more people awoke to the reality of Israel as a settler, colonial, apartheid state, which, over the nearly eighty years since its establishment, has displayed complete contempt for international law. Israel's singular belief in the rightness of its cause explains its decades-long humiliation of the Palestinian people, whose land it has taken. Anger grew among citizens, but not at levels sufficient to force the radical action needed by their governments to manacle Israel's brutal aggression. The institutional West again acquiesced in the genocide that began in 2023. It refused to call out Israel; worse, its major powers provided Israel with the arms and the diplomatic headroom to conduct the genocide. They bear equal responsibility.

Israel is a small nation. It could not have conducted a military campaign of such brutality, backed by an induced famine, without the deliberate support of more powerful nations. Israel is a country, in part, formed out of the ashes of the worst destruction of human life in modern history. In one of the most shameful acts of state treachery ever, it unleashed terror on another people that, in its purposefulness and barbarity, is close to what Europe's Jews experienced in the 1930s and 1940s. In his Knesset address on 13 October 2025, Netanyahu said the Hamas attack had left Israel no choice and that '[w]ith indomitable courage, we set out to defend our people, to defeat our enemies, and to release our hostages. Our heroic soldiers fought like lions. They fought on the front lines of civilization and barbarism. Israel achieved amazing victories over Hamas, and the entire Iran terror axis ... Iran's nuclear weapons and ballistic missile program with your enormous help, Mr President.'[33]

Another senior Israeli political figure who attended the Knesset session that morning was President Isaac Herzog. The Herzog family has a long history of public service. In a vignette that reflected tensions across Europe, two months after the 'ceasefire', the city council of Ireland's capital, Dublin, dropped a motion to rename one of its public parks that bore the name of Chaim Herzog. Ireland, along with Spain and Norway, was the first Western state to recognise Palestine after Israel's offensive in Gaza. It has been consistently strong on the optics of supporting Palestine but has failed to follow through on promised actions. Trade restrictions were promised but not delivered. One of the country's main airports has been used to facilitate US military support for Israel. These failures reflect more than the common fear of upsetting Israel; Ireland's economy has a significant dependence on America, Israel's sponsor-in-chief.

Dublin City Council's plan to rename the park that bore Herzog's name met with the standard rush to brand the promoters antisemites. Institutional Ireland reacted predictably. Taoiseach

(PM) Micheál Martin and Tánaiste (deputy PM) Simon Harris of the centre-right coalition used highly emotive language to criticise the plan. They bought the antisemitism line. They were wrong. Their focus was on Herzog's early years in Ireland, not what he went on to do. They missed an opportunity to make critical distinctions based on the facts. In their eagerness to play to the Western institutional gallery, they failed to attack all forms of racism and to distinguish between antisemitism, which is racist, and criticism of the state of Israel, which is not.

There are Irish Jews who warrant such an honour. Chaim Herzog was not one of them. On 4 December 2025, a letter from Jews for Palestine – Ireland, published by the *Irish Examiner*, pointed out that Herzog, who left Ireland in his teens, had participated in the persecution of Palestinians in the 1930s, in the Nakba (1947–49) and again in the Six-Day War. 'As military governor of the West Bank, his war crimes include the destruction of the Maghrebi Quarter in Jerusalem and the ethnic cleansing of 200,000 Palestinians after the 1967 war.'[34] These are historical facts. There should have been no hesitation in renaming this public park; Herzog's father, Isaac, could have been a more appropriate choice. He was Ireland's first chief rabbi, spoke Irish fluently and, as the second chief rabbi of Israel, though a Zionist, he was said to insist on adherence to Havlagah, the abstention from acts of revenge.

In January 2026, Micheál Martin and Simon Harris both attended National Holocaust Memorial Day in Dublin. Appropriately, in his remarks, Martin expressed sympathy over the massacre of fifteen people celebrating Hanukkah in Sydney, Australia, the previous month. In his remarks he chose to return to the question of Herzog Park to criticise once again those who had wanted to remove Herzog's name. It was inappropriate and inaccurate, conflating people's reasonable concern over the actions of the state of Israel with being antisemitic. The taoiseach wasn't alone in doing this. Most Western leaders refuse to challenge the legitimacy of this argument.

One of those to express great upset at the move to rename the small Dublin park was Chaim Herzog's son, Isaac, Israel's president throughout the genocide. In a statement on X, he said removing his father's name would be a 'shameful and disgraceful move'.[35] No questions were raised about his suitability to comment. Two years previously, just three months into Israel's genocide, President Herzog posed for photos at a military base, signing IDF missiles to be used in Gaza. In Hebrew, he wrote, 'ani somech aleichem' or 'I rely on you'. *Haaretz*, an Israeli newspaper, questioned his actions: 'What statesmanship is there in the signing of a lethal munition, which in the eyes of the world represents Israel's greatest sin in this war – sowing devastation in Gaza and killing innocents?'[36] The president also said that there were no innocents in Gaza, and that 'It's an entire nation out there that's responsible. This rhetoric about civilians not aware, not involved, it's absolutely not true.'[37] While Herzog's role restricts him from fully entering political debate, some of his actions and comments have led to him being used as an example of Israel's intent to commit war crimes.

Isaac Herzog led the Labor Party in opposition from 2013 to 2018, after a decade during which he'd served in various government positions while the party was in power. The relationship between Netanyahu and Herzog was as would be expected of members of different political parties, but their dislike of each other had intensified in the period ahead of the Hamas attack. As president, Herzog questioned the prime minister's motivation for proposed significant legislative changes to the legal system. Considered by most Israelis to be professionally weak and personally dull, in 2023 he took a surprisingly strong line against Netanyahu's proposed changes to the power of the judiciary, saying it would weaken democracy. As a lawyer, he established a consultative forum that made recommendations to protect the independence of the judiciary. When Netanyahu showed no interest, Herzog delivered a national address warning that the country could stumble into a civil war. That was eight months before the Hamas attack; a majority of the Knesset rejected his arguments.

In the first weeks of the genocide, the president had kept a low profile. It was in December 2023 that he emerged from the shadows to provide wider political support to his erstwhile opponent. As well as the occasion when he signed the IDF missile, he did an interview with a US network during which he spoke strongly in support of the IDF and the government's approach in Gaza. US TV was safe territory, somewhere he would be allowed to protest that Gaza and all of Israel's military actions were 'really, truly, to save Western civilization'.[38]

Early the next summer, 2024, he re-emerged, this time to praise his government's actions in Lebanon. This signalled the extent of Israel's colonial ambition. While the IDF was laying waste to Gaza, its support of the Zionist 'settlers' in the West Bank had increased. Israel was also pressing its interests on its northern border. Even occasional skirmishes with Lebanon allow Israel to promote the idea that it's defending against the threat of what it describes as Iran's proxy in Lebanon, Hezbollah. It was no coincidence that Sky News and US networks were the media outlets targeted by the presidential office for his media coverage. They are among the outlets where Israel knows most evil in the Middle East can be presented as originating in Tehran.

On the day of Trump's address, President Herzog was reduced to a diplomatic bystander. Protocol meant he was the first to greet Trump when he disembarked Air Force One at Ben Gurion Airport, but that was the extent of his involvement. In parliament, he sat for three hours, was hardly referenced or recognised, and passed much of his time on his phone, feigning interest in the proceedings. The only time he was referred to must have been excruciating. Trump turned to him and asked if now wasn't the moment to grant Netanyahu a pardon from the serious criminal charges he faced. 'I have an idea. Mr President, why don't you give him a pardon?' The president grinned awkwardly, then Ohana applauded madly and the government benches broke into a raucous ovation. Netanyahu, unfazed by references to his criminal indictments, stood up and acknowledged the chants of 'Bibi, Bibi'. Herzog offered a half smile, half grimace, as Trump continued, 'whether we like it or not, this has been one of the greatest wartime presidents … Cigars and champagne [a reference to the corruption charges], who the hell cares about that?'[39] Herzog knew there were many reasons to consider letting the court case proceed.

Opposition leader Yair Lapid's reaction to Trump's suggestion was also reserved. Lapid leads the Yesh Atid party, which has twenty-four seats in the Knesset (Likud has thirty-two). Given his centrist position, it was reasonable to expect that he would distance his views from Netanyahu's. It was Israel's day, however, so there was to be a broad consensus on how events since October 2023 were to be profiled globally. In his speech, the only point of real difference to his political opponents came early on: 'We believe in the principles laid in our Declaration of Independence, which says, "Israel will ensure complete equality of social and political rights to all its inhabitants, irrespective of religion, race, or sex. It will guarantee freedom of religion, conscience, language, education, and culture. It will safeguard the holy places for all religions." Those are our values. That is who we are as people, as a country.'[40] Yet Israel legislates outside those ideals. It is an apartheid state that, across a wide matrix, discriminates against the 20 per cent of its citizens who are Arab. While most of Lapid's speech was well received, his emphasis on equality was met with silence on the government benches.

Otherwise, he was in lock-step with the government that he opposes. They loved it when he said the world needed to understand that Israel was 'here to stay'. There was a clear appeal to the Judeo-Christian world. 'Our story did not end in the Bible. It began there. It continues in our laboratories and universities, in our innovation hubs. Hamas, Hezbollah, Iran, and the Houthis all read the wrong intelligence reports. The real intelligence report on Israel's intentions is found in the Book of Genesis. "And I will give you, and your descendants after you, the land of Canaan [the Promised Land], for an everlasting possession".'[41] Israel's assertion that the land of Palestine is their birthright is a constant; a fundamental across its political canvas.

Lapid's most significant intervention was on the genocide. Over the three hours of speeches, he alone used the word but did so only to rubbish the idea. 'You were misled. There was no genocide. There was no deliberate starvation. The truth is there was an army and a country fighting in the most complicated conditions imaginable against terrorists who send their own children to die for follow-up, who used their own children as human shields. The truth is that a democratic state was attacked by a fanatical terrorist organization. 1,200 people were killed in one day. Women were raped, babies were burned alive, and all that, on all the while they played with your minds, selling you the absurd idea that supporting Islamic terror is somehow a liberal value.'[42]

Lapid is in opposition to a government that he knows has slaughtered many tens of thousands of innocent civilians, but in Israeli politics, as the victims are Palestinians, it is of no concern. Even to the opposition leader it is justified. What criticism there was focused on Netanyahu allowing Hamas to remain strong in Gaza. Across institutional Israel there were no more than the faintest whispers of discontent over Trump and Netanyahu's plan. Fear prevails. Shockingly, the passivity of the West when the Jewish people faced the threat of extermination in 1930s' and 1940s' Europe is being repeated as the Jewish state brutalises the Palestinians. Fear prevails again.

Lapid continued, 'There is good and evil in this world. When you stand with Hamas, you stand with evil. When you stand with Hezbollah, you stand with evil. When you stand with the Iranian regime, you stand with evil. When you stand with Israel, you stand on the side of justice ... Israel has endured two terrible years on the battlefield and in the international arena, but in those two years, we also rediscovered our own greatness. We remember how good we can be. Our pilots who took control of the skies over Iran, our industries leading the world in technology, our civil society, which reached out to help every victim of the war.'[43]

The mendacity of Israel's political elite does not rest with Netanyahu alone; he has no copyright over promoting its utterly false narrative to the world. Arguably the most disturbing revelation of the day was that Israel's parliamentary opposition saw no fault in the government's genocidal campaign against Palestinians. Lapid was as enthusiastic about the Trump plan as Netanyahu, as willing to follow the Trump rainbow to its end. His twenty-four seats gave him the political capital to hold the government to account, but he was not so inclined. There was no public pressure to do so. When it comes to pursuing the prime minister over potential fraud, he and his party would not be found wanting. Genocide, however, was another matter altogether, for him and for those he represented.

The words, the sentiment, of the opposition leader on the occasion of Donald Trump's address, were a clear indication that the great majority of the 120 members of Israel's parliament supported the government's actions in Palestine. Were Lapid's Yesh Atid party in government, it would adopt a similar approach to the annexation of Palestinian land and the forceful removal of its people. Concerning the genocide charge, if the parliamentary arithmetic reflected public opinion, Israel as a nation was dismissing it out of hand.

MUTUAL REGARD

Personal interest has always been central to the political decision-making of the two men at the heart of the day's activities. For Donald Trump, success in the Middle East would be a valuable notch on his imaginary belt of negotiated peace deals. Netanyahu, too, had reasons to pause the 'war' or pretend to. His criminal trials at home were due to resume, and a ceasefire would allow him time to consider his next moves and give the US space to ensure its continued alignment with Israel's interests.

Trump specialises in flattery – both receiving and giving. In presenting himself as a peacemaker, he extolled the virtues of Netanyahu, who was wanted for war crimes by the International Court of Justice (ICJ). It is one thing to excoriate that court as his predecessor Biden did, but it is another altogether to lavish praise on Netanyahu, as Trump did that morning. 'I want to express my gratitude to a man of exceptional courage and patriotism, whose partnership did so much to make this momentous day possible. You know who I'm talking about. There's only one Prime Minister Benjamin Netanyahu. Bibi, please stand up.'[44]

The Knesset, with two exceptions, rose to its parliamentary feet more than twenty times over the course of Trump's typically meandering, lengthy speech. It was reminiscent of how America's political elite had behaved on 25 July 2024, when, nine months into the genocide, Netanyahu had addressed the Joint Houses. The official slaughter toll in Gaza back then was almost 40,000. With senior public servants resigning from the State Department and US medics calling out the Biden administration's failures on Gaza, US legislators still gave Israel's prime minister endless ovations as he led his people in a genocide.

Fifteen months later, with the roles and locations reversed, the number of Palestinian dead had almost doubled by conservative estimates, yet the mood between the two leaders was one of celebration of an unbreakable partnership. On this day, in Israel's parliament, except for the 2,000 Israeli fatalities referenced by Netanyahu, more than half of them soldiers, there was no reference to the enormous human cost. It was about marking a 'victory', the triumph of one combatant over another, of the sanctity of Judaism over the evil of Islam. Israel's parliament was celebrating success on the battlefield against what it portrayed as its 'terrorist' opponent.

In doing so, Donald Trump talked up what Israel had done with aplomb. It was he who legitimised it, told its legislators that their country had won, as he touted his own plan for the future, one that would benefit those who conducted the genocide. While the Joint Session of Congress of 25 July 2024 will go down as one of the most shameful occasions in US politics, 13 October 2025 has to be the most offensive display of 'diplomacy' ever by a sitting US president.

Trump's speech was riddled with factual errors, outrageous boasts about his own political decision-making, wildly inappropriate personal references and misrepresentation of the events at issue. It also exposed the scale of the challenge facing Palestine and its people, given how deeply embedded the Zionist ambition is in the political fabric of the West. The US is the most culpable of the states that contributed directly and knowingly to the butchery of Palestinians in Gaza and the destruction of their place. Though its role – and that of its regular partner-in-crime in foreign excursions of self-interest, the UK – should be a matter of shame, history suggests neither will be overly concerned about the fate of tens of thousands of Palestinians.

Israel's success in wooing the institutional West to allow it to colonise Palestine over the last century or so is based on different elements. It is rooted, though, in the decision of Britain, a giant of colonialism, to grant its mandate territories in the Middle East to the Zionists in the 1917 Balfour Declaration. Guilt over the calamitous loss of 6 million Jewish lives in the Holocaust also contributes. Israel's regular military campaigns mean that for a small nation, it contributes disproportionately to the armaments industry of Western economies, never more so than over the course of this genocide. It has mastered how best to weave these different threads into a fabric so robust that, whether you're a Democrat or a Republican president in the US, a Conservative or Labour prime minister in the UK, or an EU Commission president, you find a reason to fall in line with Zionism.

IRAN

Israel has also established itself as a bulwark in the Middle East against the perceived threat of Islam, especially Iran. It has always promoted Iran as a dangerous, rogue nation against which Israel alone can protect the West. In the summer of 2025, when Benjamin Netanyahu's government briefly paused the brutal Gaza onslaught, it expertly fabricated a threat from Iran that led to twelve days of missile trading with Tehran. The US was willing to support Israel throughout, before choosing to intervene directly as much of the world looked on, terrified.

The levels of concern across the West at that time betrayed a general ignorance of the fact that Iran does not possess nuclear weapons (Israel does) and remains, based on independent assessors, years away from doing so. Western culture is so soaked in anti-Islam, anti-Iran commentary that the perception of Iran's nuclear capacity is at odds with reality. So is the notion that Iranians are somehow inclined towards starting a nuclear conflict, which would end their civilisation as it would ours. Iran's record on human rights, on the treatment of its own citizens, leaves it open to intense criticism and sanction by other nations.

This needs, however, to be accurate and on point. It should also be ignored when the criticism issues from Israel, a nation whose shocking record on human rights and on international law should disallow it from commenting on the record of others.

Creating a narrative of Iran as a nuclear threat, as Israel does with much of the West following, devalues other criticism which is warranted. When Israel persecutes its neighbours, steals their land and oppresses them to the point of genocide, it renders its views on other states worthless. When the West has stayed silent on Israel's abuse of human rights and incarceration without trial of thousands of Palestinians, its consistent determination to condemn Iran should be viewed with suspicion.

The West's major military powers trip over each other in their rush to back Israel against Iran; even those suspicious of it are cowed by this presumed threat and grateful for Israel's apparent capacity to manage it. Israel's playbook of aggressive expansionism in Palestine and Lebanon has generally been peppered by skirmishes with the Islamic Republic. Over the course of those twelve days in June 2025, about 1,150 Iranians were killed. The toll included fourteen of its nuclear scientists and a handful of military generals; fewer than thirty Israelis were killed. Israel did not need to take action against Iran. It chose to do so to distract from its genocide in Gaza and send a message to the West that it alone was a reliable defence against the spread of Islam. With growing scrutiny over Gaza, Netanyahu knew creating alarm over Iran would dull criticism and provide renewed cause for those who supported Israel's right to take Palestine. Israel choreographed the events of summer 2025 towards that end.

The impact in Washington fulfilled Netanyahu's hopes. On 22 June, just over a week after Israel launched its attack on Iran, the US took direct action. Using B2 bombers and Tomahawk missiles, it struck nuclear sites at Isfahan, Natanz and Fordow, with immediate claims by the White House that the attacks were a spectacular success. It said the threat of Iran deploying nuclear weapons had been set back years. President Trump said its nuclear capacity had been 'obliterated'. He thanked Israel for being the first line of defence.

In his Knesset address, four months later, he was less presidential. 'With Operation Midnight Hammer – boy, that's a great name for that, what we did last June. The United States military flew seven of those beautiful B2 bombers. They looked so beautiful all of a sudden. They were always – I thought they were pretty planes. I had no idea they could do what they did. In fact, we just ordered 28 more of them … So we dropped 14 bombs on Iran's key nuclear facilities, totally, as I said originally, obliterating them. And that's been confirmed, and everybody understands it. Together, we stopped the number one state sponsor of terror from obtaining the world's most dangerous weapons. And if you think about it, if we didn't do that, and assuming we made the same deal that we have today, there'd be a dark cloud over this deal.'[45]

This is how the fable of Israel as the West's self-proclaimed defender-in-chief in the Middle East gets shaped. Israel's malevolence, its ethnocratic form of government, is shrouded in a cloak of fear about a culture the West neither knows nor wants to know. The West wants to believe that Islam's primary ambition is the destruction of the West. Iran is that threat in sovereign form.

Israel has been promoting this idea of Iran as a nuclear threat for decades. The regular imposition of sanctions on Iran over the last fifty years is, in some ways, a tribute to the world of Israeli intelligence and propaganda. None of this is to suggest that the Islamic Republic of Iran is not a supporter of states and agencies that threaten the US, but Israel has made a virtue of exaggerating the extent and immediacy of any threat. Israel's claimed special status as the bulwark against Islamism is critical to its relationship with the US and the West more generally. One story is illustrative.

The attacks on US soil by Islamist terrorists on 11 September 2001 killed 2,977 people. The immediate consequences were dire, but oddly enough, 9/11, as it became known, presented an opportunity for a fundamental change in the relationship between Iran and the West. In Iran, there were spontaneous demonstrations and marches of solidarity with the victims of the attacks in America. In a Tehran football stadium, 40,000 fans observed a minute's silence for the victims, two days after the attacks. While the public took to the streets in huge numbers, there was also an overwhelming pro-American political reaction. Two hundred and ten of the 290-member parliament signed a statement of condolence, which also condemned the attacks. Supreme Leader Ayatollah Ali Khamenei gave a sermon condemning the mass killing of human beings. He preached that such killings were catastrophic acts, whether they involved 'atomic bombs, long-range missiles, biological or chemical weapons, passenger or war planes'.[46]

President Khatami also condemned the attack and expressed sympathy with the families of the victims. Iran signalled to the US that it was ready to assist it in tracking down those responsible. Speaking at the United Nations (UN), Khatami said, '[T]he September 11 terrorist attacks in America can only be the job of a group that has voluntarily severed their own ears and tongues, so that the only language with which they could communicate would be destroying and spreading death.'[47] This was more than diplomatic niceties; the Islamic Republic of Iran wanted to assist the US and, in the process, change the prevailing narrative.

The US had no embassy in Iran, but the UK did. British Foreign Secretary Jack Straw went to Tehran, the first visit by a UK minister since the revolution of 1979, which had overthrown the Shah. Iran knew, as the West suspected, that the attacks originated in Afghanistan. Straw had direct meetings with President Khatami and Iran's foreign minister, Kamal Kharrazi. Iran shared valuable information and agreed to provide support operations for the US troops. The commitments Straw received gave George W. Bush the confidence to present the Taliban with an ultimatum and, when that was rejected, go to war in early October.

Later, after the US had established its military position of strength, discussions began about the future of Afghanistan. Iran and the US worked together to lead that process. Iran's role in the selection of a successor regime led to direct diplomatic collaboration with the US. At a UN Bonn Conference, the US worked closely with a coalition of India, Iran and Russia, and, within Afghanistan, the Northern Alliance insurgency on establishing a new administration. The Americans and Iranians agreed that Hamid Karzai was the best person to lead Afghanistan. It was a joint choice. As one journalist has pointed out, 'Washington was fond of characterizing the Iranian regime as a fundamentalist theocracy. The truth was more complex. Iran wasn't Switzerland, but at that point it was more democratic than Egypt and less fundamentalist than Saudi Arabia, two of the United States' most important allies in the region … Even the supreme leader, the successor to Ayatollah Ruhollah Musavi Khomeini, had been chosen, formally at least, by a council of popularly elected clerics.'[48]

Jack Straw is an interesting witness to these events and to how real opportunities to build relationships between the US-led West and Iran were lost through deep-seated bias. His fascinating book, *The English Job: Understanding Iran and Why it Distrusts Britain*, offers insights into the complexities of Britain's relationship with Iran and how the West is so hopelessly compromised in its dealings with that country. The shared view of the Taliban meant that, for a moment, standard animosity was put aside and it was a time when alliances could have been deepened. The evidence shows it was the US that failed to imagine such a change.

One party which could be genuinely threatened by any profound improvement of engagement with Iran was Israel. It had watched events with a growing sense of alarm and wielded its substantial influence in the US to cool enthusiasm for improved relations with Iran. Any threat of strengthening Iranian and US relations, beyond the one-off event in Afghanistan, had to be stopped. When Israel intercepted an Iranian ship carrying weapons for the Palestinian Authority, it pressurised the Bush administration to sever relations.

The 2002 State of the Union Address started that process. Just four months after 9/11 and the close cooperation with Iran that allowed him to proceed with confidence in Afghanistan, Bush described Iran as part of an 'axis of evil', alongside North Korea and Iraq.[49] This was the arrogance America has often displayed when it feels invincible. That sense of indestructibility had been hit by 9/11, but its speedy response in Afghanistan had corrected any sense of vulnerability. Iran had been of critical assistance in making that possible and had hinted at wanting a changed relationship.

Iran's religion and its nuclear programme provided Israel with the opportunity to reinforce its narrative of Iran as a threat and to present itself as uniquely positioned to protect Western interests in the Middle East. The 'axis of evil' term provided Israel with the perfect headline on which to base its rhetoric about how great a danger Iran posed. In the context of the previous few months, in the knowledge that it could not have disabled the Taliban regime without the support of Iran and of its political and religious leadership, it was a betrayal for Bush to have used that term.

The 'axis of evil' speech, as it became known, had very serious consequences; not least, it completely undermined the real progress made in US–Iran relations. President Khatami and his supporters, who had worked so closely with their White House counterparts for months, reacted with disbelief. But it wasn't just Israel that had been concerned by the two nations cooperating as they had; Iranian hardliners were also unhappy to see government ministers and officials working so closely with their American counterparts and they rejoiced in being proved correct about America.

In time, when the extent of Iran's assistance had become widely recognised, commentators returned to this speech and questioned how Iran could have been grouped with Iraq and North Korea. The Bush side suggested it had been 'overdramatised',[50] and went on to explain it away, saying the 'axis of evil' term had found its way into the final draft without the president realising its import. This does not stand up. The 'State of the Union' is a set-piece of US politics that even absent a recent crisis like

9/11 gets very significant attention. The idea that with tensions as high as they were, the president's speech would not have been subject to the most rigorous attention is hard to believe. Even if that term was removed, the rest of the speech made no effort to change the perception of a nation that had provided the US with critical support at one of the most challenging moments in contemporary American history. It seems more credible that those whose interests most needed Iran and the US to remain sworn enemies ensured that the speech would reinforce the view of Iran as evil in the American psyche. It's a status that it has retained ever since. Israel has long been the main beneficiary.

Even in his first term, President Trump had played an Iran-as-global-threat card for Israel. In 2018, he withdrew the US from Barack Obama's Iran nuclear deal of 2015, refusing to renegotiate it as he'd promised. Iran's commitment to the deal had been independently vetted by the International Atomic Energy Agency (IAEA), which found that it had committed no violations, apart from 'minor infractions' that the Iranians had been happy to address. Trump's move, motivated by his hatred of Obama, endangered the world but suited Israel's ongoing need to position Iran as the nuclear shadow in the region.

Iran is Israel's fall guy. Trump's Knesset address reinforced the idea of Israel as the West's buffer against Iran and its alleged proxies: 'This is now a very exciting time for Israel, and for the entire Middle East … the forces of chaos, terror, and ruin that have plagued the region for decades now stand weakened, isolated and totally defeated. A new coalition of proud and responsible nations is emerging. And because of us, the enemies of all civilization are in retreat. Thanks to the bravery and incredible skill of the Israeli Defense Forces and Operation Rising Lion.

You know, [pointing to IDF Chief of Staff Eyal Zamir] the guy's central casting. Let's put him in a movie. Look at him. Great job. And my people loved working with you. Loved it. They worked so well together.'[51]

Trump greatly overstretched the need for the action that Israel and the US took, suggesting, as Netanyahu had, that those few days of military action had staved off Armageddon. 'This was our last shot. They looked at it for 22 years. This was our last shot ... We took a big cloud off of the Middle East and off of Israel. And it was my honor to help.'[52] That he ordered the US Air Force into direct action against Iran in June 2025 represented the clearest evidence of how, under his leadership, the US would be an even more powerful ally of Benjamin Netanyahu than the hapless, self-proclaimed Zionist Joe Biden. Netanyahu knew it signalled how, with the right circumstances and in the right moment, this vain, utterly erratic US president could be encouraged to take bolder action.

In *Catastrophe: Nakba II*, I said Israel would, as it always has, 'play the Iran card'. It did, in summer 2025. The US followed. In early 2026, as the genocide continued in Gaza, and the destruction of Palestinian life in the West Bank reached unprecedented levels, Israel's war criminal prime minister played the next hand masterfully. The US, with neither cause nor congressional approval joined Israel in declaring war on Iran.

BOASTFUL RHETORIC

With Trump, it's rare for him to speak for more than a couple of minutes without centring attention on himself. The day's main event, the return of Israeli hostages, allowed him to return to his favourite subject and his favourite word, 'I'. 'The hostages are back. The hostages are back. It is a good feeling. Isn't that nice to say? You know, I just said the hostages – first time I said the hostages are back. It sounds, it feels, so good to say it. But when you settle eight wars in eight months, that means you don't like war. Everyone thought I was gonna be brutal ... No, and my personality actually is all about stopping wars, and it seems to work. It seems to work.'[53]

The world was becoming accustomed to Trump's frequent references to his unique ability to resolve conflicts. So much of his approach is drenched in machismo; a great deal of his behaviour is that of the schoolyard bully. These features sculpt his distinctive approach to securing anything, including peace. It was important for him to remind the Knesset that peace is achievable only through strength. It's a mantra that he knew his host, Netanyahu, shared. The Knesset speech allowed Trump to reinforce this point, in the process leaving no doubt that, more than any of Israel's partners, it was the US that had enabled genocide: 'We make the best weapons in the world, and we've got a lot of them. And we've given a lot to Israel, frankly. And I mean, Bibi would call me so many times, "Can you get me this weapon, that weapon, that weapon?" Some of them I never heard of, Bibi, and I made them. But we'd get them here, wouldn't we, huh? And they are the best. They are the best ... But you used them well. It also takes people that know how to use them, and you obviously used them very well. But so many that Israel became strong and powerful, which, ultimately, led to peace. That's what led to peace.'[54]

To so openly provide the International Criminal Court

(ICC) with evidence of US sponsorship of Israel's genocide was remarkable. Joe Biden and his secretary of state, Anthony Blinken, had placed America firmly on the side of Israel from the outset. They were equally contemptuous of international law, but they didn't brag about it; their pronouncements were few and were generally made using political language. There could be no compromise on Israel, and moves to end its campaign had to be armour-plated against the risk of being seen to abandon the cause of the Zionist lobby in the US. For Trump, this meant reiterating the justness of Israel's case. It was important to remind the Knesset that the 'war', as it erroneously became known, was not of Israel's making: 'So, as we celebrate today, let us remember how this nightmare of depravity and death all began. Two years ago, on the eve of the Simchat Torah holiday, thousands of innocent Israeli civilians were attacked by terrorists in one of the most evil and heinous desecrations of innocent life the world has ever seen; the worst slaughter of Jews since the Holocaust. The cruelty of October 7th struck to the core of humanity itself. Nobody could believe what they were witnessing. The United States of America grieved alongside you, and we mourn for our own citizens who were so viciously taken that day. And to all the families whose lives were forever changed by the atrocities of that day, and all of the people of Israel, please know that America joins you in those two everlasting vows, "Never forget, and never again."'[55]

Condemnation related exclusively to the actions of Hamas on one day in October 2023. There was not a word of concern about the actions of Israel over the 735 days since. The US, under two different presidents, representing its two political parties, had been suckered into support of Israel despite the overwhelming evidence of its malfeasance. Trump dispensed with even the appearance of diplomatic norms in previewing his proposed 'ceasefire plan' at the parliament of the aggressor, the oppressor in the crisis that he likes to claim he 'fixed'. It was a shamelessly arrogant display of political brawn over intellect and of money over morals. On the question of sponsoring a genocide, his boastful rhetoric spoke volumes.

In choosing to preface the events in Sharm el-Sheikh with a visit to Jerusalem and an address to the Israeli parliament, the US president was making a statement. The gathering in Egypt would mark the official signing of the agreement, but there was to be no misunderstanding: its terms would benefit Israel. Trump's administration was doing what every US president who claimed to have established a basis for peace has done: determining the shape of the proposed 'fresh start' exclusively through the Israeli lens. It bears repeating that 'Gaza will be a deradicalized terror-free zone that does not pose a threat to its neighbors' is the first clause of Trump's agreement.[56] Over the course of his address, while the Palestinians were barely referenced, Israel's interests were promoted as paramount; its status as the great friend and ally of the US in the region was proudly proclaimed.

There was no equivocation on where the balance of interest lay in advancing the peace plan and in moulding a new beginning. Trump talked up the moment and the extraordinary potential of the region, but in doing so, laid the fault for the wasted decades on the Palestinians and their supporters: 'It should now be clear to everyone throughout the region that decades of fomenting terrorism and extremism, Jihadism and anti-Semitism have not worked. They haven't worked. They've been a disaster. They've just killed. They've killed. They've backfired completely and totally. They've just totally backfired. Everything that you thought, take it worst case, it's turned out to be worse than that. They have not worked.'[57] Even allowing for the apparent limitations of his competence, a disinterest in history and the strength of Israel's grip on the US body politic, Trump's profile of the 'decades of fomenting terrorism' was a gross distortion. It was also potentially inflammatory.

Other US presidents have said stupid things about Israel and betrayed the depth of their alliance with Zionism. Some have had senior officials misrepresent the truth to protect the special relationship between the two countries. In the summer of 2024, Anthony Blinken did not share information provided to him showing how Israel was inducing famine conditions in Gaza. It was a serious failure, but right back through every administration since the state of Israel was formed, and certainly since the emergence of the big pro-Israel lobby groups in the US in the 1960s, Palestine's cause has been ignored. Still, it's hard not to consider Donald Trump's speech to the Knesset on 13 October 2025 as the nadir.

'I said, "This piece of land [Gaza] is very small. It's unbelievable what you do with that tiny ..." You look at a map, even, of just not the world, the Middle East, and you have this little dot. And think of what you've done, it's incredible. It's incredible. But the world is loving Israel again ... the world wanted peace, and Israel wanted peace. Everybody did. Everybody did. And what a victory it's been, right? ... The timing of this is brilliant. And I said, "Bibi, you're gonna be remembered for this far more than if you kept this thing going, going, going, kill, kill, kill. It would ... not be the same." And I just want to congratulate you for having the courage to say, "That's it. We've won and now let's enjoy our lives, and let's rebuild Israel, and make it stronger, and bigger and better than it's ever been before. We're gonna do that." Took a lot of guts.'[58]

What were Palestinian minds to think of a US president describing their near annihilation as a great victory for the country that has oppressed them for decades and wants to eradicate them? What were Palestinian hearts to do but drop in despondency at the callousness of a man who leads one of the most powerful nations on earth congratulating the prime minister of their oppressor on a 'victory'? What were young Palestinians to make of a US president standing shoulder to shoulder with a political leader indicted for war crimes and telling him he had won? What were Hamas fighters to do when the self-proclaimed leader of the free world said that Israelis should enjoy themselves and become stronger and better than ever? Peace through strength indeed. When one side has all the strength, any peace can only be one-sided.

TO THE VICTORS GO THE SPOILS

Proceedings in the Knesset on 13 October 2025 showed there was only one winner from the violence of the previous two years. It was not the people whose rebel army had, on one day, in one place, struck out at the colonial power. The winner was the colonial power that had engaged in a savagely brutal genocide in response. Settler-colonial Israel, with the support of its monied sponsors and the supine extras in the cast of Western nations, had 'won'. The US president, who, with his predecessor, Joe Biden, had led the West's sponsorship of the genocide, said so. Not only that, but he said it in exactly those terms, in Israel's parliament, and went further, congratulating Israel for what it had done.

President Trump was, in fact, so full of love for his hosts that he encouraged them to enjoy themselves and to rebuild Israel! As Israel was untouched, having barely endured a scrape as it pounded Gaza, his reference to 'rebuilding' could only have meant expanding its territory. The president of the US appeared to be giving Israel the right to rebuild Gaza, to which it has no entitlement, as part of building outwards the state of Israel. He was greenlighting the ultimate Zionist ambition. This led to the other essential strand of his address: how to rebuild Gaza in a way that would generate an economic windfall for all, bar one, of the participants.

Money or, to sanitise it, commerce, was always going to be a big factor in any deal. Trump, who always wants to make a buck, knew that in Netanyahu he had an Israeli leader enamoured of money too. While some of his Cabinet were genuine Zionists, the economics of any peace would mean more to Netanyahu than ideological considerations. For him and Trump, realising a peace dividend meant something different to the norm.

Among those waiting in Egypt were the other parties to Trump's plan. The president appeared determined that there could be no misunderstanding about why: 'I have many Arab countries, very wealthy countries that came up and said, "We'll put up tremendous amounts of money to rebuild Gaza." And I think that's going to happen. The power, they want dignity. They want to come forward, and they want to say, and I wanna say who they are because, uh, what they're doing is going to be, I think, something that you're gonna be very impressed with, Bibi.'[59]

Monied Arabs could be spoken of warmly in the Knesset but

not those whom some Israeli government ministers describe as the 'subhuman' Palestinians. The countries Trump was speaking of were keen to work on the redevelopment of Gaza. They were the kind of Arabs who would gift a US president a jumbo jet but would also help an Israeli prime minister. With the backdrop of a genocide that had killed tens of thousands, displaced millions and wilfully destroyed the land and infrastructure of the people whose land it is, Trump had a simple message for Israel: 'You've won, and now you can build, and you can do things that you never even thought possible.'[60] Nowhere were the Palestinians referenced.

It was exactly the kind of sentiment that prevailed after the First World War. The idea of winners and losers contributed to changes in Europe and decisions that generated such resentment that the conditions emerged which allowed the Holocaust. Yet this was Trump's way of building peace. It should have been no great surprise. He is known to have a low tolerance of 'losers', so it was a case of to the victor go the spoils. Donald Trump did not doubt what lay ahead for the victorious Israelis: 'When you put that genius into doing something else … It's gonna be a miracle. The miracle in the desert. It's gonna be amazing.'[61]

Even those who, against all the evidence, wanted to believe the US would find a way to correct things could only have shuddered. Those eternal optimists must have been shocked at the moves being made to reward Israel. The renowned American commentator, Norman Finkelstein, a Jew, had a typically blunt take on it: 'Israel just devoted two years plus to turning Gaza into a parking lot. Can anybody in his or her right mind believe that suddenly they're going to start chanting "Om", give peace a chance, singing "Kumbaya", linking arms and rebuilding Gaza, with those people, with the people of Gaza? It was just so stupid how anyone could possibly believe these things.'[62]

Monday, 13 October 2025 was when a US president told Israel that it could proceed to 'enjoy' the benefits of the 'war' that it had just 'won'. It was the moment when two men devoid of principle or conscience wallowed in the prospect of transforming the wasteland their countries had made of the Gaza Strip into a global idyll. It would become a place where fortunes would be made and people would travel to and never know or be bothered by its past.

America's Democratic Party also stands accused. The complete absence of moral leadership on Israel by Biden, Kamala Harris and Blinken provided Netanyahu with the opportunity to commence the planned obliteration of Palestine. Furthermore, it left Donald Trump to inherit a Washington that allowed him to proceed as he wished on Israel, knowing the Democrats could hardly criticise him. These were the ideal circumstances in which to construct something that appeared new and refreshing, but which would reward Israel. If, in the process, other allies of Trump were to benefit as well, so much the better.

The abandonment of a moral compass on Palestine is what has long been expected of American presidents. Trump just takes it to excess. He saw beyond his constitutional responsibilities; there were potential riches for America and other sovereign nations through the parties he was bringing to the table. This would also appeal to his pal, Bibi. For Trump, the real value of the deal lay not just in the glory of pulling it off, but in adding to his imagined long list of peace deals already secured as president. What he could foresee through his deeply compromised Arab friends were personal benefits beyond his term in office.

Seven Arab countries were referenced in Trump's imagined new Middle East. Palestine wasn't one of them. 'From the very first day that modern Israel was founded, we have stood together through thick and thin, setbacks and through victory and defeat, through glory and heartache. We have built industries together, we have made discoveries together, we have confronted evil together, and we have waged war together. And perhaps most beautifully of all, we have made peace together. And this week, against all odds, we have done the impossible and brought our hostages home. So now we're going to forge a future that is worthy of our heritage. We're going to build a legacy that all the people of this region can be proud of. New bonds of friendship, cooperation, and commerce will join Tel Aviv to Dubai, Haifa to Beirut, Jerusalem to Damascus, and from Israel to Egypt, from Saudi Arabia to Qatar, from India to Pakistan, from Indonesia to Iraq, from Syria to Bahrain, Turkey to Jordan, the United Arab Emirates to Oman and Armenia to Azerbaijan, another war that I just settled.'[63]

The idea of an economically strong region with Arab nations working with Israel to create prosperity was not at all alien to the Netanyahu cabal. The proviso, as it always has been, is that this cannot include Palestinians. The Zionists believe they have no place in any regeneration of the land because all of the land belongs to what they term 'Greater Israel'.

The 'commerce' piece was where the real victory lay. 'We are going to have hope, harmony, opportunity, and happiness here in the spiritual and geographic center of the entire world. That's what you are. Israel, America, and all of the nations of the Middle East will soon be safer, stronger, greater and more prosperous than ever before. And I want to thank you all once again for this exceptional honor … And I love Israel. I'm with you all the way. You'll be bigger, better, stronger, and more loving than ever before.'[64]

President Trump was giddy with excitement at what could be done with Gaza now that Israel had secured its 'victory'. This was perhaps the greatest real estate play he'd seen, and with allies in the petrostates of the Gulf, he saw only good times ahead for Israel and the region. So, just after the second anniversary of the start of a genocide, the holder of the West's most powerful political office had his ego stroked by Zionist leaders intent on obliterating the people of Palestine and any vestige of their culture and heritage.

Amongst the debris and, as yet, unaccounted for human remains lay mosques, museums, art galleries, cemeteries – all the features of the rich civilisation which is of that place. Millions of tonnes of rubble could be cleared, new homes and infrastructure could be built, but the people whose land it is, the people whose rebel army fought Israel, as generations before them had done, were not to be a factor. Trump said their suffering was their own fault and had resulted from a Palestinian fixation on trying to 'finish' Israel, something he described, without a hint of irony, as a 'bitter hatred'. It had, he said, not weakened Israel but stirred it to annihilate Hamas and its followers. The US was, he proclaimed, proud to have helped!

Israel's government and opposition benches were as one on the need for the complete removal of the people of Palestine. The majority of Jewish Israelis believe there are no innocents in Palestine. Norman Finkelstein concludes that this indicates the most accurate description of Israel is as a Jewish supremacist state. '[T]he aspect that most manifests its Jewish supremacist character is the worthlessness it attaches to Palestinian life.'[65] Brutal as his conclusions are, there's no disputing their truth. The humiliation of Palestinians for decades has needed the support of the majority of Israel's Jewish citizens. Some in the West like to think Israel's brutality is solely the fault of Benjamin Netanyahu. It is not. As reflected in the composition of its parliament and in the view of the majority of its citizens over the course of the genocide, the people of Israel support the actions of the state. Israeli society, never liberal or outward-looking, has become increasingly conservative and racist in the twenty-first century.

◆◆◆

It was 3.35 p.m. when the presidential motorcade left the Knesset and retraced its steps to Ben Gurion Airport. Within half an hour, the huddle of Air Force One's early morning arrival was replayed on the airport tarmac. The last embrace and word were with Benjamin Netanyahu, who had one more reason to be thankful to Donald Trump. President to president, he'd publicly asked for Israel's prime minister to be granted a pardon for his alleged crimes.

The airport is named after David Ben-Gurion, Israel's first prime minister, who was the first to sign Israel's Declaration of Independence, which he helped compose. Ben-Gurion was unrelenting in his pursuit of the expansionist ideal of Greater Israel and unafraid of declaring its implications: 'Let us not ignore the truth among ourselves ... politically we are the aggressors, and they [Palestinians] defend themselves ... The country is theirs, because they inhabit it, whereas we want to come here and settle down, and in their view we want to take away from them their country.'[66] A year earlier, in a letter to his son, Ben-Gurion addressed the implications of realising the Zionist dream: 'We must expel Arabs and take their place. Up to now, all our aspirations have been based on an assumption – one that has been vindicated throughout our activities in the country – that there is enough room in the land for the Arabs and ourselves. But if we are compelled to use force – not in order to dispossess the Arabs of the Negev or Transjordan, but in order to guarantee our right to settle there – our force will enable us to do so.'[67]

History may not interest this US president, but the undeniable colonial ambition of Zionism is known to many who have shaped US Middle East policy for decades. None of this had any bearing on events in Jerusalem on 13 October 2025. The Knesset, with a handful of exceptions, enthusiastically received Trump's peace proposal. The US–Israel alliance was intact. Visiting Israel had been prioritised ahead of attending a gathering of world leaders because this US president knew his political welfare depended on it. Delivering for Israel was very important to the evangelical-supported Zionist movement in the US. The agreement, limited as it was, had been hopelessly compromised.

With protocols completed on the tarmac just after 4 p.m., President Trump boarded the aircraft, and by 4.13 p.m. the White House press pool reported 'wheels up'. Next stop Sharm el-Sheikh.

'My life is ruined. I'd rather die here than move south. Even if we could afford it, my wife couldn't survive in a tent with no basic conditions and a newborn baby who is underweight. When we left home, we took nothing, only clothes. I knew it was the last time. I said goodbye to our house and our neighborhood. Being displaced feels like my soul has left my body ... We are now displaced, without hope, under bombardment and destruction. There is no safe place or humanitarian zone in the Gaza Strip. Every place is attacked.'

Ahmad Miqdad
(11 September 2025)

TWO

ALL THE WORLD IS ISRAEL'S STAGE

THE PAST

Colonialism is such a feature of the West's history that facilitating the establishment of the state of Israel was not problematic. At the time, Gaza and the West Bank were recognised as being under Egyptian and Jordanian control respectively. The founders of the new Jewish state, established in 1948, had other ideas, but they waited twenty years before fully pursuing their real colonial ambition. After the 1967 Six-Day War, Israel occupied Syria's Golan Heights, and took the West Bank and East Jerusalem from Jordan. It seized the Sinai Peninsula and the Gaza Strip from Egypt.

Arab states had, until then, ignored the claims of the Palestinians, whose land was now either effectively lost (the state of Israel) or occupied by Israel in contravention of international law (the remainder). Estimates of the loss of life in the Six-Day

War are between 750 and 1,000 Israelis and 12,000 to 18,000 Arabs (Syria, Jordan, Egypt), a marked disparity that's been a consistent feature of every period of armed conflict involving Israel since. The West's military support of Israel has provided it with the firepower to enable it always to behave as the schoolyard bully, something it does with aplomb.

This has never been so marked as during the genocide that commenced in October 2023; nor has it ever previously happened at the same time as anything like the Russia–Ukraine conflict. The contrast in how the West has approached the two situations is marked. Support for Israeli aggression against Palestine, while being hand-in-glove with Ukraine in combating the aggression of Russia, is stark. However, some see such comparisons as erroneous, with geopolitics making the case straightforward: 'Ukraine is seen through the lens of Cold War-era containment, while Israel is viewed as a vital ally in a volatile region.'[1]

Some who believe the West has a monopoly on justice argue that Israel is fighting forces of evil. This is a lie. Israel has been illegally occupying Palestine since at least 1967, and, in parallel with Russia in Crimea, it has rejected all interventions by the UN and other parties seeking its withdrawal. The land Israel targeted with such menace throughout 2024 and 2025 is not its land. Under international conventions and international law, it is the land of Palestine.

Trump is a president with an aversion to the written word and too much detail in oral briefings. One biographer said of him, 'Donald Trump doesn't read anything, and let me accent that – anything. Nothing … then there's the second hurdle – that not only does he not read; he doesn't listen. So it becomes from

Day 1, the crisis of the presidency: You can't tell him anything.'[2] Trump himself said in one interview: 'I like bullets [bullet points] or I like as little as possible. I don't need, you know, 200-page reports on something that can be handled on a page.'[3] There was little hope that the long and well-documented history of Palestine's abuse by both Israel and its Western sponsors would permeate the closed mindset of America's two-time president.

Israel's unrelenting bombardment of Palestine slaughtered many tens of thousands of civilians, using arms supplied by the same Western nations that chose to support Ukraine's fight against colonial Russia. Israel is the invader, not the invaded. Israel is the occupier, not the occupied, and Israel is the oppressor, not the oppressed. The denial of support of Palestine, for the protection of its people and its territory from the illegal occupation and genocide of Israel, is racist. The West's support of Ukraine against Russian aggression highlights this, but it has been in evidence for decades. America's forty-seventh president has added a different layer to the discrimination. While he could never bring himself to relate to the people of Palestine, there was a different Arab cohort who presented him with no such challenge – those who could gift him a Boeing 747 or provide capital to his son-in-law's business.

SHARM-EL-SHEIKH

Within a couple of hours of leaving the Knesset, the Trump entourage arrived at the Sharm el-Sheikh Conference Centre for the official unveiling of his twenty-point plan. The flight from Jerusalem took about an hour, and once in Egyptian airspace,

Air Force One was greeted by an escort of six American-made F-6 military aircraft. Three planes on each side guided the president's flight along the Nile before it landed in Egypt near the southernmost point of the Sinai Peninsula.

Sharm el-Sheikh is a major tourist destination that has twice been occupied by Israel – once in 1956 and, again, from the time of the Six-Day War until the peninsula was returned to Egypt under the Camp David Accords of 1978. In September 1999, it had hosted the signing of the Sharm el-Sheikh Memorandum on the return of Gaza and 41 per cent of the West Bank to 'limited self-rule'. That agreement, which met the deadline for Israel and Palestine to enter permanent-status negotiations under the Oslo Accords, was signed by Palestine Liberation Organization President Yasser Arafat and Israeli Prime Minister Ehud Barak.

In 1995, with Israel under more moderate leadership, Oslo II had been signed, which proved to be a death sentence for its then prime minister, Yitzhak Rabin; a Zionist assassinated him for his efforts. Rabin was succeeded by Benjamin Netanyahu, who showed no inclination to implement Rabin's plan. By the time he was replaced by Labor Party leader Ehud Barak in 1999, there was little optimism that the original intent of the Oslo Accords could be realised. The Sharm el-Sheikh Memorandum of that autumn, signed by Barak and Arafat, referenced that a 'permanent agreement on final status issues' was to be reached within twelve months.[4] Instead, it only marked the end of a lengthy and unsuccessful Oslo process.

That catalogue of missteps would not have bothered Trump, but the absence of a representative of Israel on this occasion should have done. Mahmoud Abbas, leader of the increasingly marginalised Palestine Authority, was there, although he was barely referenced as Arab leaders from the region were feted. Netanyahu reportedly declined an invitation due to the Jewish holiday of Simchat Torah, though it was also understood that some Arab nations had objected to his attendance. Understanding what happened is important in appreciating the interdependence between the US and Israel. The official, real-time press pool reports were revelatory:

Sent:	**Reports:**
October 13, 2025 *12:26 IDT*	**WH Travel Pool Note #8: Bibi to Egypt** As we await POTUS 'speech' at the Knesset, your pooler can confirm on background from a WH official and an Israeli official that Netanyahu is now going to Egypt. From WH official: POTUS brokered the call with Egypt, and Netanyahu was invited to Egypt.
October 13, 2025 *13:43 IDT*	**WH Travel Note #15: Bibi NOT going to Egypt** Your pooler has received an update from the Prime Minister's office indicating he will NOT be going to Egypt, despite the invitation.

	STATEMENT FROM PM OFFICE: Prime Minister Netanyahu has been invited by US President Trump to participate in a conference to be held today in Egypt. The Prime Minister thanked President Trump for the invitation but said he would not be able to attend due to the proximity of the holiday. The Prime Minister thanked President Trump for his efforts to expand the circle of peace, peace based on strength.
October 13, 2025 *14:20 IDT*	**WH Travel Pool Note #17: CORRECTION** CORRECTION: The White House ONLY confirmed that Netanyahu was INVITED to Egypt, not that he was attending. Apologies for the confusion.[5]

Over the course of two hours the messaging changed. The press corps was first told that Israel's prime minister was going to be at the official signing at the request of Donald Trump. This was confirmed by both White House and Israeli officials, who also stated that the agreement had been 'brokered' by the president. Ninety minutes later, the account was updated to state that the Jewish holiday prevented Netanyahu from travelling. A subsequent clarification, a further forty minutes later, indicated that the US had never said he would attend, only that he was invited. The truth was that he was going to be there until Turkish President Recep Erdoğan objected. As Turkey, Egypt, Qatar and the US were the four nations signing the agreement, and as its government maintains ties with Hamas, Erdoğan's view prevailed. It precluded Netanyahu from participating. The Jewish holiday was a convenient way for the Americans to lessen any risk of criticism from the Israeli/Zionist lobby when it became clear Netanyahu would not be there.

Trump's presidential motorcade had left Sharm el-Sheikh airport, until 1982 an Israeli Air Force base, within twenty minutes of Air Force One's arrival. The much longer-than-anticipated Knesset session left Trump and his team little time for formalities before the planned signing of the Trump plan. The leaders of many of America's main allies and some Arab states had been waiting at the conference centre for his arrival. Most were, as ever, eager to do his bidding.

The White House press pool log noted that Trump and President El-Sisi of Egypt took a photo together at 5.55 p.m., then answered some questions from the press. Trump talked up Egypt's importance, the vital role it had played in the negotiations, curiously referencing that El-Sisi had 'a lot of respect from Hamas'.[6] US Secretary of State Marco Rubio, who rarely misses an opportunity to praise Trump, said it was the most significant moment for peace in the Middle East in fifty years.

The first part of the official duties at Sharm el-Sheikh was the most important. It was the formal signing of the 462-word plan, carefully crafted by the US administration and, as its text clearly indicates, heavily influenced by the government of Israel. The twenty-point plan outlined the terms the Trump White House had referenced days earlier when the ceasefire was announced. It was prefaced by a declaration formally signed by Trump, El-Sisi, Erdoğan and the Emir of Qatar, Tamim Bin Hamad Al Thani.

The plan was heavy on grandiose but loose commitments, including:

- That 'both Palestinians and Israelis can prosper with their fundamental human rights protected, their security guaranteed, and their dignity upheld'
- A recognition of 'the deep historical and spiritual significance of this region to the faith communities' with roots there and an equal respect for them all, including Christianity, Islam and Judaism
- To address 'the conditions that enable extremism' by using 'education, opportunity, and mutual respect as foundations for lasting peace'
- To resolve 'disputes through diplomatic engagement and negotiation rather than through force or protracted conflict'
- To ensure the 'region is a place where all can pursue their aspirations in peace, security, and economic prosperity, regardless of race, faith, or ethnicity'
- That 'peace, security, and shared prosperity' would be 'grounded in the principles of mutual respect and shared destiny'

Following the necessary protocols for the four signatory nations to sign the agreement, a public event was held. Other key allies of the US stood, to varying degrees of attention, behind Trump and President El-Sisi. Following introductory remarks by the host, Trump was again centre stage and addressed everyone in attendance for half an hour. It was, he said, a momentous occasion marking an agreement that no one had thought it would be possible to achieve: 'Together, we've achieved what everybody said was impossible at long last. We have peace in the Middle East … We have achieved together in recent days a change that really is historic, and it's gonna be remembered forever … But the momentous breakthrough that we're here to celebrate tonight is more than the end of the war in Gaza. It's, with God's help, it'll be the new beginning for an entire beautiful Middle East. From this moment forward, we can build a region that's strong and stable, and prosperous, and united in rejecting the path of terror once and for all.'[7]

Occasions like this are understandably laced with optimism. Achieving peace in the Middle East has been the holy grail of American presidents for decades. To portray its significance as he saw it, Trump had to go into hyperbolic overdrive. In truth, were he even half right in his estimation of the agreement's significance, then it would be truly historic and, for him, career-defining. Over the history of Palestine–Israel, other less self-absorbed US presidents have thought the same, but few have been in such a rush to claim it as a completely new start for the Middle East. It neither represented that, nor was it, as the hundreds of Palestinian fatalities in the days, weeks and months ahead proved, as he claimed, the dawn of peace in the region.

LESS IS MORE

In 1998, when Ireland's Good Friday Agreement was signed, neither the British nor Irish governments hesitated to promote its importance and to project what it represented for the island of Ireland. The other 'parties' to the Agreement, involving the main protagonists in the decades-long conflict, voiced their belief that it represented the best way forward. The process in South Africa in the 1990s that brought an end to apartheid rule involved various milestones, each generally marked by cautiously optimistic language, without risking the overreach that could compromise progress towards a lasting outcome.

The Sharm el-Sheikh event overlooked that key dimension. Palestinian Authority President Mahmoud Abbas's attendance was diplomatic tokenism. The interests of Palestine were hardly acknowledged, even though Israel had, just hours earlier, already held its own Zionist-oriented event where the initiative's true purpose was on full display. Trump's plan started with the protection of Israel's interests, for the simple fact that its interests are those of the US.

Nelson Mandela often referenced how the West's concerns over apartheid were rooted in its own needs: 'It is a typical attitude of countries which really do not approach the problem of South Africa from the point of view of the liberation struggle in South Africa, [but] which approach these problems from the point of view of their own interest.'[8] Mandela had a keen understanding of the Western mindset; he knew its institutions' narrow perspectives were always centred on what was best for them. Although he had a particularly jaundiced view of the US, it might have surprised even him that some leaders openly placed their personal interests within the political framework of their policy initiatives.

In Sharm el-Sheikh, Trump thanked President El-Sisi for giving him Egypt's highest honour, the Order of the Nile. Only one other US president, Jimmy Carter, had received the pure gold collar. That was in 1979, after he helped negotiate a peace between Egypt and Israel. Carter, who had tried more than many world leaders to shift Israel's Zionist mindset, would have been horrified by the vulgarity with which Trump managed proceedings.

President Trump loves awards and craves public approbation. A teetotaller, praise is his fix of choice. Even performing formal duties as president, he'll find a way to reference someone's endorsement of him. With the world watching, he interrupted his own speech to ask Pakistan's prime minister, Shehbaz Sharif, to come forward to the microphone. 'Do you wanna say what you said to me the other day in the … Come, would you like to say what you said the other day? I think it's; it was so nice. Please.'[9]

This was, by the US president's own claims, the most momentous day in the Middle East for generations, but as he addressed all the leaders present, he called on only one of them to speak, someone not central to what was announced or to the process that might follow. Other leaders watched, unsure why Sharif had been asked to speak.

In Gaza, less than fifty kilometres away from the beauty and opulence of Sharm el-Sheikh, parents searched for the bodies of missing children, and children for those of their missing siblings or parents. But their plight was of no concern to this US president. Even Arab leaders present seemed reticent to address the humanitarian reality. The host, Egypt's president, Abdel Fattah El-Sisi, mixed sycophantic praise of Trump with a warning that only the creation of a Palestinian state could resolve the conflict.[10] The Emir of Qatar, Sheikh Tamim bin Hamad Al-Thani, said his focus was on 'supporting the Palestinian people and alleviating their suffering, particularly in the besieged Gaza

Strip.'[11] This was not Donald Trump's concern. No one was invited to address the conference on this most fundamental point. Trump chose instead to give a platform to Pakistan's prime minister. While tens of thousands of Gazans were still being denied aid by Israel, were foraging for food and water, their fate, their hurt, their cause was not what Trump wanted highlighted. People the world over, who had protested and demanded action, needed optimism, but America's president was uninterested in their expectations. In the moment when Jewish voices globally, who'd risked opprobrium and worse for standing with Palestine, wanted to hear words of empathy for its plight, they were to be denied. None of that concerned President Donald J. Trump.

Sharif was as peripheral a political figure to events as Pakistan had been to the agreement. But there was a reason why Trump had asked him to speak. It was evident from the start. After a few unctuous words where he promoted Trump as a leader who had worked 'tirelessly and relentlessly to make this world a place of peace and prosperity', he continued, 'I would like to nominate this great president for [the] Nobel Peace prize.' He spoke for almost five minutes, with no mention of Palestine or Israel. 'I genuinely feel that he is the most genuine and most wonderful candidate for [the] Peace Prize, because he has brought not only peace in South Asia, saved millions of people their lives, and today, here in Sharm el-Sheikh, achieving peace in Gaza, is saving millions of lives in the Middle East. Mr President, I would like to salute you for your exemplary leadership, visionary leadership. And I think that you're the man this world needed most at this point in time.'[12]

In thanking Sharif, Trump's vanity and shallowness were on full display. In his excitement America's president forgot himself and suggested he hadn't known what was going to be said. 'Wow, I didn't expect that ... That was really beautiful and beautifully delivered. Wow. Thank you very much.'[13] The praise Sharif had given Trump privately apparently only had value if the whole world knew of it.

Many US presidents have failed Palestine, but none have so blatantly placed their own personal needs ahead of addressing Israel's oppression of the region. It was impossible to observe Trump's performance and not conclude that the agreement that they were gathered to sign had a purpose other than ending Palestine's suffering. This president was its architect-in-chief; hopes for it were slim. Coming just hours after the Knesset, it was a reminder of how money, power and ego are Trump's – and Netanyahu's – primary motivators.

What followed was a tick-box exercise in which, with varying degrees of interest, the US president referenced the other leaders in attendance at Sharm el-Sheikh. Two of his favourite hardmen were there: Hungary's Viktor Orbán and Narendra Modi of India. In referencing another one of the right-wing cohort, Italy's prime minister, Georgia Meloni, Trump was Trump. 'Where is she? There she is. You don't mind being called beautiful, right? 'Cause you are. Thank you very much for coming. We appreciate it. She wanted to be here, and she's incredible, and they really respect her in Italy.'[14]

The Arab states were referenced, as were leaders of other, less critical, Western and Asian nations. The ever-marginalised Palestinians were placed among this bundle: 'Also with us is President Prabowo, a very incredible man of Indonesia. President, come on. Great job. President Abbas of the Palestinian Authority, see we have them all.'[15] Mahmoud Abbas, the only person in the room representing either party that was the subject of the agreement, was granted the shortest reference. The President of Indonesia was brought forward for a nod, but not the person who nominally represented Palestine.

Perhaps, as the US had refused even to consider recognising Palestine as a state, its absence throughout the process and the tokenism displayed in Egypt that day were not surprising. It's usually a basic premise of such matters that, as well as having a lot of the detail in place before making anything public, the different parties to the process are given equality in any public announcements. This was demonstrably not the case here. The emptiness of this particular process was reflected in both Israel's absence from the formalities and the attention paid to its Parliament and people earlier in the day. Sharm-el-Sheikh was a pageant, one reflecting how the president of the US didn't need Israel in attendance to leave no one in any doubt as to whose interests they were there to protect. It also reflected the paucity of the document that the four leaders had signed and the twenty-point plan that Trump believed had, magically, brought peace to the Middle East.

AN UNBREAKABLE BOND

The US has remained in thrall to Israel over the course of its genocide of Palestine. Its support did not waver over the two years, the first under the Democratic presidency of Joe Biden and the second under the Trump administration. The bond has been as strong as at any time since the 1970s. It supported Israel as it doubled down on its intention to realise the Zionist ambition of a Greater Israel that would include all of Palestine, (at least) some of Syria (it occupies the Golan and Mount Hermon) and parts of Lebanon. Over the first twenty-four months of the genocide, the US supplied Israel with almost $22 billion of military aid.[16] Since October 2023, America has been an active participant in Israel's genocide in Gaza. The Biden administration ignored reports from the State Department that Israel's conduct had the hallmarks of a genocide and that it was allowing famine conditions to take hold. Biden's team refused to accept reports by Médecins Sans Frontières (MSF) that the hospital infrastructure was being targeted. On the day Benjamin Netanyahu addressed Congress, Biden and Harris received the detailed testimony of an independent group of US medical professionals that Israel was killing and torturing Palestinian medics.[17] That too was ignored. President Trump's first year in office saw no change. That the US's decades-long commitment to Israel's colonial project now includes Democrat and Republican administrations sponsoring a genocide makes it hard to see the US brokering any equitable outcome. It is also difficult to see how one could be reached without its involvement.

Many Americans hold an exalted opinion of their nation's place in the world. There's an institutional belief, absent any evidence, that it represents a uniquely positive force in world affairs. Yet the West is not the powerful sphere of influence it once was; Europe and the US account for 13.2 per cent of the global population and economic shifts mean 'the global order has been steadily moving toward a "post-American World" or "post-Western World" for some time'.[18] The US still has the world's largest military, which clearly can lend weight to its role in 'conflict resolution', but even this capacity is compromised by its belief in its sovereign wisdom and its predilection for 'regime change'. America's economic interests are generally also a factor in its decision-making. US involvement in the Middle East is driven by the stranglehold of the Zionist lobby on its politics, the strong economic ties and Israel's strategic location. US self-interest demands that it support Israel, and the conduct of the Trump administration around the heavily choreographed 'ceasefire agreement' has served only to reinforce that conclusion.

Robert Fisk has addressed this more directly than most. In *Night of Power*, his last book before his death, he wrote: 'The craven genuflection of the American political elite toward Israel is as shameful as it is unworthy of a great nation. Strength and cowardice do not have to walk hand-in-hand, but that is the nature of the American–Israeli relationship. US foreign policy in the Middle East belongs to Israel to such an extent that American policy is now Israeli policy.'[19] Reflecting on his work just months before Trump announced his ceasefire agreement, Fisk's widow, Nelofer Pazira-Fisk, wrote about the positive role the US had played in Ireland's (Good Friday) peace agreement. 'But in the Israeli–Palestinian conflict, the United States, unfortunately, is an accomplice.'[20] That description goes well beyond what Pazira-Fisk correctly described as America working with Israel in suppressing voices of dissent.

Sharm el-Sheikh did see a change of emphasis from earlier in the day at the Knesset, though not towards the oppressed Palestinians. In Jerusalem, President Trump lavished praise on Israel and told Netanyahu to enjoy the moment because he had 'won'. Hours later, the plaudits were for the US. 'And it's gonna be a great tribute to really the United States. I mean, the United States has worked very hard in the Middle East. So it would be a tribute to us and to Jared [Kushner] and to Steve [Witkoff], and to all of the people, Marco [Rubio], all of the people that have worked so hard on that.'[21]

The US and money were Trump's focus in Sharm el-Sheikh. This was not a peace or ceasefire agreement to address wrongs. It wasn't about establishing a means by which parties responsible for human rights abuses or war crimes could be held accountable. The motivation wasn't to erase or even ease past trauma. This concerned how those involved in brokering and supporting the process could help ensure its sustainability and benefit from their efforts. There was to be no hiding what this was about, no subtlety. 'So I hope everybody's now joining up. Now we have no excuses. We don't have a Gaza, and we don't have Iran as an excuse. That was a good excuse.'[22]

It wasn't a mistake, a clumsy off-script remark. This stunning comment was scripted. 'We don't have a Gaza' meant that this ravaged place, home to two million Palestinians, would no longer be an obstacle to whatever scheme Trump and his allies would decide upon. His intentions were laid bare; the moment when any small hope that humanity was a fragment of his motivation evaporated. In history, there have been opaque peace agreements drafted to hide the real intentions. This one did not have that failing; there was no attempt to conceal that commerce was the plan's primary driver. President Trump wanted to assure the nations whose support he needed that, as the plan's originator, he could guarantee it would yield them a meaningful return. He said the participation of the four signatories to the agreement was on that basis, and that others could become involved if they chose to do so. Unsaid, it was safe to assume Israel would be a big part of the plan.

Trump's ignorance or indifference to facts has rarely been so manifest. That the land belonged to Palestine didn't matter to him, so neither should it to all those others who were getting involved. When he did, for the one and only time, refer to the Palestinians, it was to reassure them that peace would bring them a return to some form of normality. That did not mean the exploitation of their land would be for their direct benefit: 'for the people of Gaza, the focus now must be on restoring the basics of a good life'.[23] The idea of returning to how things were betrayed the US's disinterest in the plight of Palestinians. 'We don't have a Gaza' meant that the irritation it represented would no longer prevent real progress. The plan was to create a commercial bonanza for the US, its Gulf partners and, of course, Israel. The consolation for Gazans was a return to the basics of life.

In *Catastrophe: Nakba II*, I looked at what life was like for Palestinians on 6 October 2023, the day before the Hamas attack. Returning to life before the genocide would mean living in a place – your homeland – where the coloniser limited the supply of food and other critical supplies so that 80 per cent of you relied on humanitarian aid. It meant living where only 4 per cent of the groundwater was fit for human consumption. It would mean living in what is often described as the world's largest concentration camp, knowing that less than 5 per cent of you have permission to move in and out.[24] In the West Bank, Israel's methods were more subtle, but, from 2022, increasing numbers were being killed, and land was being settled (stolen) at a markedly increased rate.

The Trump administration's casualness about life for the Palestinians post any 'peace' should have registered alarm across the world. It did not. In July 2025, Israel's minister of defense, Israel Katz, had spoken about the creation of a 'humanitarian city' in Rafah in southern Gaza. Briefing Israeli reporters, he said the IDF would secure the area from a distance and that 600,000 Palestinians would be accommodated in the camp, with a plan to increase this to 2 million over time. Palestinians would be free to emigrate voluntarily, provided they accepted that they could not return.[25]

That plan never evolved, but that it was spoken of publicly showed that Israel will do whatever is necessary to expand its territory. This expansion requires either continued attrition and annexation-creep as characterised by the last fifty-eight years, or finding the means to force Palestinians to leave in great numbers. Israeli public opinion was no less committed to completing what had been started in Gaza. Around the same time that Defense Minister Katz was briefing the media, the Israeli daily newspaper, *Haaretz*, published an opinion poll that showed 82 per cent of the Jewish population would support the expulsion of all Palestinians from Gaza.[26] This was the highest figure yet, although all opinion polls over the course of the genocide consistently showed that a majority of Israelis wanted a complete expulsion.

Donald Trump's words in Sharm el-Sheikh revealed everything about his ambition. 'We're gonna have a lot of money coming into Gaza and a lot of rebuilding and building. It's not so much rebuilding. It's really building, cleaning up and building. And I'm pleased to announce that numerous countries of great wealth and power and dignity have come forward to me just today and over the last week to say they want to help in the reconstruction of Gaza, putting up whatever money is necessary. And the money is, of course, it's a lot of money, but it's not much compared to the value or the wealth of these tremendous countries.'[27]

For the Gazans, it was about 'the basics'; for America's partners, it would be about much more. President Trump believed the Palestinians should be grateful that, after two years of genocide, the US, other Western countries and some Arab states were committing to rebuilding Gaza. What was on offer to the inhabitants was a consolation prize of 'the basics of a good life' and the Palestinians knew Israel didn't think them worthy even of that. There was no mention of their colonised land being returned to them. There was no mention of self-determination. There was no mention of human rights or of the need for those who had slaughtered their family and friends to be held accountable. There was no reference to how Israel and its genocide-sponsors would undertake to make Gaza safe and commit the hundreds of billions of dollars necessary to rebuild an entire societal infrastructure that had been obliterated. There was no mention of how the tremendous economic value Trump talked of unlocking would be released for those whose land it was. The word 'reparation' appeared nowhere in Trump's speech – but how could any of these imperatives have been referred to when they are not referenced anywhere in the ceasefire plan?

The Trump plan was Israel's plan, the only one it would countenance. Israel did not want peace. Its government wanted to continue its genocide. Indeed, the hard-right-wing elements in the coalition government wanted to accelerate the killing of Palestinians in the West Bank as well as Gaza; as Ministers Ben-Gvir and Smotrich said, the job must be finished. Ben-Gvir said, 'I call on the Prime Minister, it is time to come to sense [*sic*], to return to intense fighting, to conquer, to crush, to win.'[28] Despite threatened resignations by these hardline ministers, the Trump plan progressed at pace in response to activities involving France and Saudia Arabia at the UN.

THE NEW YORK DECLARATION

The UN's New York Declaration on the Peaceful Settlement of the Question of Palestine and the Implementation of the Two-State Solution, signed on 29 July 2025, had attempted to address the fundamental issues at stake in the region politically. It carried the inherent risk of running into the sand, as had every such attempt to find a solution since 1948. That was its weakness. Its strengths were its focus on Palestine and the involvement of some international heavyweights. France, the UK, Italy and Spain, as well as the EU itself, committed to it, as did Saudi Arabia, Egypt, Turkey and Jordan. The US did not. As a socio-political document, the Declaration had to propose a determination. Its second clause referenced, as many have over time, 'the effective implementation of the two-state solution'.[29]

There are those among Palestine's most powerful supporters and the most knowledgeable writers on the subject, Omer Bartov and Ilan Pappé among them, who argue that the opportunity for a two-state solution, originally agreed in the Oslo Accords, has passed. It has certainly become less viable with the massive acceleration in the establishment of Jewish settlements on occupied lands and Israel's continuing refusal to budge on either the recognition of the rights of Palestinian refugees or resolving the status of Jerusalem. Still, Clause 6 of the Declaration referenced taking 'irreversible steps' towards 'the realization of an independent, sovereign, economically viable and democratic

State of Palestine'. The language of the document was pointed, the urgency of what was being proposed equally so: 'This must include the immediate lifting of restrictions and opening by Israel, the Occupying power, of border crossings ...'[30]

Israel's reaction was entirely predictable. Anger dominated. The government expressed its usual irritation at the UN and dismissed anything that could provide a roadmap to Palestinian statehood. The following week, after a lengthy Cabinet meeting, it gave its formal response, setting out five essential conditions for bringing an end to its military operations:

- Disarmament of Hamas
- Return of all hostages
- Demilitarisation of Gaza
- Establishment of an alternative civilian government in Gaza not led by Hamas or the Palestinian Authority
- Israel to exercise overriding security control over Gaza[31]

This amounted to a statement of diplomatic conflict.

America and Israel's views aligned on the New York Declaration. Both were hostile towards it – the US because its president saw himself as the global peace tsar, and Israel because any threat of an emerging independent Palestinian state needed to be stopped at source. To give added weight to its demands, as Israel dismissed the Declaration, it also announced a full offensive on Gaza city. This created the environment in which Team Trump, giddy at the prospect of adding the Middle East to its imagined tally of peace deals, could continue with its plans for something very different.

The US State Department had quickly moved to shut down

the optimism that had followed the announcement of the Declaration. Speaking off the record, a US State Department official told *Agence France-Presse* 'our focus remains on serious diplomacy, not performative gestures. Our priorities are clear: the release of the hostages, the security of Israel, and peace and prosperity for the whole region that is only possible free from Hamas.'[32]

Weeks earlier, in an especially aggressive move against Palestine, US Secretary of State Marco Rubio revoked the visa of the president of the Palestinian Authority, Mahmoud Abbas, ahead of the UN General Assembly in New York. The visas of eighty other Palestinian Authority officials were also cancelled. That same week, the Trump administration suspended a humanitarian programme that brought injured Palestinian children to the US for urgent medical treatment. Team Trump wanted Israel to know whose side it was on. In off-the-record briefings, Trump's administration continued to stress there could be 'consequences for those who take measures against Israel'.[33] It was menacing. That was the intention.

The New York Declaration was adopted by the UN on 10 September 2025; it was endorsed by 142 votes to 10, with 12 abstentions. Israel and the US were, unsurprisingly, two of the ten to vote against. The pressure on Israel increased when those previously among the most resistant to upsetting it – the UK, France, Belgium, Portugal, Canada and Australia – either completed the formal recognition of Palestine or publicly committed to do so.

The Trump peace proposal would shift the narrative away from the principles of the Declaration. It evidenced a completely different idea about what needed to be done and why. Inherent in its pitch was that Israel was not the issue. It portrayed the 'problem' as nothing to do with the occupation of one land by another people, but one of combating terror, in this case, that perpetrated by Hamas. The overriding theme was concern at the radicalism of the Palestinians and their hatred of Israel. Trump's plan did have elements that the Israelis would rather not have considered, but they approved of its emphasis on the Palestinians as 'dangerous' and on the need for them to be deradicalised. This characterisation, this profiling of Palestinians as terrorists or subhuman, which Israeli ministers often used, allowed the US to position itself as the sole arbiter of how peace could be realised.

There was another thread of concern around this time for the US–Israel axis. Over the decades of diplomacy and putative peace agreements, divisions within the Palestinian movement contributed to the difficulty in achieving progress. Israel always claims that peace is unattainable because it is of no interest to the Palestinians, certainly not to its armed factions. History suggests otherwise. Almost exactly a year before the New York Declaration, Palestinian groups had attempted to forge unity within their own ranks. Facilitated by China, fourteen Palestinian groups, including Hamas and Fatah, met in Beijing and agreed on the 'Beijing Declaration on Ending Division and Strengthening Palestinian National Unity'. A key feature was a commitment to form a government of national reconciliation to govern Gaza and the West Bank. This would, according to the published document, take the form of an interim national unity government to 'deploy all efforts to lift the Israeli blockade on Gaza and ensure the unimpeded delivery of humanitarian aid'.[34] It also stated the Palestinians' right to resist the Israeli occupation in accordance with international law and the UN charter, and to prevent the displacement of Palestinians from their land. The negotiations were witnessed by envoys from Egypt, Algeria, Saudi Arabia, Qatar, Jordan, Syria, Lebanon, Russia and Turkey. Palestine's right to self-determination had elicited strong support. Yet this Declaration failed to get the global attention it warranted.

Fatah and Hamas had not worked together since 2006, so the move was seen as positive by the UN and other international parties. Not by Israel and not by the US. Israel regards any signs of unity within the Palestinian Arab world with suspicion. It threatens the Zionist project. Indeed, Israel funded Hamas for years through Qatar with the intention of maintaining divisions. The more pronounced they were, the better it was for Israel.

◆◆◆

Weeks after the New York Declaration, the US brought forward its own plan. The reaction internationally was revelatory. Despite being involved in Beijing and being co-sponsor of the New York Declaration, Saudi Arabia backed it. Just months earlier Crown Prince bin Salman had said the plan he had co-sponsored with Emmanuel Macron of France was delivering 'unprecedented mobilization' for Palestinian statehood.[35] Now he pivoted to become an important supporter of Trump's move. Previously bin Salman had always been resolute in ruling out any normalisation of relations with Israel 'without an "independent Palestinian state"'.[36] When the vote on the New York Declaration was taken, Saudia Arabia said it confirmed the international consensus on the Palestinians' right 'to establish an independent state based on the 1967 borders, with East Jerusalem as its capital'.[37] Saudi Arabia had never deviated from that position until Trump's plan.

In the weeks following the New York Declaration at the UN, the US and Israel had worked on their very different approach. The Trump Peace Plan did not reference an independent sovereign Palestine or the Palestinians' right to self-determination. The territorial area at the heart of self-determination is the occupied (stolen) territories, including East Jerusalem. Acceptance that the territory at issue is all the land occupied and controlled by Israel since 1967 is critical. Trump's markedly pro-Israel peace plan was very different to that which Saudi Arabia and France brought to the UN. The New York Declaration had said, 'We agreed to take collective action to end the war in Gaza, to achieve a just, peaceful and lasting settlement of the Israeli–Palestinian conflict based on the effective implementation of the two-State solution, and to build a better future for Palestinians, Israelis and all peoples of the region.'[38] This was one of the red lines for Israel. The corresponding clause in the Trump plan says simply that Gaza must become a deradicalised, terror-free zone that poses no threat to its neighbours. It is oriented towards the oppressor.

In Trump's proposal, security threats and violence were portrayed exclusively as a Palestinian problem. Any and all positives for Palestine were contingent on certain behavioural criteria being met, as determined by Israel. Most independent experts concluded that it was a weak ceasefire, unlikely to deliver a path to peace: 'True peace will require reconciliation, justice, and self-determination, and this plan, in its current form, contains none of the above.'[39]

None of these machinations should be considered without reference to the marked increase in visible public support in the

West for Palestine. It has always been there, if more manifest in some countries with a history of colonial oppression than in others. However, it has never been more widespread or more visible than since late 2023. Israel's genocide has hardened public opinion in the West like never before. The longer the genocide continued, the more people understood its cause and recognised the fundamentals of Israel's oppression and refusal to see Palestinians as their equals. More and more national governments across the West were left in no doubt about what the public thought and what was expected of them. The New York Declaration reflected this.

Sharm el-Sheikh, in contrast, was a diplomatic scam. It was America choosing to believe, as it has always done, that it knows best and that it alone has the means of improving people's lives. In the Middle East, that view is Israel-centric. The number of America's evangelical Christians supporting Israel makes it even less likely that any US administration will lead an effort towards realising a Palestine-oriented peace. Trump's ambassador to Israel, Mike Huckabee, is a notable evangelical who has long supported the Zionist ideal of Greater Israel. Resources are currently being thrown at further strengthening the bonds between these evangelicals and Zionism. The '1,000 Preachers Project', which brought 1,000 US pastors to Jerusalem in December 2025, was a collaboration between Israel's Ministry of Foreign Affairs and the Friends of Zion Museum in Jerusalem. Its express purpose was 'to provide training and prepare participants to serve as unofficial ambassadors for Israel in their communities'.[40] Christians United for Israel (CUFI) is by far the largest pro-Israel group in the US. Even if its claim to have more than ten million members is exaggerated, its reach is immense. In July 2025, the presence of thousands of its members on Capitol Hill protesting Israel's cause brought a reaction from a few hundred Jewish and Christian protesters concerned by CUFI's growing influence.[41]

Many right-wing Christian groups have lobbied as hard as AIPAC for the government to continue its support of Israel. CUFI has added considerable weight to the pro-Israel lobby over the last decade. Georgetown professor and peace activist Eli McCarthy outlines how such influences can be destructive: 'We're seeing again how U.S. government leadership prioritizes geopolitical power and economic benefits over international law or the dignity of all people – and that's being laid bare in Gaza right now under both Trump and Biden … groups like CUFI are a key driver of that dynamic. Their theology gives political leaders religious cover to justify war, occupation and bombing campaigns – and too many Christian leaders go along with it.'[42]

The Zionist lobby in the US is becoming more assertive about there being no compromise on America's support for the state of Israel. That's not going to change unless there's a seismic shift in how US politics is structured. While that was evident throughout the first year of the genocide with Biden in power, Donald Trump's real estate instincts mean Palestine's hopes of a shift in the American approach to its cause are, in the medium-term, practically nil.

It is why the greatest irony of all in President Trump's performance in Egypt was his emphasis on his so-called 'Board of Peace'. It was as if the branding of the board overseeing management of the inequitable proposal would distract from the warped approach it was taking. And, of course, it was also about him: 'They said, would you be the chairman? I say, I'm pretty busy too, but whatever we can do to have peace in the Middle East, it's worth it. But everybody wants to go on the Board of Peace. So we're probably going to enlarge it. We're gonna get, and the leaders, the top people, the top leaders, they want to be on the Board of Peace.'[43] Trump couldn't find enough superlatives to promote this board as transformative, though without any recognition of the rights of Palestinians, peace will remain elusive.

Trump's Board of Peace later received UN sanction through a mandate signed in mid-November. It was given authority to support the reconstruction, economic recovery and ultimately the administration of the Gaza Strip. The mandate noted this as part of a peace plan for the aftermath of 7 October attacks and what it termed the Gaza War. Why the UN chose to give any credence to a plan devoid of any basis for a resolution remains a mystery. Why it granted formal recognition – UN Security Council Resolution 2803 – to a document that represented an abandonment of Palestine needs to be explained. The plan it endorsed made no reference to accountability for the crime of genocide and was entirely lacking in any consideration for the right of the Palestinian people to self-determination. Still, the UN, an organisation openly mocked by this US administration, chose to support it.

The way Trump closed his Sharm el-Sheikh address, marking the formal signing of the plan, made the subsequent UN decision all the more perplexing. 'If we do [this] together, we will reach the Middle East's incredible destiny, a safe and prosperous and beautiful crossroads of culture and commerce, faith in humanity and geographic center. This will be the geographic center of the world.'[44] The speech lacked any substance. The avoidance of political outcomes and its consistent focus on deriving commercial value from rebuilding Gaza were stark. Palestine was not the issue. This was about corporate America and its allies in the Gulf states. Israel's interests were being put first, just as with every intervention made by the US since 1948.

The drafting of UN Security Council Resolution 2803 without any input from people representing the interests of Palestine, appears to have been deeply political. It was not grounded in international law. The UN document stated that a ceasefire, negotiated by the US, was in place, ignoring the fact that at the time the resolution was being considered, over 300 Palestinians had been killed in the Israeli bombardment that had continued apace over the intervening month. Indeed, on the day the resolution was passed, Israeli airstrikes killed twenty-eight Gazans. The wording of the original agreement was altered to make some vague, highly conditional offer of statehood, based on the reform of the Palestinian Authority and the satisfactory rebuilding of Gaza. Only then 'the conditions may finally be in place for a credible pathway to Palestinian self-determination and statehood'.[45] The plan was woefully defective, and not only because it proposed that those who needed to undergo 'reform' were the representatives of the oppressed rather than the state that had, for generations, been oppressing them.

Resolution 2803 was also, as the UN's own special rapporteur on Palestine, Francesca Albanese, pointed out, in breach of international law. The ICJ was clear: self-determination is an inalienable right of the Palestinian people. Albanese described 2803 as 'a security-first, capital-driven model of foreign control' that 'consolidates Israel's unlawful presence in the occupied Palestinian territory and legitimatizes ongoing violence'.[46]

No conditions were placed on Israel. Nowhere was there reference to accountability for a genocidal campaign that had slaughtered tens of thousands of people, more than 80 per cent of whom, according to Israel's own records, were civilians. And yet, even this meaningless commitment to a future state of Palestine was too much for the Israeli political establishment. The reaction of some of Netanyahu's Cabinet forced him to temper his welcome of the resolution with strong words that reinforced his implacable opposition to the idea of Palestinian sovereignty – ever.

Albanese's reference to the Security Council's resolution as the UN's endorsement of a 'security-first, capital-driven' ceasefire plan is incontestable. The way President Trump promoted his plan to the Knesset and to world leaders in Egypt on 13 October revealed it as a commercial enterprise poorly disguised as a grand diplomatic intervention. The conduct of the political leadership of America and Israel that day displayed globally the enormity of the challenge facing the Palestinians. Recognition of them as a people has to start with the recognition that a genocide has been committed against them. There was none. With the West so critical to its pursuit of nationhood, is it ever likely to be recognised as such?

PEACE FOR BUSINESS SAKE!

Jared Kushner was one of those who received praise for his role in the ceasefire agreement, not least from his father-in-law, President Trump. It seemed Trump's daughter Ivanka's decision to convert to Judaism, which the president himself referenced in his Knesset speech, was paying off in terms of Middle East diplomacy. It was easy to see how Kushner's presumed business contacts could be used by the president, especially if the future for Gaza was less about Palestine and more about real estate. In that context, Jared Kushner's relationship with the Gulf states might prove more important than his Jewish faith.

In Trump's first term, the closeness of his political management to his commercial interests was a constant source of debate. Kushner was often the focus of that attention, both in the media and across the political opposition to Trump. Perceived conflicts of interest were regularly debated, and there were cases where Kushner's work for the White House overlapped with the family's business interests. Today, Kushner owns Affinity Partners, founded in 2021, shortly after his father-in-law's first term as president finished. It focuses on investing in Israeli and US companies. Soon after its launch, the Saudi Arabian Public Investment Fund placed $2 billion under its management, a very substantial commitment for a new, unproven business. On the establishment of Affinity, Jared Kushner said that he would no longer be involved in politics. It was a definitive declaration.

Six months later, in December 2021, a spokesman told Reuters that Kushner planned to create 'an investment corridor' between Israel and Saudi Arabia.[47] The term had a ring to it. It is one that Israeli Prime Minister Benjamin Netanyahu has regularly used on international platforms. This all signalled the prevailing closeness of the Trump camp to the Saudis and some of the Gulf petrostates.

What was notable was the speed with which a significant financial commitment was made to a fund that was only six months old and had no track record. The Saudi commitment of $2 billion was made just six months after Donald Trump's first term as president ended. More notable was that it required the personal intervention of Crown Prince bin Salman, who overrode the advice of advisers to the Saudi Arabian Public Investment Fund that the investment should not be made. *The New York Times* reported that the panel charged with assessing all the fund's investments had cited several concerns to support its negative assessment. They included Affinity's lack of experience, the possibility that Saudi Arabia would be responsible for 'the bulk of the investment and risk', and that due diligence had found the firm's operational capacity 'unsatisfactory in all aspects'.[48] It also considered its proposed asset management fees excessive and thought 'public relations risks' could arise from Kushner's prior role as a senior adviser to his father-in-law.[49]

During the first Trump administration, Kushner had been the lead person protecting Mohammed bin Salman from scrutiny over the assassination of Saudi journalist Jamal Khashoggi in 2018. Khashoggi, a forceful critic of the regime, was ambushed in the Saudi consulate in Istanbul in an attack the CIA concluded with 'high confidence' was ordered by the Crown Prince, as reported by most media. This, along with a huge arms deal made with Saudi Arabia and a bet on Trump returning to power, was likely the reason the Saudi fund backed Kushner. Even though Kushner had announced he would no longer be involved in politics, concerns were raised in Washington.

In September 2024, as Trump's campaign for re-election was gaining momentum, a committee of the US Senate revealed Affinity had received $87 million in fees from the Saudi fund without making any return. Some months later, just weeks after Trump had been re-elected, Kushner announced that Affinity had raised an additional $1.5 billion from investment funds controlled by Qatar and the UAE.[50] Affinity is a shareholder in an Israeli asset management firm, Phoenix, that has faced scrutiny for investments in West Bank Settlements. The Trump administration argues that there is no conflict of interest. It insists that Kushner's diplomatic work in the Middle East, even though three Arab states account for 80 per cent of his investment firm's funds, is not problematic. White House press secretary Karoline Leavitt consistently references Kushner as someone committed to serving his country and has commended his work in what she profiles as helping to secure world peace. It's true that Kushner's relationship with Benjamin Netanyahu, coupled with his business ties to Qatar, the UAE and Saudi Arabia, could only have facilitated the Trump ceasefire, but at what cost? Where were the lines drawn between the interests of peace, human rights, international law and those of private enterprise?

When you review the broader agreement and the dynamic of 13 October 2025, it's impossible to imagine that the business interests of Trump and possibly those of some Arab leaders did not supersede concerns about the people of Palestine. This is critical to what emerged. The intention of the monied Arab states in choosing to work with Trump and Israel on a long-term plan for the region has to be interrogated. The intersection of corporate America and the primacy of Israel's wishes is a longstanding dilemma for Palestine's leadership.

When you look at Trump's foreign policy priorities, there's generally a business angle. Money is rarely off this president's radar. In the visitor's gallery in the Knesset he'd singled out a pro-Israel billionaire funder of his campaigns, Miriam Adelson, as someone who ensured Israel's welfare would be protected.

Days later, she publicly promised $250 million towards any effort Trump would make to seek an unconstitutional third term. Adelson is known to have invested very heavily in backing settlement of the West Bank. She also owns *Israel Hayom*, one of Israel's daily newspapers, allowing her direct influence on public opinion.

Another of his backers is Ronald Lauder, of Estée Lauder. As president of the World Jewish Congress, he delivered a powerful speech at its annual conference in the US Capitol in December 2025. He bemoaned the failure to appreciate the rise of antisemitism for the threat it represents. The speech was emotive, with one key message that Israel's infamous capacity to use propaganda was failing and that it was time for 'billions' to be invested in social media. His message was clear: 'Today our enemies have pushed their indoctrination … all the way down from kindergarten through 12th Grade … we are in the fight of our lives.'[51] Lauder has an estimated net worth of $5 billion. In the 1970s, he went to business school with Trump and, in 2018, described him as 'a man of incredible insight and intelligence'.[52] Lauder's obsession with the state of Israel has no limits. Protecting it, at all costs, is a priority. In his address to the World Jewish Congress, he announced the creation of a 'new fund' to actively oppose and defeat any candidate, at any level of US government, who runs on an anti-Zionist platform.

There is a direct link between these individuals and groups with vast sums at their disposal and the support of political and institutional America for the Zionist cause. It has always been a factor in American presidencies, but with Trump it is more marked, with a real prospect that his family is benefitting too. Money is at the heart of this president's approach. With vast Arab wealth potentially involved, it makes any moves led by Trump more open to doubt, meaning it is more difficult for Palestinians to trust the motivation of the peace brokers, especially the US.

◆◆◆

Israel has long proven itself to be an untrustworthy partner in peace agreements. Egypt discovered this in the Camp David process. Egypt had made a partial troop withdrawal and discussions were ongoing when Israel launched a major offensive on southern Lebanon, codenamed Operation Litani. The Litani river, a vital resource for agriculture and electricity in Lebanon, runs from the Bakaa valley through the centre of the country until it turns west to the Mediterranean about 10 kilometres north of the city of Tyre. The land from the Israeli border to beyond Tyre has long been coveted by Zionists but is a demilitarised zone under the control of the UN. In 2026, it became clear that Israel would use the burgeoning Israeli–American war on Iran to re-engage its ambition for Lebanon. Israel is skilled at using wider or related events as camouflage for its illegal colonisation.

Saudi Arabia had also been treated to a diplomatic hustle by Israel. In 1980 and 1981, Israel annexed East Jerusalem and the Syrian Golan Heights. In 1981, Crown Prince Fahd offered a peace proposal that would require Israel to withdraw from territory occupied in 1967 and to recognise the right of Palestinians to return. It would mean recognition of the state of Palestine. As Israel supposedly considered this, it launched another invasion of Lebanon, this time killing 20,000 civilians and forcing 500,000 Palestinians to become refugees. It is clear that Israel had long since abandoned any idea of accepting its sovereign borders.

Evidence for Arab nations that working with America and Israel would lead to a peace that would protect Palestine's interests is scant. The esteemed professor of modern Arab politics at Columbia University in New York, Joseph Massad, warns that Israel's treatment of Jordan, Egypt and, more recently, Qatar, should signal the risks associated with normalising relations with Israel. 'What is astonishing is that, despite this dismal historical record, pro-normalisation Arabs continue to entertain hopes that Donald Trump's efforts to expand normalisation with Israel will bring about regional stability and peace. That Israel has bombed Qatar, is now bombing Syria and Lebanon, whose leaders openly court normalisation, and continues to occupy more land, has hardly made a dent in this pro-normalisation propaganda.'[53] Normalisation was also a critical part of Donald Trump's Middle East endeavours in his first presidential term. For instance, he delivered agreements on the development of peace, diplomacy and friendly relations between the UAE, Bahrain and Israel as part of the Abraham Accords of 2020, which served only to push Palestine to the margins. These Gulf states were strategically targeted, using the threat posed by Iran, to focus them on their own security and the economic potential of being part of a US–Israel axis.

The truth is that economics mean that Trump has always prioritised working with the Gulf states. For many Arab states, Palestine has become an irritation, one that pulls at their heartstrings but inhibits the economic nirvana promised by a US-tailored regional plan, where any such plan would be centred on Israel. The US has been cultivating this line of attack on the administrations of the more prosperous Arab states for some time. It's not a new line, but it has rarely had the same singular focus as it does now.

In early 2019, Prime Minister Netanyahu's office leaked a short video of the foreign ministers of the UAE, Bahrain and Saudi Arabia speaking at an event in Warsaw, Poland, chaired by senior US diplomat Dennis Ross. Separately, Ross interviewed Netanyahu at the same event. That the four men spoke at the same seminar was surprising, but the intent of Israel and the US was not. Ambassador Ross's message on social media later that day said it all: 'I conducted back-to-back discussions first with three Arab ministers and then with Israeli PM Netanyahu. Same room, same views of Iran's aggressive, threatening posture in the Middle East, and unmistakable convergence about what should be done to counter it.'[54]

Again, Iran was being presented as the single obstacle to a secure, peaceful and prosperous Middle East. It has never been within the bandwidth of US politics to consider that the problem is Israel's steadfast opposition to the creation of a secure and stable region that would meet the needs of all its people equally. There was surprise that these Gulf states and Israel were meeting in Poland, and Netanyahu's office removed the video after twenty-five minutes. But by then the job was done – the Israeli public had seen an emerging Zionist–Arab consensus founded on a shared view of Iran, not Israel, as the obstacle to a prosperous Middle East.

The Islamic Republic of Iran was the 'stick' wielded by first-time President Trump once he'd removed the US from Obama's nuclear deal. His interest in fostering relations between Israel and the Gulf states has always been more about the 'carrot' of the economic potential. It would be beneficial not just for Israel and the US, but also for the Trump family. For Trump, the business of politics is business; that includes the family's business. This is what makes 13 October 2025 so remarkable. In the long history of inept Middle East peace efforts by the US, Trump's was the worst. Its motivation was economic, not social. Its objective was financial gain, not political equity. Its motivation was greed, not morality; not justice or a more peaceful world. Its winners were to be the oppressors; its losers those who had tried, against all the odds, to fight that oppression.

It wasn't new for the Palestinians to be abandoned by the Zionist-compromised West, or that some among their Arab brothers were wavering. That October day showed that money, the currency that has prevented the West from acting morally on Palestine for over a century, had turned some sovereign Arab heads too. The leaders of powerful Arab and Islamic nations attended, posed for photographs and smiled benignly as the American president painted his picture of a thriving Middle East that would allow the Palestinian people to again enjoy the basics of a good life. This was how it would be. Their homeland, the territory they'd been denied the right to call their own, would be exploited by a coalition of Western and Gulf wealth and political power. Their 'prize' would be to live free from bombardment and imposed starvation, and to be able to enjoy the basics of life, free from persecution. It wasn't said, but it was implied in every word and in every gesture – they should be grateful.

The more brutal and sustained an assault on oppressed people, the more likely they are to accept any offer, no matter how limited and demeaning, once it ends the destruction. Israel has long worked towards humiliating the Palestinians. In his words and in his approach on 13 October, President Trump told the Palestinians that now was the moment to 'settle'.

CORRIDORS OF POWER AND COMMERCE

One feature of a Donald Trump presidency is arrogance on such a grand scale that the president and those closest to him appear oblivious to it. On 29 September, on the day that Trump and Netanyahu first announced the ceasefire agreement, Kushner's Affinity Partners made another announcement. Kushner and the Saudi sovereign wealth fund announced that, along with independent private equity firm Silver Lake, they'd agreed to pay $55 billion to acquire and take private (delist from the New York Stock Exchange) the global video game publisher Electronic Arts.[55] Yet, there was little or no concern in Washington about the significant role the president continued to give his son-in-law in Middle East diplomacy, despite him being so directly involved in Saudi Arabian business interests.

Economic self-interest has always been a critical factor in US foreign policy. Almost anywhere that America has been active, its own financial interests are pivotal to its decisions. What's unusual about the Trump presidency is that these choices could involve benefits for the ultimate decision-maker. In September 2023, just two weeks before the Hamas attack, Netanyahu addressed the UN in New York. He held up a map of the region, one without Palestine, and explained how the Middle East could become a 'corridor of peace and prosperity'. It would, he said, start in Asia, go 'through the UAE, Saudi Arabia, Jordan, Israel, to Europe'.[56] Palestine wasn't mentioned, nor did he explain how the economic corridor would reach Jordan if it didn't go through Palestine.

Setting the map aside, Netanyahu told his audience that this economic plan could pave the way to peace with Palestine. Years before the much vaunted 'comprehensive' peace plan, it was clear all that interested him was economic prosperity. For Israel only. There was no role envisaged for Palestine in this proposed corridor of peace and prosperity. Palestine wasn't even on the map; it had no economic role, but it could benefit from peace provided it met Israel's conditions. It alone was placed on notice: 'It has to be said here, forcefully. Peace can only be achieved if it is based on truth, it cannot be based on lies.'[57]

This was the Israeli position on 22 September 2023. The economic emphasis in his words to the UN were not new. On business, Netanyahu and Trump are in an echo chamber. In January 2020, Trump had launched his 'Peace to Prosperity Plan', which was promoted as a serious initiative even though it included recognising Jerusalem as the capital of Israel and tried to create the impression that the settlements in the West Bank were consistent with international law. That plan, whose architect was Jared Kushner, was widely condemned as an attempt to support Israel's annexation of the West Bank. Netanyahu had even announced from the White House podium that his government would move to that end immediately.

At the time, the Associated Press published a damning column. It said the plan 'sides with Israel on key contentious issues that have bedevilled past peace efforts, including borders and the status of Jerusalem and Jewish settlements, and attaches nearly impossible conditions for granting the Palestinians their hoped-for state'.[58] Fifty former European prime ministers and government ministers signed an open letter to Britain's *Guardian* newspaper decrying the plan as contrary to 'the most fundamental principles of international law'.[59]

It's telling that almost six years later, the US, with Trump back at the helm, brought forward another similar plan. Again, it prioritised economic considerations and made any realisation of Palestine's rights dependent on a set of fantastical demands. The 2020 deal prompted widespread scorn because its terms were so one-sided and it would have led to Israel being rewarded for its decades-long abandonment of international law. The 2025 ceasefire plan Trump rehearsed in Israel and unveiled in Egypt had many of the same features, but the global reaction was more restrained, perhaps on account of the despair people felt over the prolonged genocide. Its threat is more profound, however, and the relative silence, therefore, a great deal more serious.

Remarkably, within weeks, the UN Security Council gave oxygen to this deeply flawed, inequitable plan when its special resolution was passed. It appeared that much of the West had been so de-energised by the two years of savagery in Gaza that, like the Palestinians themselves, what was being offered represented progress. The West's collective conscience, largely absent over the course of the genocide, appeared ready to settle for anything that might ease its guilt.

◆◆◆

The detail of the 2020 'Peace to Prosperity' plan had beggared belief. Included were provisions detailing how, after four years of good behaviour that garnered the approval of both the US and Israel, Palestine would be granted nationhood with conditions.

Any state would be contiguous with the state of Israel, which would retain 30 per cent of the West Bank. The provisions which the Palestinians had to accept were extreme. They included refraining from joining any international organisation without Israel's consent and taking no action against any Israeli or US citizen before the international courts or security services. 'Once these measures are completed the United States will encourage other countries to welcome the State of Palestine as a full member in international organizations. However, the State of Palestine may not join any international organization if such membership would contradict commitments of the State of Palestine to demilitarization and cessation of political and judicial warfare against the State of Israel.'[60]

Hamas and the Palestinian Authority expressed their disgust. Hamas said it was an attempt to 'liquidate' the Palestinian's right to nationhood, while Mahmoud Abbas said, 'All our rights are not for sale and are not for bargain.'[61] That first Trump plan may have shocked many observers, but as we have seen already, America has form. The demands made of Palestine are generally hostile and pretty much always unattainable. This suits Israel as, through a prolonged diplomatic dance, it continues to take more and more Palestinian land.

Trump also has form. But however corporate the 2020 plan was, what Trump proposed just a month after his reinauguration still stunned most commentators. In early February 2025, he declared that the US would take over the Gaza Strip and would 'own it' and be responsible for it, pledging to turn it into 'the Riviera of the Middle East'. In making this announcement in the White House, flanked by Netanyahu, Trump said that the two million Palestinians living there would be moved permanently to Jordan and Egypt. Later, his own social media platform, Truth Social, posted a video showing what Gaza's 'Riviera' would look like. When his suggestion about relocating Gazans met with heavy criticism, he protested that the lives of Palestinians would be transformed.

Later, Secretary of State Marco Rubio said that any relocation would be temporary, although Trump posted that a permanent relocation would mean the Palestinians having 'a chance to be happy, safe, and free.'[62] Such a solution would represent the end of Israel's egregious theft of Palestinian land, including in the West Bank, which had been pursued with markedly increased aggression during the course of the genocide in Gaza. Israel killed over 1,000 Palestinians in the process, as the IDF became a greater presence to ensure the Zionist settlers could do as they pleased.[63] As with its Gaza genocide, Israel's violent accretion of land in the West Bank did not stop the US from prioritising the aggressor's interests in any post-conflict scenario.

All Trump's plans lacked detail. That is not unusual; sometimes it is necessary to advance the chances of success or to avoid increasing pressure in the early stages of a peace process. It was widely reported, however, that in this case, the absence of any detail was because there was none. It was classic Trump. David Schenker, a former assistant secretary of state for the Middle East, said, 'The administration took its victory lap after the initial cease-fire and hostage release, but all the hard work, the real hard work, remains.'[64]

◆◆◆

Away from the 13 October hype around Trump's 'Comprehensive Plan to End the Gaza Conflict', some observers were alarmed by the involvement of former UK prime minister, Tony Blair. Once Trump's plan started to gain media attention in the West, it was Blair's involvement that generated most comment. The Israeli newspaper *Haaretz* revealed that over the two years of Israel's genocide, Blair made frequent visits to Israel, seven of them for meetings with Netanyahu in 2024.[65] The former British prime minister also met regularly with Ron Dermer, a former Israeli strategic affairs minister and someone who attended Trump's Knesset address. Blair and the consulting business he runs, the Tony Blair Institute, have a reputation for working in the shadows, but his level of interaction with Israel's genocidal government concerned many.

Despite the relative success of his time in government, Blair was not popular in Britain, being widely considered untrustworthy, and he is hated across the Arab and Muslim worlds. A central figure in the successful ceasefire and peace achieved in Northern Ireland, something he has traded on since, he is still a divisive figure. The perception is of a polished, articulate man interested in and motivated by money. It was that which, more than anything, generated suspicion around his involvement.

One of the main architects of the Good Friday Agreement in Ireland, the deputy leader of the Social Democratic and Labour Party, Seamus Mallon MP, dealt directly with Blair over a lengthy period. While the outcome of those negotiations was positive, Mallon, who was deputy first minister of Northern Ireland from 1998 to 2001, had a perspective on Blair that would temper confidence about his motivation. Mallon was a tough, uncompromising constitutional republican, who had old-fashioned values about truth. He found Blair wanting in that regard. 'I began to realise that in his political dealings he was amoral and didn't know the meaning of the word "honesty".'[66] Lord Chilcot, who spent seven years leading the state inquiry into the Iraq War, concluded that Blair had not been 'straight with the nation'[67] when he joined the UK with the US in the invasion of Iraq.

In late 2025, the digital newspaper *Politico* obtained a haul of documents, some of which originated from the Blair Institute, that showed the lack of depth to the Trump plan. They highlighted how the Palestinian Authority wanted 'to shape events in Gaza despite Israel's opposition.'[68] The firmness of Israel's opposition to any Palestinian involvement illustrated the immensity of the security challenge alone. Israeli opposition to working with the purely constitutional Authority, which has low levels of support in Gaza, should have been enough to prompt concern. If Israel could not even work with the Authority, how could accommodations be reached with Hamas, which, despite the horror of the genocide, still has high levels of influence there?

An International Stabilisation Force (ISF) proposed by the plan was paramount, especially as it was estimated that Hamas remained well resourced in many areas of Gaza. Hamas is more than a rebel army; it has elected political representatives who have managed Gaza for two decades. According to the documents reviewed by *Politico* in November 2025, it still controlled more than 40 per cent of the territory and had 7,000 security personnel overseeing the great majority of Gazans who lived in that area. Hamas quickly dismissed Trump's plan, saying it provided no basis for disarming.

The *Politico* report revealed what must have been an alarming picture for those tasked with delivering on Trump's promises. Yet Secretary of State Rubio seemed confident that the proposed ISF would be able to exert control over Hamas. In a memorandum sent to the UN, a body Trump's administration would rather not deal with, the US sought its approval for a two-year mandate for the ISF. The UN has its own peace-keeping force, the UN Interim Force in Lebanon (UNIFIL), that serves as a buffer between Israel and Lebanon, but in late November 2025, it chose to sanction the move to establish the proposed ISF. The Palestinian Authority also approved, while Hamas denounced it as imposing 'an international trusteeship on the Gaza Strip that Palestinians and "resistance factions" oppose'.[69] The composition of the ISF would, of itself, prove to be contentious. Israel would have a say in that but not Palestine. Turkey, for example, had expressed a willingness to provide troops, but Turkish involvement was reported to be unacceptable to Netanyahu and Israel.

Politico also reported that the documents showed tensions in terms of where ultimate control of Gaza would rest: 'The Palestinian Authority expects to run, secure and control the enclave, as it did prior to 2007, when Hamas ousted it by force. The Palestinian Authority currently governs parts of the West Bank. But the Israeli government rejects the Palestinian Authority and is opposed to it having it [*sic*] rule Gaza. Trump's 20-point peace plan says the Palestinian Authority can only participate once it has reformed itself.'[70] The idea that the Palestinian Authority would be acceptable to Gazans was questionable; that it needed to 'reform' before it would be acceptable to Israel was bizarre. Nowhere in the documents was there reference to the Beijing Declaration and Hamas's interest in merging its political work with that of the Authority – the kind of move that, however embryonic, would undermine Zionist ambition.

What was noteworthy about longer-term governance was how Israel objected even to Palestinian interests being overseen by, arguably, its weakest link. The Western narrative was dominated by a view that the longer the Israeli bombardment continued, the more the popularity of Hamas would wane among the Palestinians. It was often argued that the greater the loss of life and destruction of Gaza, the more Palestinians there and in the West Bank would resent Hamas's decision to attack Israel on 7 October 2023. The evidence does not yet bear that up; the likelihood is that it never will.

Two years into the genocide, in polls conducted across Palestine shortly after Trump's ceasefire plan had been published, satisfaction with Hamas was at 60 per cent, twice that of the Palestinian Authority.[71] Interestingly, and consistent with a trend over the last number of years, Hamas outpolls both the other Palestinian groups even in the West Bank, where it has no meaningful presence and no administrative roll. In a sign of the strength of peoples' resolve, after suffering over two years of slaughter, in the same poll a clear majority – 69 per cent – was opposed to the disarmament of Hamas. When the poll was split between the West Bank and Gaza, it showed 87 per cent of Gazans, in the weeks after Trump's plan was unveiled, believed Hamas should not disarm (55 per cent in the West Bank). Blame for what they were suffering was attributed to Israel at 54 per cent, the US at 24 per cent and only 14 per cent blamed Hamas.[72] This continuing support for Hamas is a significant problem for those who see the Palestinian Authority as the only possible 'partner' towards a fresh start. Furthermore, when those surveyed were asked who they'd vote for in a presidential election between Khalid Mishal of Hamas and Mahmoud Abbas, Mishal received more than twice as many votes as Abbas.

Polls also showed that the man many think could unite the Palestinian factions, Marwan Barghouti, would easily win any such contest. The leader of the West Bank resistance movement Tanzim, a small armed group within Fatah, Barghouti was imprisoned for life in 2002. That his popularity has increased in the more than twenty years since is why Israel refuses to release him. Barghouti is a man who could move Palestinians to peace. As Norman Finkelstein points out, such a figure might not be of interest to Israel. 'I think Israel, as a number of commentators have pointed out, is becoming an insane state. And we have to be honest about that. While the rest of the world wants peace, Europe wants peace, the US wants peace, but this state wants war, war, war.'[73] Another 'giant' of Jewish intellectual thought, Gideon Levy, a member of the editorial board of *Haaretz*, agrees. In March 2026, in an opinion piece entitled 'Everyone in This Country Has Gone Insane', he wrote, 'Where was it determined that wartime is also a time for stupidity? Who wrote that when the canons roar, the muses are not only silent but ought to be ashamed? … That is how it is after two and a half years without real journalism, without even minimal coverage of the war in Gaza.'[74]

The representation of Palestinian interests being splintered has benefited Israel and its considerable propaganda machine so far this century, and it also allows many countries to obfuscate on offering outright support. The Palestinian Authority represents the Palestinians internationally. Fatah, the ruling party in the West Bank, has civil control of those parts that remain unoccupied by Israeli 'settlers'. Since the elections in 2006, it has had no presence or involvement in Gaza, which is under the control of Hamas, its parliamentary party and significant guerrilla army. This diffuse representation needs urgent reform if the cause of Palestine is to gain further strength and, ultimately, its people are to be governed in peace.

These reforms need to be worked out by the Palestinians, not imposed by outsiders. The need for international help and counsel is not questioned, but the Palestinian people themselves must lead this. The weakness of the apparently fractured representation is a convenient excuse for not advancing Palestine's cause, so it is critical that they find the space and means to reform politically. This is the one condition that could reasonably be put to them by the international community uniting behind a full, lasting and Palestine-oriented peace. The 2024 Beijing Declaration represented an important enough step in that regard to be of concern to Israel. The international community rallying behind that, along with the release of Barghouti, could have made a very material difference.

THE BUSINESS OF POLITICS IS BUSINESS

Donald Trump's ceasefire plan addressed only Gaza. It was dealing with only one piece of the colonial jigsaw, the one Israel had chosen to destroy as it fiddled with the other pieces. The world's focus has been only on Gaza, the tiny strip of land that is home to about 2 million Palestinians. The bombardment, the destruction of the place, the slaughter of its people with bombs and by starvation was so intense, so shocking, it was hard to step away to consider Israel's wider malevolence.

Another weakness of the Trump plan was that, reflecting its sponsor's limitations, it didn't consider the history of Israel's colonialism. Trump's glory-avarice means that only two things really matter to him: being recognised as great and being wealthy. Achieving peace in Gaza was a prize that could deliver on both counts. The interests of the Palestinians were relevant only insofar as they might contribute to meeting his and Israel's needs. The Trump vortex was exclusively Israel-focused, so its lens was never going to be wide enough to see the Palestinian perspective.

This is not an exclusively Trump problem, nor, in the US, is it a failing only of Republican administrations. This has been the great limiter of US policy in the Middle East for generations. However, a government led by Trump's ego was even less likely to see the Zionist wood from the Palestinian trees, making real progress virtually impossible. The Trump plan is not conflict resolution. The parties were never going to come together with a shared wish for peace and recognition with, as these things require, each moving somewhat to achieve it. The West is so tied to Israel that all the evidence is that it will never call it to account. The Palestinians, on the other hand, were supposed to do the West's bidding. Palestine's choice was no choice at all. It must continue the fight against its oppression or fully engage in a process organised, coordinated and managed by the US, whose primary objective is the protection of Israel.

The party sponsoring the 'ceasefire deal' was bound to Israel. The party sponsoring the 'ceasefire deal' was the one that could have prevented the genocide but instead chose to fund it. Worse, its president openly and unashamedly talked up the economic benefits of the proposed peace plan for the US and Israel. With other nations, including some Arab countries, the US had unveiled a plan for Palestine that would allow them all to turn a buck and would prioritise the interests of the oppressor and occupier.

Trump and Netanyahu always understood the wider non-political value of the Gaza Strip. They are autocrats dressed in a stained, ragged cloak of democracy, men who like to pontificate, especially about their own gifts. They are politicians for whom allies are those who share their penchant for bullying any weaker party. They like them even more if they have money. Trump's Gaza Riviera may have been ridiculed at the time, but not everywhere. It may have raised political eyebrows in the West, but some nations in the Middle East, which know the expanse of Gaza's coastline, had taken note.

Even though Donald Trump was long gone from the White House in 2023, Benjamin Netanyahu returned to this favoured subject when he addressed the UN that year on the potential economic welfare of the Middle East. It was an interest that could be shared by Israel and Arab states – absent Palestine. This economic alliance, combined with a shared resolve on Iran, was a constant in all of his major speeches.[75] Netanyahu referenced the Abraham Accords, concluded during Trump's first presidency, which he often claimed demonstrated Israel's focus on commerce as the way to establish a bright future for the Middle East. No less certain of his own acumen than Trump, he reminded delegates of what he'd always said and how, for years, his approach to peace had been 'rejected by the so-called experts. Well, they were wrong. Under their approach, we didn't forge a single peace treaty for a quarter century. Yet in 2020, under the approach that I advocated, we tried something different, and in no time, we achieved a remarkable breakthrough. We achieved four peace treaties working with the United States. Israel forged four peace agreements in four months with four Arab states: the United Arab Emirates, Bahrain, Sudan and Morocco.'[76]

The real focus of the Abraham Accords was trade, which, for Netanyahu, represented the way forward, reflected in significant levels of business and cooperation. The benefits were there for all to see, and the Accords had, he said, 'ushered in another dramatic change. It brought Arabs and Jews closer together … We see it in lessons that are given to Arab students about the Holocaust in the UAE. There's no question, the Abraham Accords heralded the dawn of a new age of peace.'[77] Netanyahu was praising the UAE for amending its curriculum so that children would learn of the Holocaust, knowing that Israel's Ministry of Education prohibited the Nakba and the events of 1948 from being taught in schools. In 2010, under a previous Netanyahu government, the ministry prevented a civic group from holding workshops for teachers on Palestine. It banned schools from distributing a booklet on the Universal Declaration of Human Rights.

The Abraham Accord agreements had no relevance to what is at issue between Israel and Palestine. Israel was not conducting a genocide on any of the four nations that joined the Abraham Accords; it has neither occupied their land nor routinely slaughtered and incarcerated their people.

In his 2023 UN address, Netanyahu also argued that those who had opposed him believed Israel needed to establish peace and support the self-determination of the Palestinians before it could pursue a broader ambition. Yet, he claimed, Palestine was little more than an irritation, one given far too much attention: 'See, the Palestinians are only 2% of the Arab world. As long as they believe that the other 98% will remain in a war-like state with

Israel, that larger mass, that larger Arab world could eventually choke, dissolve, destroy the Jewish state … But I believe that we are at the cusp of an even more dramatic breakthrough: a historic peace with Saudi Arabia.'[78]

Was this the turning point for Netanyahu and Trump? Their reasons may not have been the same, but an outcome where the cause of Palestine would no longer inhibit the wealthy Arab nations from aligning with Israel would suit them both. Trump's courtship of the petrostates hadn't ended with his defeat in 2020. In fact, the break in his White House tenure provided space for his team, including various family members, to fan out across the region. They set about building deeper relationships, creating corporate momentum that would be valuable whether or not he won re-election. When he did, it offered Trump an opportunity, and not just to gain that next notch on his peace-belt. Were he to bring the catastrophe in Palestine to an end, however crudely, it would provide the perfect platform on which to realign interests in the Middle East. With Israel central to that, Palestine would have to be managed off the map permanently.

Israel would have no difficulty in working closely with established, monied Arab states that could provide unrivalled resources and opportunities. It could form Netanyahu's beloved 'economic corridor'. The Palestinians could be absorbed into the success or leave. The key, as always, was the Palestinians' preparedness to accept their fate and commit to living in peace. Netanyahu had told the UN that, 'Such a peace will go a long way to ending the Arab–Israeli conflict. It will encourage other Arab states to normalize relations with Israel. It will enhance the prospects of peace with the Palestinians. It will encourage a broader reconciliation between Judaism and Islam, between

Jerusalem and Mecca, between the descendants of Isaac and the descendants of Ishmael.'[79]

In that 2023 speech, the map Netanyahu held up indicated clearly that peace for Palestinians would involve recognising that Israel would cover the territory from the River Jordan to the Mediterranean. In this, as well as the emphasis on economic growth and prosperity, his speech, a month before the Hamas attack, foreshadowed how Donald Trump would position Palestine two years later. Netanyahu spelled it out: the Palestinians were not to be trusted. They could never hope to participate in a thriving Middle East without embracing a peace that was based on Israel's truth, rather than its lies. The bar set for Palestine by Trump's 2025 plan was the same. That bar, one that is equally tied to each man's analysis, involves peace being based on Palestine accepting that Zionist 'truth'.

Netanyahu also portrayed himself at the UN as a man who wanted the world to understand that not just peace but prosperity was available to everyone, perhaps even the Palestinians, if only they would recognise Israel's right to all of its homeland. Israel, it was implied, already met the highest standards of international law and mores. Yet over 2024 and 2025, it has been as wilful a state aggressor as any the contemporary world has seen. If any other country had behaved as it did, it would have led to a Western alliance behind those whose land had been invaded and annexed. There would have been action taken by the world's powers over the many tens of thousands who had been slaughtered. On this, the US and its Western allies have been found hopelessly wanting. America, which has engaged in some of the most spurious acts of protecting the oppressed overseas, has never once shown such faux ambition for Palestine.

On 13 October 2025, when the Knesset hosted President Donald J. Trump, he used similar language and imagery to Netanyahu's to portray how the region could function and how economic prosperity could flow. In the two years between Netanyahu's address to the UN and Trump's to the Knesset, Israel had 'softened up' the region for exactly the kind of economic rollout Netanyahu had set out in September 2023. Money talks. The Middle Eastern economic boom that Trump and Netanyahu had prophesied years before could now include one of the world's most ambitious rebuilding projects in Gaza. The commercial value of the forty kilometres of Mediterranean coastline, so coveted by Trump, was reason enough to put the normal considerations of international conduct to one side.

◆◆◆

When the captain of Air Force One called 'wheels up' in Sharm el-Sheikh to begin the homeward journey to Washington, DC, President Trump and his inner sanctum could reflect on a successful day. A full cast of the expected world leaders had been present in Egypt for the formalities and to do his bidding. Trump's America was forging a new beginning for the Middle East, one focused on unlocking part of the region's untapped economic potential, which could be opened to Western exploitation. That was the purpose of his original proposal back in 2020. He and Netanyahu had spoken of it for years. Now it was in hand.

The press pool reported that the motorcade left the conference centre at 8.42 p.m. on the ten-minute drive to the airport. 8.55 p.m. – wheels up.

‘[M]y mother, my brother Ahmad, 12, and I went together … When we approached [the aid distribution site], the army suddenly opened massive fire. It was unbelievable … When the shooting stopped, we moved again towards the distribution site. I was in front, and behind me, my mother was holding Ahmad’s hand. Then the shooting resumed, and a bullet hit my mother in the head. I turned around and saw her lying on the ground. I thought she had fainted; I couldn’t imagine she’d been killed.’

Mirvat Zidan
(17 June 2025)

THREE

NURTURING A GENOCIDE

Air Force One's flight back to Washington necessitated a stop to refuel, so after take-off from Sharm el-Sheikh, it headed directly north towards the UK. There was a synergy in choosing to refuel Trump's plane in Britain. It was the UK that had, as it always did, most swiftly followed America's lead on the big decisions over the two years of the genocide to this point. Its government had been as strong as the US in constantly referencing Israel's right to self-defence. Then Prime Minister Rishi Sunak chose to stress that point without any guardrails around proportionality, human rights or international law. So another of the West's self-declared gatekeepers of law and order had left the gate wide open.

Although the quantum of the UK's arms shipments was less than America's and certain European countries, it did supply them. Its wider military commitment, especially the flying of intelligence missions over Gaza, demonstrated its unwavering commitment to Israel's cause. The UK is always a friend to Israel. As a genocide unfolded, Britain chose to support the colonial oppressor, not the oppressed. When it came to the cause of Zionism and the rights of the Palestinians, it was ever thus.

The US/UK synergy hadn't been on show in Sharm el-Sheikh. As he was doing his rollcall of leaders, President Trump humiliated Prime Minister Keir Starmer. Reading from a script, he said, 'And ... United Kingdom. Where's United Kingdom? Where's our friend?'[1] When Starmer muttered that he was behind him, Trump turned around and beckoned him towards the lectern. 'Come here,' he said in his most condescending manner. They shook hands as Trump asked if everything was 'going good'. Keir Starmer responded, 'Very good,' but just as he reached the lectern Trump turned away from him and said, 'It's very nice that you're here.'[2] Starmer, looking bemused, had no choice but to turn on his heels and return to his place.

Trump likes to embarrass those he thinks might want or need the limelight. It is his to share, or not, as he sees fit. Starmer's muttered acknowledgement of his presence was that of an unsure schoolboy during rollcall. Trump hadn't even used his name, referring only to the UK. Starmer had walked forward before realising all Trump wanted was an acknowledgement he was there. The slight looked deliberate, but it could just have been Trump's standard poor manners that had left Britain's prime minister looking lost.

As was the case for Trump with Biden, Starmer had inherited Britain's involvement in Israel's genocide. That inheritance may have suited Trump, but, while that will not have been the case with Starmer, it didn't appear to greatly bother him. Over those two years, whether under a Conservative government with a small working majority of forty-six seats or Labour with the third largest majority of modern times, the UK stood four-square with Israel. Its commitment was never in question, even as evidence of Israel's war crimes and genocide became incontestable.

Britain's responsibility for the persecution of the Palestinian people goes back a great deal further than its unconditional support for Israel since October 2023. Its cowardice sowed the seeds of what the indigenous people of Palestine have experienced for generations. Just as 7 October 2023 would not have happened without the conditions Palestinians were experiencing forcing some to rebel, Israel's genocide is rooted in the historic failure of the West to corral its colonial intent. There have been many occasions in the almost eighty years since Israel was founded when its ambitions to expand its territories could have been reined in by the West. None were taken. So, circumstances have played out as some prophesied, though even the most pessimistic of observers could not have predicted the descent into the barbarity of the genocide unleashed since October 2023.

BRITAIN'S GIFT TO ZIONISM

In 1917, a lengthy memorandum from British Cabinet member Edwin Montagu to Foreign Secretary Arthur Balfour warned of serious consequences if an imminent government decision to transfer British Mandate Palestine to Zionists went ahead. It was a detailed, expertly argued treatise on the perils attached to what the government in which he served appeared ready to do. Allowing for its clarity and the energy with which it was offered, it still seems unlikely that Montagu could have envisaged just how calamitous the decision would prove to be. Despite the strength of his appeal, he could hardly have conceived of the fate that would befall the Palestinians.

At the time, the Great War was ravaging Europe; it would take around twenty million lives. Men like Montagu, with liberal views, were a rarity in British politics. He was a Jew but strongly anti-Zionist. He was a considerate person. Later, as secretary of state for India, he played a significant role in the Government of India Act, which committed Britain to granting India self-government under its terms. He was fearless in his condemnation of the government's plan to assign British Mandate Palestine to the Zionists, arguing that forcing Muslims and Christians to allow Jews to 'be put in all positions of preference' would have dire consequences.[3]

Montagu was merely recognising the inherent dishonesty in what was being proposed. In the late nineteenth century, the founder of modern Zionism, Theodor Herzl, had acknowledged this, warning that Palestine would have to be taken by stealth. The sole dissenting voice at Cabinet, Montagu was also its only Jew. He warned that giving land that was not theirs to the Zionists would fuel antisemitism and that once they had a land of their own, 'Jews will hereafter be treated as foreigners in every country but Palestine'.[4] While he could not stop it, he succeeded in having a clause to protect non-Jews in Palestine included in the final version of what the government approved. The Balfour Declaration had the effect of granting what was British Mandate Palestine to the Jewish people for their homeland.

In the course of its genocide a century later, all those who dared question Israel's conduct have been painted into the antisemitic corner by its hasbara brush. Hasbara, the Hebrew for 'explaining', is Israel's public diplomacy or global propaganda and it is critical to its management of international opinion. The hasbara budget for 2026 was set at a record $700 million, a huge increase on prior years, reflecting the work Israel faces in quelling public dismay at its actions.[5]

Montagu had foreseen the impact the creation of a state of Israel would have. As the Hungarian journalist Arthur Koestler described, what happened in 1917 was that 'one nation solemnly promised to a second nation the country of a third'.[6] A Zionist, Koestler had no love of the Palestinians but argued, nonetheless, that Britain's action was unprecedented. History would prove neither man was wrong in their concerns.

THE ANTISEMITISM TROPE

Antisemitism has had an impact in the UK, certainly on its politics, for decades. Accusations of it have bedevilled the modern Labour Party, which, while otherwise successful under Tony Blair's leadership, lost much of its left-wing character and draw. The dawn of what became known as 'New Labour' under Blair was about broad popular appeal rather than ideology. Blair's membership of Labour Friends of Israel (LFI) brought him into contact with Michael Levy, who became one of his main supporters. Levy, who described himself as a Zionist, was on the Jewish Leadership Council and used his influence to raise over £15 million for the Labour general election campaign of 1997. Later Blair appointed him to the House of Lords (the upper house of Britain's parliament) and in 2000, at a sensitive time in the region, he used Levy as his 'special envoy' to the Middle

East. Levy 'had acted as a fundraiser for former Israeli Prime Minister Ehud Barak as well as lobbying for Israel in the UK'.[7] The obvious conflict of interest appeared not to concern Blair and during his premiership from 1997 to 2007, Labour's ties with Israel strengthened.

Levy's appointment to the Lords was among a number of cases investigated by the Metropolitan Police in what became known as the 'Cash for Honours' scandal. As part of that investigation, he was arrested in 2006 and again in 2007; no charges were brought. Known as Lord Cashpoint, Levy provided considerable sums of his own, as well as accessing wider Jewish backing. This contributed to Blair becoming more pro-Israel. Josh Paul, who resigned from the US Department of State over its support of Israel, had dealings with Blair and warned that he would 'prioritise economic progress over political progress and Palestinian self-determination'.[8]

Labour's dependence on more traditional funding sources reduced. The trades unions, their power reduced by Margaret Thatcher, became less relevant. The shift was reflected in the policies of Blair's government and, more gradually, a decline in the importance of Labour's traditional support base. Thatcher was widely reported once to have said that New Labour was her greatest achievement, something many analysts agreed with.[9] She was an admirer of the Jews but tougher on Israel than Blair; unafraid to remind them of their responsibility to act in accordance with international law. As prime minister, she distinguished between support for the Jewish people and criticising Israel. She was an admirer of much of what Israel stood for, but throughout her career she also spoke of the Palestinians' right to self-determination. In 1982, she condemned Israel's support of Lebanese Christian militia conduct in Lebanon as 'pure barbarism'[10] and ordered an embargo on arms sales that was to last over a decade. At the same time, the US President, Ronald Reagan, another a supporter of Israel, also expressed outrage at its bombing of Beirut in 1982, halting a shipment of cluster bombs as a result. It seems, then, that the two great allies, led by deeply conservative figures, were more circumspect on Israel.

Blair didn't have Thatcher's backbone or capacity to challenge allies. When it came to the UK's support of Israel, under his premiership it was more robust than ever.

◆◆◆

The only concerted effort to move Labour back to a less Israel-centric position came when Jeremy Corbyn was its leader between 2015 and 2020. Corbyn had always supported Palestine. While a number of issues contributed to the failure of his leadership, it was the charge of being antisemitic that brought him down.

Palestine activists were drawn to Labour under Corbyn. They had been opposed to the pro-Israel approach of Blair's New Labour; with Corbyn at the helm, criticism of Israel became more of a feature of Labour's commentary. Most of it was warranted, but it provided the Zionist lobby with the opportunity to conflate such criticism with antisemitism. Errors, no matter how inconsequential, made by Labour under Corbyn were amplified by the Israeli lobby. Allegations that he'd facilitated a culture of antisemitism in the party, and by some that he himself was antisemitic, ended his leadership.

What is relevant here is less the rights and wrongs of the saga and more the extent to which the Zionist lobby can influence political events. Corbyn was always a vocal critic of racism in British politics, but he did make some comments and interventions that allowed his opponents to paint him as being antisemitic and, therefore, racist. Describing Hamas as 'friends', irrespective of the wider context, was not politically smart. However, it did not make him antisemitic.

Jeremy Corbyn's suspension from Labour in 2020 and the years of controversy preceding it meant his successor, Keir Starmer, had to take a strong position on antisemitism. It was a task he appeared comfortable with – claims about antisemitism running wild in Corbyn's Labour were overstated, but the underlying truth was lost in the political chicanery. In his fine book, *Complicit: Britain's Role in the Destruction of Gaza*, Peter Oborne explores this in detail. Oborne writes that from the moment Starmer was elected party leader, despite having consistently defended Corbyn against the antisemitism charge, he styled himself as a crusader whose priority was to tackle racism against Jews. He argues that Starmer was going to take Labour to the right and 'support for Israel was one ingredient in the glue that helped bond [advisers and allies] together'.[11] Oborne goes on to reference how Palestinian activism was dismissed as a 'creature of the hard left' by Labour's new leadership cohort.[12]

Israel's standard errant behaviour involving its apartheid governance, its theft of land in the West Bank and its skirmishes with Hezbollah in south Lebanon, needed to be monitored and criticised. Corbyn did so, correctly. From day one, Starmer, instead, chose to put Israel back on the long leash Blair had kept it on for years. Starmer, who became prime minister in year two of the genocide, simply absorbed Israel's hasbara that any and all criticism of it amounted to antisemitism. The clean break from Corbynism meant political criticism of Israel in Britain was pushed to the fringes. Little attention was paid as the settler-colonial Israel went about its business with the stealth advocated by Theodor Herzl. Palestine's struggle was becoming more challenging, but the manner of its oppression didn't garner much sympathy in Westminster. Those who spoke of the inequity or of Israel's continuing accretion of Palestinian land were simply criticised for being antisemitic. This managed conflation of any criticism of Israel with antisemitism continued to have the desired effect.

◆◆◆

Corbyn had understood the gravity of Britain's role in Palestine's fate and the moral imperative that followed. That it was a century ago didn't change the fact that the Balfour Declaration's endorsement of Zionism had been catastrophic for the indigenous population. In Britain, Balfour gave a status to Zionism among Jews, spurring 'growth in organized membership: from 7,500 in 200 Zionist societies in 1914 to 30,000 in 600 societies in 1918. One year later, the number of members reached 149,000.'[13] Edwin Montagu called Zionism, a 'mischievous political creed' and saw it as a threat.[14]

The Balfour Declaration facilitated Jewish immigration to Palestine, and Zionists did not delay in setting out to take the land's riches and cultivate a nation exclusively for the Jewish people. Palestinians suffered immediately, in ways similar to what future generations would endure. The nature of suffering, the scale of loss and the scale of deprivation varied over time, but the fundamentals remained the same. Imperial and imperious

Britain knew best when it came to land and to its devolution. In those early years of the twentieth century, what it granted to the Zionists laid the ground for the Nakba, the catastrophe, that was to befall the people of Palestine in 1948.

What Britain did was an act of white-colonial fraternity. A European nation granted territory in the Middle East to a group of foreigners seeking land, without consulting the local population. Some historians dispute the designation of the land as Palestine, given its complex history, but none can argue that the Palestinian claim is without merit. In 1917, Palestine had a population of about 700,000; 82 per cent were Muslim and just 6 per cent Jewish. While each side can build a theoretical narrative around the distant past, 'there is no objective reason why Israelis and Palestinians must fight each other';[15] the reason they do has nothing to do with events of the Middle Ages or the Roman Empire. What's relevant is the last hundred years.

Montagu's memorandum to Balfour had set out the problem pretty starkly. Two years later, in a confidential Cabinet memorandum of 1919, Balfour himself addressed some of the issues arising from the declaration that bore his name. Contrasting it with the policy of the Allies towards Syria, he wrote, 'in Palestine we do not propose even to go through the form of consulting the wishes of the present inhabitants of the country … The four Great Powers [US, UK, France and Italy] are committed to Zionism. And Zionism, be it right or wrong, good or bad, is rooted in age-long traditions, in present needs, in future hopes, of far profounder import than the desires and prejudices of the 700,000 Arabs who now inhabit that ancient land.'[16]

The document set out how Britain and the Zionists, to whom they granted Palestine, were to proceed in realising that objective. It recognised the implications for the indigenous people, 'Whatever be the future of Palestine, it is not now an "independent nation", nor is it yet on the way to become one.'[17] Balfour was acknowledging the move was racist, one that placed the needs of Zionist settlers ('of far profounder import') ahead of those 700,000 Arabs whose land he acknowledged it is. His words would not be out of place in Israel's Knesset of the twenty-first century.

Another five years later, in March 1924, Balfour travelled to Palestine. The independent Arab newspaper *La Palestine* published a special English edition. It quoted the Bible, 'For we wrestle not against flesh and blood, but against principalities, and powers, against the rulers of the darkness of this world, against spiritual wickedness in high places.'[18] It used the phrase of French writer, Emile Zola, 'J'accuse', as its headline for an article challenging the British government, the League of Nations and the government of Palestine over their collective responsibility in allowing a Jewish minority to control the lives of the Arab majority. In another section entitled 'Zionist Colonisation', it said, 'In spite of Zionist attempts to acquire large tracts of land, it is open to doubt if these will be successfully colonised.'[19]

Those words, published a hundred years before Israel's genocide, were an attempt to draw the attention of the British to their responsibility for the treachery afoot. Pointing Zola's 'J'accuse' towards Britain and most of the West is as salient now, a century on. Western powers, starting with Britain, stood by as the Palestinians were subjected to humiliation upon humiliation. Over those hundred years, numerous opportunities to correct the wrongs done to them have been lost; some by design, some through ignorance and others through misplaced fear. The

West's abandonment of Palestine, of its people, has been evident for decades, but never has it been so morally absent as over the course of Israel's recent genocide.

◆◆◆

Zionists had been taking land from Palestinians long before the Nakba of 1948 and the establishment of the state of Israel, but largely by more traditional commercial means. Land purchase had been tabled by leaders as a means of expanding the territory of the Zionist project. Paying for land was, initially, not alien to that endeavour. The Zionist movement was well resourced, and by 1926, less than a decade after the Balfour Declaration, the Jewish population of Palestine had grown from 6 to 18 per cent as the number of little colonies grew dramatically. It plateaued then until the rise of fascism in Europe. The persecution of Jews had an immediate impact; various sources show that in 1935 alone, 60,000 Jews arrived from Germany and other places where Jews were being persecuted. This influx continued and dramatically changed the dynamic.

From 1934 to the end of the Second World War, there was a steady influx of Jewish immigrants, many of them highly skilled, well-educated and financially well-off. The threat to the Palestinians grew and tensions increased. Even then, much of the 'settlement' took the form of land purchase at deflated prices accompanied by the expulsion of the people who'd lived there for generations. By 1940, the Jewish population had grown to 31 per cent.[20] In today's Palestine, there's no purchasing involved – those who come to take what isn't theirs see it as an entitlement – theirs just for the taking.

From the arrival of the first settlers, Jewish communities appeared considerably more prosperous than their Arab counterparts. Much of the wealth was held overseas. This had been the case since the earliest settlements in the late nineteenth century and continued well past the establishment of Israel. Some was acquired through the active sponsorship of very wealthy Jews, but there was institutional support too. 'The World Zionist Organisation established financial and land purchasing institutions',[21] which continued to play a role in the acquisition of land for decades.

However, all was not always as it appeared. The Jewish colonies that were seemingly most prosperous were often in debt and heavily subsidised. In an interview (published by the Zionist Press Bureau), Baron Edmond de Rothschild (with whom Balfour had engaged on the 1917 Declaration) said, of the colonies he'd established, 'To this day I receive letters from the majority of the colonies with requests for money; for this person or the other for his personal needs; for the repair of a road, the building of a well, the construction of a hospital or a school. There is no end to these proposals – always loans of considerable sums to cover budget deficits in Galilee, Samaria, and even Judea … If, after years of work and effort, the colonists cannot attain to the situation of the Egyptian, Arab, or European farmers, the fault lies with them …'[22]

It is not an isolated account. Zionist propaganda ignored this truth in creating the legend of the Jew going back to the land of Palestine. That narrative claims the land was barren, uncultivated by the native Arabs who were portrayed as backward and incapable of making the land productive. It's a false Zionist legend, promulgated for generations, which continues to find willing political endorsement today. Western politicians and some commentators reference Israel and the Zionists as having cultivated the lands of Palestine. This is offensive and at odds with the facts. In 1948, about 5 million dunams, or *c.* 5,000 square kilometres, of Palestine was cultivated, providing for its people.

This key truth is unhelpful to those in the West who need to undermine Palestine's self-sufficiency in order to build the case for Israel. In an address to President Isaac Herzog on the seventy-fifth anniversary of the establishment of Israel, EU Commission President Ursula von der Leyen said, 'Seventy-five years ago, a dream was realised with Israel's Independence Day … You [Israel] have literally made the desert bloom.'[23] In 2017, then Democratic Senator Kamala Harris said pretty much the same to a meeting of AIPAC, lauding 'Israeli ingenuity that has truly made a desert bloom.'[24]

The obvious inherent racism and historical inaccuracy of such statements, which were pointed out at the time, didn't stop Keir Starmer later using the same fable. In 2021, he told the annual LFI lunch that early Israeli leaders were 'democrats who made the desert flower'. More seriously, the aspirant prime minister offered the same audience policy hostages to fortune, by saying that Labour was opposed to BDS and, bizarrely, referencing Israel's 'rumbustious democracy, its independent judiciary, and its commitment to the rule of law … [and] vibrant media.'[25] Starmer's determination to put distance between his leadership and Jeremy Corbyn's was such that his profile of Israel bore no relation to reality. When he delivered that speech, Israel's judiciary was in a battle with legislators to retain its independence. That the country had long excluded international law as relevant seemed a matter of indifference to a Labour leader who'd served as Britain's director of public prosecutions (DPP).

More seriously, Starmer described an ethnocratic, apartheid state as a robust democracy. Here was evidence that more than a century after it gifted the land of Palestine to the Zionists, institutionally, the UK remained firmly behind Zionism. These remarks were made shortly after Starmer had become Labour party leader. There's been no lessening of that commitment since he became prime minister a year into Israel's genocide.

◆◆◆

The hasbara that misrepresents the truth about Palestine before the foundation of Israel contributes to the West's refusal to stop Israel's colonial ambition. Its status, one long granted by the US, Britain and Europe's major powers, is as the West's only friend in the region. This is a product of colonialism, geography, security, commerce and racism. It's so all-consuming that it has engulfed any concern for the Palestinians. Palestine's autonomy, its right to exist and the welfare of its people have been sacrificed to the need to serve Israel. Israel is regarded as the West's strategic buffer against Iran and Islam. Israel profiles itself in a manner that plays to a political cohort in the West that views the Muslim world with suspicion and fear.

Israel's twenty-first-century genocide is a ramped-up version of the incremental destruction of Palestine and the terrorising of its people. Hamas's brutal attack on Israel's soil on 7 October 2023 was a release of the pressure valve of oppression. That was the fault, not just of Israel but of its collaborators in the West who, for decades, stood firmly in its corner. Western powers may have hoped the settler-coloniser might be content with the land they already held, but that has never looked likely from the moment the state of Israel was founded as the embers of the Nakba still burned.

The Nakba or Catastrophe was horrifying. It resulted from the wild colonial ambition of the Zionists, whom Western powers had supported in their intention to build a Jewish nation state in Palestine. The West was as indifferent to that horror as it is to today's genocide. The 1948 Nakba was the point at which the threat hanging over the indigenous Palestinian Arab population for thirty years, since the Balfour Declaration, struck. In late 1947, the Zionists, using the declaration as a form of licence, started a series of massacres and violent attacks. When they ended, with about 500 towns and cities destroyed, 15,000 Palestinians dead and 750,000 displaced, there was an opportunity for the Zionists to change forever the dynamic around ownership and control. The Palestinians had fled in such numbers that great tracts of land, their dwellings and farm buildings, were abandoned. Once the occupiers took control of this land and property, they refused to relinquish them. They claimed, as they have done ever since, that they were being held for security reasons. Israel's refusal to acknowledge the Palestinians as refugees, denying them the right to return, was critical to the Zionist ambition. It remains so.

The new state enacted legislation authorising it to take over abandoned land and property wherever it wished. The 1953 Land Acquisition Law retrospectively gave legal character to all the abuses inflicted on the Palestinians over the course of the Nakba, or what Israel determined as 'a state of emergency'.[26] This new law had a broad and destructive impact on the fate of Palestine. It was later used to allow the direct intervention of the state in the administration and management of all property interests of

Palestinians. This gave rise to what is euphemistically known as the 'settler movement'. The state had to make the land it had taken profitable, so it chose to establish settlements populated by its citizens and Jewish immigrants from Europe.

This period of settler-colonialism by the infant state of Israel highlighted its status as a rogue nation. It believed then and does today that its origins exempt it from the international rule of law or the codes of behaviour set down by the UN. It set out its stall and, despite becoming a member of the UN in 1949, has behaved with complete autonomy ever since. The UN, as an institution, and the international community, chose to leave well enough alone. This was a fatal error.

What the Zionists learned from the Nakba was that if they took the land by force and then policed their control of the stolen property, Palestinian resistance was limited. They saw too that the international community would occasionally protest, but not often and never meaningfully. The people of Palestine were poor; they were farmers with limited resources and no administration to protect them. The Zionist movement in the Middle East may have been young, but it was organised and it moved with purpose to advance the cause of a Jewish state. That their belief was, in part, maniacal, rooted in a literal interpretation of the Old Testament, gave them the certainty of their rights. This remains the case with many of today's settlers. What they have done in the West Bank over the first two years of the genocide in Gaza amounts to the largest land-grab since Israel began appropriating the holdings of Palestinians.

Zionists have been emboldened by the international community's indifference. Israel's sense of exceptionalism is rooted in the inherent racism of Western culture. That is powerfully evident today in the actions of Israel's right-wing government and how it manages the West's reaction to its excesses. The West remains easy prey to the power of the Zionist lobby. And while there is one unified voice representing Israel, the Palestinian cause has long been fractured. It has also never got to grips with how the West thinks. In his seminal work, *The Hundred Years' War on Palestine*, Rashid Khalidi emphasised this: 'Compared with the sophisticated grasp the Zionist leadership had of European and other Western societies, of which most of them were natives or citizens, Arab leaders had at best a limited understanding of the politics, societies and cultures of the countries of Europe, to say nothing of the nascent superpowers.'[27]

The history of Palestine since 1948 is littered with conflict, wars and uprisings (Intifadas), and with peace initiatives, including the Oslo Accords, Camp David and a number of less high-profile initiatives from 2008 to 2011. This history is critical to understanding how it can be that the nations of the West chose either to actively sponsor Israel's genocide or simply to look on silently. It helps us to understand how, despite words of support and countless UN resolutions, the Palestinians have long been abandoned. It is fundamental to a recognition that Israel is a product of the West. The West created Israel in its own likeness, and it has continuously nourished Israel's settler-colonial ambition.

Israel had done many shocking things to the Palestinians since its foundation, but nothing it ever did met with disapproval or any serious sanction. What I call Nakba II, Israel's genocide in the third decade of the twenty-first century, is the most violent attack on the rights of the Palestinians ever, including the original Nakba of 1947–48. Within months of commencing Nakba II in October 2023, the state of Israel knew the West would be indifferent, even if it chose to wipe all trace of Palestine off the map. It is unlikely that Netanyahu's government ever doubted it. On 13 October 2023, courtesy of Trump's 'celebration', they knew for certain that they need not have worried.

Over the decades the West has had numerous opportunities to act and change the dynamic. Those failings may seem as nothing against its deliberate sponsorship of a genocide, but they should not be overlooked. Those moments represent why the circumstances exist that allow Israel to behave as it does. After the 1948 Nakba, the next pivotal point came towards the end of the 1960s, when, as an established presence in the Middle East and a firm ally of most Western powers, the state of Israel asserted the full scale of its ambition.

WHAT MIGHT HAVE BEEN

President John F. Kennedy was largely pro-Israel, but he had a greater understanding of the Palestinian cause than most US politicians. At the age of twenty-one, he'd been sent to Palestine by his father and wrote to him about the Zionist plan being touted by Britain in the late 1930s: 'it theoretically presents a good solution but it just won't work'.[28] Proud of his Irish ancestry, even a young Kennedy would have been well aware of the detritus of British colonialism. Nonetheless, he was a pragmatist, who understood that Israel was an essential ally of the US.

Later, some years into his presidency, Kennedy's early political enthusiasm for Israel seemed to be on the wane. In May 1963 he tried to discourage France from assisting Israel's development of nuclear weapons. Records of a White House meeting show that French Foreign Minister Maurice Couve de Murville acknowledged France's mistake and undertook that, going forward, it would 'only lease [it] uranium, not sell it'.[29] Unlike most presidents since, Kennedy was not content to just ask America's allies to intervene, he was also prepared to act directly. Two months after his White House meeting with de Murville, and just days after Israel had appointed a new prime minister, Levi Eshkol, Kennedy wrote to Eshkol about Israel's Dimona nuclear facility. The letter was friendly but direct. Kennedy apologised for writing so soon after Eshkol took power, but in the letter, headlined 'Secret', he emphasised the issue's crucial importance to the welfare of both Israel and the US. He set out a proposed schedule of visits to Dimona by US scientists, which he wanted to happen six-monthly. He also made a quite explicit threat: 'As I wrote to Mr. Ben-Gurion [Eshkol's predecessor], this government's commitment to and support of Israel could be seriously jeopardized if it should be thought that we were unable to obtain reliable information on a subject as vital to peace as the question of Israel's effort in the nuclear field.'[30] The content and tone of the letter were unusually combative.

Arguably, the most provocative and far-seeing decision on Israel that Kennedy made was to thwart the power and influence of the already growing Zionist lobby in America. He was acutely aware of its political significance and not shy about using it. During his 1960 presidential campaign, he addressed the American Zionist Organisation of America [a forerunner of AIPAC]. The speech was enthusiastic, punctuated with very positive perspectives on the Zionist mission, but it also referred to the need for a 'reconsideration of the Arab refugee problem'.[31] That continues, today, to be a particularly sensitive point for

Israel. The potential of Greater Israel would be fatally damaged if Israel were forced to acknowledge Palestinians' right of return. Kennedy did express the standard support for Israel in his speech but also warned that the US would 'act promptly and decisively against any nation in the Middle East which attacks its neighbor' and that the region needed 'water, not war … tractors, not tanks … bread, not bombs'.[32]

Two years after his election, Kennedy sought to establish greater transparency in the Zionist agency's work. On 21 November 1962, the American Zionist Council received formal notification that the government had determined it was no longer entitled to an exemption from registration as an agency of a foreign government and would be obliged to register under the Foreign Agents Registration Act.[33] It seems the decision, contemporaneous with his moves on the refugee issue, represented Kennedy's belief that Israel's growing influence on US politics was excessive. His motivation may also have been about the perception, bordering on paranoia, gripping Washington about the growth of communism. Some historians believe that while he remained pro-Israel, JFK believed that the Arab people could be a counterweight to the perceived communist threat.

While Kennedy approved a weapon system sale to Israel, he had an appreciation of the ills of colonialism and the risk that Israel was betraying signs of territorial entitlement. Something even more energising than nuclear power for Israeli politicians of that time was the rights of Palestinian refugees. A few months before his death, in a move consistent with what he'd told the Zionist lobby in 1960, Kennedy's administration was preparing to press the case for the right of return of Palestinian refugees. Israel was outraged. Israeli newspaper archives of a now defunct daily newspaper, *HaBoker*, show Ben-Gurion's government reacting furiously to a US plan to call for the implementation of Article 11 of UN Resolution 194, the right of return of Palestinian refugees.[34] The archives state that the Cabinet drafted a response saying that the refugees had 'fled of their own free will'.[35]

On 21 November 1963, the day before JFK's assassination in Dallas, Texas, *The New York Times* reported that an American resolution calling for the UN to resolve the predicament of Palestinian refugees was approved, with Israel the only dissenter of the eighty-four voting nations. The paper also reported, consistent with what Israeli archives show, that Israel had summoned the US ambassador to inform him of its 'extreme distaste today for the United States' position in the Palestine-refugee debate'.[36]

That rare effort by a US president to deal in uncomfortable truths, whatever its motivation, perished with Kennedy. What seems likely is that, had he not been assassinated and had he served a second term, he would have made use of the next opportunity that arose for the West to recalibrate its relationship with Israel. Palestine's interests would have been better served by John F. Kennedy being at the helm when the Six-Day War occurred four years later, during which Israel took the West Bank, including East Jerusalem and Gaza.

◆◆◆

In November 1967, French President Charles de Gaulle addressed a concern felt by many Western nations at a news conference in Paris resulting from this war. He said that while some powers, including France, were pleased to see the state of

Israel established, it had a responsibility to act morally towards its neighbours. He said that meant that it must live within the territory it had been granted. De Gaulle spoke prophetically about what he feared in that moment. '[T]he action taken by doubling its [Israel's] population through the immigration of new elements suggested that the territory it had acquired would not be sufficient for long and that it would be inclined to expand it, to use any opportunity that might present itself.'[37]

The UN is the global body responsible for monitoring such things. A decade after the Six-Day War it passed Resolution 32/5, which called on Israel to 'desist forthwith from taking any action which would result in changing the legal status, geographical nature or demographic composition of the Arab territories occupied since 1967, including Jerusalem'.[38] Nowhere else have the limitations of the UN been as exposed as they have in the face of the disdain with which Israel has treated the organisation over its eighty years of membership. There should have been no surprise that two decades after it had become the UN's fifty-eighth member state, Israel refused to countenance Resolution 32/5 or to consider addressing its policy of settler-colonialism.

Israel's Zionists were not going to be dictated to by anyone with regard to what best suited their ambition for God's chosen people, least of all an international agency that was only as old as itself. The Israeli authorities completely ignored 32/5, as they have pretty much all of the hundreds of UN resolutions dealing with the issue of settlements since. For as long as some of the UN's most powerful member states, especially the US, choose to help Israel, it cannot enforce the steps necessary to curb the latter's settler-colonialism.

The first signs of Zionist contempt for the UN were evident

at its meeting to consider Israel's application for membership. The motion referenced a report of the UN Security Council that Israel, which it termed a 'peace-loving State', had 'unreservedly' accepted the obligations of membership and committed to honour them from day one.[39] However, the record of the proceedings indicates that Israel had no real intention of complying. In the debate on its membership, its representative was asked about the fate of Palestinian refugees, given the resolution previously passed on repatriation. The response was 'another method of settling the question would be resettlement of the refugees in neighbouring countries'.[40] The official record of the debate, held almost eight decades ago, clearly establishes the intentions of this newly elected member of the UN: either to ignore its obligations completely or, if necessary, to pay lip service to them. Nothing has changed since.

It is accepted by most analysts, even the most pro-Palestine, that any resolution that could be credibly brought forward now would be predicated on a form of territorial realignment. This is a reason the Six-Day War is so important. It's what makes the events of that time so relevant to the future. The year 1967 marked Israel's full descent into the geopolitical abyss, the point at which it expressed contempt for the international order or rule of law. Every year since that it has been allowed to behave as though its boundaries are not what they were in 1948, but what it presumed to make them in 1967. That the West has never prioritised challenging this abuse demonstrates the stranglehold of the Zionist movement.

Each of the fifty times, to 2025, that the US vetoed UN motions sanctioning Israel, it did a great deal more than weaken the UN's status; it showed itself to be a cipher of a nation of ten million people. Security Council votes matter. The small state of Israel has dominated its ledger since the foundation of the UN; the bulk of such votes have been resolutions critical of that state. It is the only country with a standing agenda item at the UN Human Rights Council, requiring that its human rights record is debated at every session. Its settler colonialism has been on full public view for decades, but the West has chosen to ignore it. In the face of Israel's consistent aggression toward Palestine, the West has allowed the annexation-creep to continue and increase. In the process, it has rendered meaningless the UN and any moral code it espouses.

The 1967 war is critical to events since October 2023. It contextualises the wider Western conduct over the course of the twenty-first century genocide. Ever since that war, the West's collective indifference to Palestine has been marked. Two decades after Israel's foundation and formal recognition on the land of Palestine, that short war was its clear statement of intent. Israel wanted more land and it would take more. The events of June 1967 resulted in Israel gaining complete control of the land of British Mandate Palestine and meant that its territory more than tripled to over 68,000 square kilometres. After the Sinai was returned to Egypt in 1982, Israel's control across Palestine remained secure.

It was then that Israel registered, beyond any debate or question, its colonial intent and signalled, as it has most resolutely ever since, that it would be patient but that it would not stop. UN Resolution 242 followed in November 1967, calling for the 'withdrawal of Israel armed forces from territories occupied in the recent conflict'.[41] Western inaction over the five plus decades since has convinced Israel that nobody is going to prevent it from realising a Greater Israel. Resolution 242 remains on the UN's books to this day.

The leadership of the US was unconcerned in 1967. John F. Kennedy may have been considering policy change early in the decade, but Lyndon B. Johnson, who replaced him and then won re-election, was not. Israel was already providing significant funds to the Democratic Party. Kennedy had benefited but held the view that the Palestinian cause had to be addressed. Johnson and his closest advisers and confidantes couldn't have cared less about Palestine. His administration was wedded to Israel, and if that meant they needed to be hostile to the Arab cause, so be it. Most were Zionists. US public opinion was pro-Israel, and the already confident Zionist lobby became ever more arrogant in its pursuit of political support.

The 1967 war saw Israel sweep aside their Arab combatants, Egypt, Syria and Jordan. As would became the norm, the unprecedented levels of arms provided by the US facilitated this military victory. President Johnson also granted Israel significant economic aid. Johnson's presidency altered the dynamics of the US–Israel relationship, providing levels of military and financial support that have largely been sustained ever since. In a brilliant essay on the subject, Ronan Mainprize wrote that when Joe Biden first embraced Benjamin Netanyahu after 7 October 2023, 'he did so as a clear continuation of Lyndon Johnson's policies'.[42]

The Six-Day War had two profound and lasting impacts. Israel occupied considerably more of Palestine than it did before it started, and the US–Israel alliance, strong since the state had been founded in 1948, was considerably strengthened. It may seem like a long time ago, but when Israel conducted its genocide in 2023–25, those interconnected facts contributed to the ease with which it could slaughter Palestinians and destroy their land.

THE GREAT MARCH OF RETURN

Refugee status goes to the very heart of Israel's obsession with keeping Palestinians in their place. From its establishment, it has refused to recognise that Palestinians have a right to return. That recognition would undermine the Zionist view that the land is theirs. It's critical to Israel's cause, to the belief of Zionists, that the Palestinians have no rights to any of the land Israel has taken from them. This total belief drives the oppression and the inevitable and understandable outbreaks of rebellion. Importantly, even when those who have done the most to take the fight to Israel – Hamas – joined with more peaceful elements, Israel chose to fight peaceful protest with gunfire.

The period of what became known as 'The Great March of Return' is important in the context of Trump's plan and the West's acquiescence to Israel. It is also important because of the frequency with which Israel claims Palestinian resistance always takes the form of violence. While it rings hollow coming from Israel, many in the international community argue that it is forced to act as it does because the Palestinians' only interest is in violent resistance. The Palestinian civil protests of 2018 and 2019 show that it is Israel that feels most threatened by peace.

A joint report of B'Tselem and the Palestinian Centre for Human Rights records: 'On 30 March 2018 – Land Day – Palestinians in the Gaza Strip began to hold regular protests along the perimeter fence [erected by Israel], demanding an end to the blockade Israel has imposed since 2007 and fulfilment of the right of return.'[43] Known as the Great March of Return, protests by tens of thousands, including women and children, took place on Fridays and continued until the end of 2019. They were largely peaceful. There were no reports of arms being used, although some of tyres being burned and stones being thrown at the IDF patrolling the other side of the fence. However, it was clear, and largely accepted by most Israeli media, that the objective of the exercise was a display of civil disobedience.

Many accounts said the activities took place 400 metres from the fence and included stalls and various arts and sporting activities. IDF sources argued that the protesters were nearer, with international news agencies putting them at more like 200 to 300 metres. However, Israeli security services acknowledged there was no risk of the fence being breached. Yet, over the course of these protests, Israeli snipers regularly opened fire, killing and injuring Palestinians.

In May 2018, Donald Trump's recklessness, in his first term, contributed directly to the loss of innocent lives. Seventy-three Palestinians were shot dead on 14 May as the marchers protested the relocation of America's embassy from Tel Aviv to Jerusalem. A month earlier, the then ICC prosecutor Fatou Bensouda warned that, 'Any person who incites or engages in acts of violence including by ordering, requesting, encouraging or contributing in any other manner to the commission of crimes within ICC's jurisdiction is liable to prosecution before the Court …'[44] She warned both sides against breaches. The government of Israel ignored her. The UN Human Rights Council made similar noises in early 2019, demanding that Israel investigate cases which could constitute 'war crimes or crimes against humanity'.[45] The chair of the commission of inquiry, Santiago Canton, didn't mince his words, but they were wasted. Israel ignored him too.

IDF snipers active during this period were among those who came forward to provide detailed evidence. In May 2021, *Hamakor*, an investigative programme on Israel's Channel 13, broadcast in Hebrew the testimony of a number of snipers from the field. Their instructions were to 'open fire' whenever they encountered ringleaders or 'major instigators' of violence. It was up to each individual soldier to decide who qualified for shooting. One soldier described it as being, '"the eye of God". That's what they call it. You decide who's going to walk in the morning and who isn't. You decide who's going to have a knee afterwards and who isn't.'[46] Another recalled that they were pressured to shoot so, 'I'll stop looking for the right person ... and start looking for the right person for the situation because I have to shoot somebody, but it could be that he didn't really do anything. It could be that he was standing looking at the view, saying, wow what a pretty sky.'[47]

This abuse happened on Benjamin Netanyahu's watch as prime minister, but he rebutted all criticism. He said the marchers' intentions – even though they were unarmed – was to breach 'the border fence, and kidnap and murder Israelis that are 100 metres away and communities that align the fence and so on.'[48] None of the evidence supported this narrative. Neither did the soldiers' testimonials: 'They have no way of getting through there. You have a ton of ramparts, a ton of covers ... There's no single person who can, especially during a riot, get through.'[49] An international commission of inquiry confirmed that over the period of the protests, 214 Palestinians were killed, 46 of whom were children. Eight thousand eight hundred children were among the total number of 36,143 Palestinians injured. An estimated 22,500 children required psychosocial support due to trauma from the events.[50]

This prolonged period of disturbance can be overlooked in reviewing the conduct of Israel over the decades since its foundation. Juxtaposed against other periods of sustained violent oppression – the two Intifadas (1987–93 and 2000–05) or Israeli offensives like Operation Cast Lead in 2008–09 – the Great March of Return might appear less noteworthy. But its importance lies in the nature of the Palestinian action, and how Israel still chose to react with violence. It was a restrained form of protest against decades of oppression, yet it was met by lethal force. There are those, even among critics of Israel, who blame Hamas or other factions for Israel's excesses. There are some who understand the levels of oppression but still refuse to countenance the Palestinians' right to fight. Why would you not fight if, even when you protest peacefully, you're met with brutal violence?

This is why the Great March of Return is important. There's no credible witness who has argued that the thousands of civilians who took part represented a threat to Israel or the hundreds of IDF soldiers on the Israeli side of the Occupation Fence. The evidence, even that provided by soldiers who were there, indicates there was no control over how they combatted the imagined threat. With Israel, its right is always to fight fire with fire and, as has been noted by the most experienced commentators, to do so with excessive force.

◆◆◆

In 1972, the Northern Ireland Civil Rights Association organised a march in the city of Derry in northwest Ireland to protest against the British government's ongoing use of internment without trial. Tensions were very high in Derry and Belfast, as thousands of nationalists were resisting with increasing intensity over the inequalities that were such a part of Northern Ireland's social order. Internment of great numbers of agitators was the thin end of a wedge thick with discrimination against the nationalist people.

In August 1971, eleven people had been killed over three days by the British Army during operations in the Ballymurphy area of Belfast on Ireland's northeast coast. It was a time of great unrest, the very early phase of the period that would become known as the Troubles and would run for thirty years. Belfast was the focal point. Shootings, many fatal, were daily events, and there were often multiple explosions and incidents of arson, as well as non-violent acts of civil disobedience. Paramilitary groups, both loyalist and republican, were becoming more organised, more active and more prepared to kill, sometimes indiscriminately. Tensions were very high when, in carrying out a wide sweep of Ballymurphy to take republican (nationalist) suspects for internment, the army was met by resistance and opened fire. It claimed that the victims were all republican gunmen.

The wheels of justice move really slowly in such circumstances. It was 2021 before the results of an independent inquiry established that 'all of the deceased ... were entirely innocent of any wrongdoing on the day in question'.[51] While acknowledging the widespread tension in the city at the time, the inquiry chair, Justice Keegan referenced that there were a number of occasions when 'the use of force was clearly disproportionate'. It seems proportionality is often beyond the oppressor.

What happened in the Bogside in Derry six months later was more shocking. On Sunday, 30 January 1972, about 12,000 people in Derry marched to protest the continuing discrimination against the nationalist community. The same regiment that had been involved at Ballymurphy, the Parachute Regiment, was sent in; within hours, twenty-six unarmed people had been shot, thirteen of whom died that day. There was verified evidence of brutality, with frightened civilians being chased down and beaten, and armoured vehicles running down others on the street. The British government claimed the soldiers had acted in self-defence, while the Irish government appealed to the UN for the support of peacekeepers in Northern Ireland.

What the events of that day presaged was the strengthening of armed resistance and a lengthy period of sustained violence that cost a great number of innocent lives. Within days of Bloody Sunday, British Prime Minister Edward Heath ordered an inquiry by Lord Chief Justice Widgery. His report, produced within two months, found the soldiers had acted reasonably, in self-defence. While even some British establishment figures dismissed the Widgery Report as a whitewash, it was decades before a new process was established, in 1998, as part of the Northern Ireland peace process.

The Saville Inquiry took twelve years to complete and involved interviewing almost a thousand witnesses. Its findings were powerfully destructive of the idea that marches or gatherings of civil disobedience are, inherently, a threat to law and order. The conclusions were damning of those there to keep the peace. It said people were killed because the soldiers had lost control, that no warnings were given before shots were fired, that none of the victims had been armed, and that none of the paratroopers had 'fired in response to attacks or threatened attacks by nail or petrol bombers [as had been claimed]'.[52] The report also said that soldiers had lied to cover up their wrongdoing. The testimonials to Israel's Channel 13 by the IDF snipers who took part in the killing of Palestinians during the Great March of Return stand in stark contrast.

It is easy to brand as terrorists all those who take up arms to fight back against oppression. Israel has mastered the black art of propaganda which, along with its representation of any challenge to its behaviour as antisemitic, has allowed it to demonise those Palestinians who have taken up arms. Israel is a terror state; even Palestinians who simply marched peacefully in protest at their oppression were gunned down. Israel knows it can ignore any concerns of the international community or institutions like the UN about its behaviour. It knows there's no chance of being held to account. Its conduct and its freedom to do whatever it wants, whenever it chooses, makes it impervious to criticism. Its management of the Great March of Return was to crush it and wait for the international blowback, which, when it came, was limited. It was ignored and the West forgot about it. This was not Tiananmen Square or downtown Hong Kong, so there wasn't even a modicum of diplomatic tut-tutting. The dead were Palestinians – not our concern.

It was another important sign that the West's need of Israel would always protect it from any intervention to curb its aggressive colonialism. It was this that John F. Kennedy recognised. In a letter to a friend who had warned him against the partisanship of US politics in the Middle East, he wrote, 'I wholly agree that American partisanship in the Arab–Israeli Israel conflict is dangerous to both the U.S. and the free world.'[53]

Israel knows that even if there is condemnation it will be limited and will not be followed by action. This has never been more manifest than since the end of that last great act of civil defiance by the people of Gaza in 2018–19. The violence meted out to the Palestinians who took part was such that the great symbolism of the exercise – the idea of being free to return – was lost. That aspiration holds the key to their future. It is that aspiration that most threatens the Zionists. It is that aspiration that drives the repulsive language of Israeli politicians who profile Palestinians as some class of lower humans, incapable of managing themselves. Why therefore would you grant them their rights? The West has failed them, failed to protect them and to fight on their behalf.

A BEHOLDEN BRITAIN

In 1948, Britain, which alone had birthed the problem of Zionist aspirations for Palestine, saw that error take sovereign shape as the world completely abandoned the indigenous people. It knew, even then, that trouble lay ahead. It was cowardly; in such a rush to create distance from any involvement that, just a fortnight later, it had withdrawn all its troops from a territory it had controlled since 1917. Once its administration of Palestine on 14 May 1948 came to an end, it was as if it had never been there. The most critical part of its mandate should have been the preparation of the Palestinians for self-rule, but this was abandoned. This pattern was repeated by Britain continually, right up to and including its support for Israel's genocidal campaign against the Palestinians since October 2023.

Britain has chosen to be in lockstep with the US in most moments of international conflict; when it comes to Israel, they're always of the same mind. President Biden's rash and irresponsible commitment the day after Hamas's attack, that he would provide unprecedented levels of support, set the tone. He said he would make 'no effort to urge restraint from Israel … Israel has the right to respond, indeed it has a duty to respond to these vicious attacks', setting the tone for all that followed.[54] An emboldened Netanyahu led a chorus of bloodlust from his government ministers, and the first Israeli strikes on Gaza happened on the evening of the Hamas attack.

UK Prime Minister Rishi Sunak had more time than Biden and could have reacted differently; he could have been supportive but in a more measured way. That seemed to escape him. The brutality of Israel's intentions was already clear by the time he offered full support without any constraints. It was twelve days after Hamas had killed 1,200 in its attack on Israeli soil that he travelled to Tel Aviv. By then a Royal Navy task force was in the Eastern Mediterranean, and the RAF was providing surveillance information to the Israelis.

There was never any doubt that Britain would support Israel, but, as with America, the lack of any conditionality should have been of concern. Israel has form in these matters; there has never been a conflict where its reaction has been proportionate. The UK knew this; the first fortnight after 7 October should have worried it about what lay ahead. Sunak arrived in Israel shortly after an airstrike on the al-Ahli Arab hospital in Gaza city killed hundreds. It was also within hours of the departure of President

Biden, who'd travelled to meet Netanyahu. Already taken aback by the scale of Israel's immediate response, the president tried to rein in Israel's thirst for vengeance. 'While you feel rage, don't be consumed by it,' he counselled.[55] It was too little too late.

When Sunak met Netanyahu, the official Palestinian death toll was already estimated at 3,500, while 12,000 were injured, and the UN was reporting that almost half the population of Gaza was homeless. Yet the prime minister's comments made no reference to the plight of the Gazans. Nor did he call for proportionality or warn of consequences if Israel did not abide by international law. The backing of Israel's two firmest allies, the two military powers that always seek to work together on international affairs, proved resolute, even as Israel's most right-wing government chose to take the Middle East towards the abyss.

Sunak's official statement called for leaders 'to come together to avoid a further dangerous escalation of conflict'.[56] It was no more than standard Whitehall guff. Later he stood alongside Benjamin Netanyahu as he described Hamas as 'the new Nazis' they had to fight together. The British prime minister said solemnly that the UK would stand in solidarity with Israel in what Netanyahu had called 'its darkest hour'. The UK government's statement may have referenced the need to avoid any escalation, but Sunak chose to follow his host's highly emotive words by telling him, '[W]e [the UK] will stand with your people and we also want you to win.'[57] Netanyahu had profiled Hamas provocatively; Britain's prime minister chose not to distance himself or his country from these remarks.

Exhorting an oppressive coloniser to 'win' showed how strong Israel's hold remains. It is a word that should never have entered Sunak's lexicon on Palestine; it is the word Trump used as an accolade in the Knesset more than a year later. To tell the people of Israel that the British wanted them to 'win' sanctioned not just what had occurred over the first twelve days of Israel's actions, but the genocide that followed. It meant, of course, that Britain wanted to see the Palestinians 'lose', which, given their already dire situation, suggested the UK was happy to aid the genocide from the start. This amounted to a great deal more than providing the nourishment for Israel to become genocidal; it was tantamount to telling it to go out and do its thing.

Rishi Sunak's Conservative government, which displayed many old-fashioned Tory characteristics, was approaching its end. Yet its successor, a Labour party with unprecedented opinion poll leads and a former DPP and expert on international law, Keir Starmer, as leader, couldn't find a different pitch. Starmer's then shadow foreign secretary, David Lammy, and attorney general, Emily Thornberry, also law graduates, were as resolute in their support of Israel as Starmer himself. Labour did not condemn Israeli ministers who advocated for a complete siege of Gaza, including cutting off humanitarian aid. This absence of any moral code was extraordinary and distressing in equal measure.

The bizarre appointment by the ailing Tory government of former Prime Minister David Cameron as foreign secretary in November 2023 changed nothing. Brexit had exposed Cameron's weakness and a period out to pasture hadn't improved his performance. Millions of Palestinians were to suffer as he made error after error, each reinforcing Israel's position and making life considerably tougher for the Palestinians. The worst was when, in January 2024, he suspended future payments to the UN Relief and Works Agency (UNRWA). It was a shameful decision based on nothing more than Israeli propaganda claiming, without evidence, that UNRWA staff were assisting Hamas in its military operations. UNRWA has been critical to Palestine since it was established by the UN in 1949. In *Catastrophe*, I describe it as 'irreplaceable', 'a bulwark of the Palestinian defences against that Zionist mission'.[58] This is precisely why Israel has long had an antipathy towards it. Cameron's decision was inept and wrong.

Many Western nations chose blindly to accept the lie about UNRWA, also responding by cutting aid to the agency that pumped blood into Gaza's veins. When an independent report in April 2024 found that Israel's allegations were largely unfounded, Britain chose not to follow others and restart funding. It remained tied to the American position, resolute in its refusal to back UNRWA. The only parliamentary challenge came from the Scottish National Party, which, apart from criticising the Tory government, paid out an additional £250,000 from Scotland's development aid budget to UNRWA.

After the Labour Party won the 2024 election, the new foreign secretary, David Lammy, restored the funding, but this did not mark any wider change in approach. The loss of funding over those six months was of direct benefit to Israel in weakening the agency of 13,000 employees in Gaza who worked to alleviate the suffering of its two million people. This blind, unquestioning acceptance of the Israeli line on the one agency that has served the people of Palestine revealed much about the stranglehold Israel has on the West. It exposed the West's partiality.

◆◆◆

As it did about UNRWA, Israel lied about the Hamas attack. The facts of 7 October 2023 were undoubtedly horrific but not enough for its intended response. On the basis of the kind of ratio applied to previous violent events, 1,200 people killed would not allow the Zionist government to pursue its ambition to rid the region of Palestinians for all time. It needed to portray the Arabs as barbarians. So the attack was made about a great deal more than the loss of life and hostages taken. It was embellished to exaggerate the conduct of the perpetrators.

Hamas has published two reports on the attack, defending it, while at the same time acknowledging failures and indiscipline. Neither report, the brief one months after the attack or the more detailed one two years later, alter the fact that it committed war crimes. Its reports have been criticised by some human rights bodies, but, however flawed, they amount to more than the sovereign state of Israel has done. At the time, Israeli authorities said the scene included babies burned in ovens, some removed from their mothers' wombs, and beheaded bodies. This was largely fabricated, but it worked. As media analyst Marc Owen Jones has said, 'If you can activate people's sense of disgust, they're more likely to support dire retribution against Palestinians.'[59] The mounting expressions of outrage by world leaders outdid each other, with most matched by commitments to support Israel no matter what.

The change in the British government in July 2024 brought little shift in the policy towards Israel. Britain's political left had long abandoned its principles, though, since the Blair premiership, considering Labour to be left wing is possibly moot. The Starmer government did introduce a partial suspension of thirty arms export licences in September of that year. This represented less than 10 per cent of relevant licences, but Prime Minister Netanyahu was still furious, accusing Britain of threatening

Israel's security and 'sending a horrible message' to Hamas.[60] Whenever its allies offer even the slightest admonishment or propose any form of constraint, Israel reacts like the sovereign adolescent it is.

This small adjustment was the only point at which it appeared UK policy might shift. The move to reduce licences happened around the same time as payments to UNRWA were restored and the British government dropped its opposition to the ICC's arrest warrant against Netanyahu. However, figures published by the research and advocacy group Action on Armed Violence (AOAV) showed that over 8,500 separate munitions (including bombs and missiles) were sent to Israel after the announced partial suspension.[61] The new government's support of Israel continued apace and, most critically, it ensured the UK remained in lockstep with Washington.

Britain's greatest military assistance to Israel was in gathering military intelligence invaluable to the pursuit of its genocidal ambition. Surveillance is one of the most sophisticated and essential areas of modern warfare, especially for a regular army fighting a guerrilla force on its own turf. In 2025, there was only a small reduction in Britain's surveillance of Gaza for the IDF compared to what had been carried out in the first full year of Israel's genocide. The sophistication of the aircraft and systems means that from thousands of feet above Gaza every movement can be tracked, with all the information then provided to the IDF. How the IDF then uses that information is outside Britain's control. The available evidence suggests this is where UK government officials and politicians should face the most serious charges of supporting a genocide. UN Special Rapporteur Francesca Albanese cites an AOAV report for reference purposes in her report on Gaza to the UN in October 2025.[62] AOAV saw no appreciable change when Labour won the general election. Its report acknowledges that the Ministry of Defence (MoD) claimed the flights were only to locate hostages, but most independent military intelligence experts have dismissed this claim. As journalist Iain Overton says, 'Each revelation exposed the same pattern: Britain watching Gaza from the air while disclaiming any part in what was happening below.'[63]

One of the more notorious bombings of the IDF's genocidal campaign was on 8 June 2024, when it attacked Nuseirat camp in an attempt to rescue hostages. Four were recovered but 270 Palestinian civilians were killed in the process. In the fortnight before that raid, the RAF flew twenty-four missions over the area.[64] All of these intelligence-gathering missions involved Shadow R1 reconnaissance aircraft from the RAF base Akrotiri in Cyprus. It's known that when thirty civilians were killed after another bombing of Nuseirat on 12 December 2024, the bombing happened a day after another RAF mission had circled the camp.[65] Two days earlier, Prime Minister Starmer visited the camp in Akrotiri and told personnel, 'we're really proud of what you're doing. We can't necessarily tell the world what you're doing here.'[66] Starmer cultivates an image of an eloquent if understated lawyer who understands the importance of language and tone. Choosing to address troops aiding a genocide, on camera, was unwise; describing himself 'proud' was plain stupid.

Some of the heaviest periods of RAF activity coincided with major Israeli assaults, including on Rafah and Khan Younis, and AOAV reported that surveillance operations continued through the limited ceasefire of early 2025. It points out: 'Responsibility for the flights spans two governments. Rishi Sunak's administration authorised 361 of them before Keir Starmer took office, with a further 245 missions conducted since.'[67]

◆◆◆

Like the US, British politics has a number of different pro-Israel lobby groups. The most important are the Conservative Friends of Israel (CFI) and LFI, each of which is decades old and wields influence on political decision-making on Middle East affairs. The levels of direct and indirect interference are significant.

In his book *Complicit*, Peter Oborne shows how, when it comes to international law, the pressure of the lobby ensures that Israel generally gets a free pass. He describes a speech of Prime Minister Sunak to the CFI's annual lunch in London.[68] The 650 in attendance included 200 Conservative Party MPs and peers (members of the House of Lords). It was a hundred days into the genocide and at least 25,000 Palestinians were dead. Sunak referenced the scale of human suffering, but there was not one single word of admonition of Israel. Empathy for Palestine was scarce. There were no requests to hold back on the slaughter, but there was a promise to crack down on those protesting against it. Sunak stressed his intolerance of BDS movements, completely rejected the merits of the genocide case being advanced by South Africa, and generally reassured his audience that Britain would never be found wanting in its support of Israel. Sunak played to the Zionist gallery, pledging zero tolerance of antisemitism, implying, as Israel's propaganda textbook demands, that to be critical of the state of Israel is to be racist. The British establishment is so in thrall to Zionism that not even the ongoing slaughter of tens of thousands of civilians could temper Sunak's backing of Israel. Even allowing for the occasion, with the backdrop that was playing out live on people's phones, the prime minister's speech on 22 January 2024 was shameful.

The Labour party's commitment to Israel is no less. The LFI 2025 list of parliamentary party members who were also LFI members included Keir Starmer and most of its front bench. One was Yvette Cooper, who, after the election, became home secretary. In June 2025, she announced a decision to proscribe the British pro-Palestinian campaign group Palestine Action, saying it had 'committed acts of serious damage to property with the aim of progressing its political cause and influencing the government'.[69] The immediate backdrop was damage done to some planes at RAF Brize Norton. There was an irony in a newly minted Labour home secretary taking legally questionable action that the Conservatives had avoided. Within days people protesting against the decision were being arrested, some of them elderly. The UK was arresting those who protested a genocide, while it was providing substantial military aid and support to the state responsible for it. The home secretary was promoted for her troubles. In September 2025, Keir Starmer appointed her as foreign secretary.

The repercussions of the decision to proscribe Palestine Action continued through the autumn and into 2026, as four members of the group, who'd been imprisoned for various offences, went on hunger strike. Their demands were: better conditions in prison, the right to a fair trial, action to be taken on the UK subsidiary of Israeli military defence firm Elbit Systems, and for the government to remove the designation of Palestine Action as a 'terrorist group'. They carried on for up to seventy days until one of their demands, the one relating to Elbit Systems, was agreed to, again demonstrating the value of civic action.

◆◆◆

Iran is another important strand to Israel's relationship with the British political elite. Just a month before 7 October 2023, Prime Minister Sunak wrote to the membership of the CFI. In a one-page letter to its *Informed* magazine, he gave considerable space to Iran. 'Iran's aggressive actions continue to threaten international peace and security. We will continue to work with Israel and our allies to ensure Iran never acquires a nuclear weapon. The UK will also stand lockstep with Israel in its efforts to counter Iranian-backed terror groups, which have dangerously expanded into the West Bank over the last year. This is harmful to both Israelis and Palestinians.'[70]

Britain's Ambassador to Israel, Simon Walters, stoked this portrayal in a letter he wrote to the CFI: 'In the UK we have become acutely aware of the threat the Iranian regime poses. The Embassy will continue to work with Israel on countering the Iranian threat and raising awareness of the risk Iran poses to the region and the UK.'[71] So, compromising any sense of independent thought on such an important matter, both a British prime minister and a senior civil servant gave credibility to the decades-old Israeli narrative that it uses routinely to bolster its own importance.

Even admitting Israel's hold on political life in the UK, it was surprising that a senior public servant would express such partisan views. Days before Christmas 2025, the same ambassador wrote an article for CTech, an Israeli global news platform, about the UK budget. Titled, 'If you build in Britain, we will back you', the article said that, in 2025, trade between the UK and Israel had increased to £6.2 billion, as 'Israel rose to 8th place in Europe [*sic*] in terms of investment in the UK, per capita'.[72] Referencing the opportunities open to Israeli business to do considerably more trade with the UK again illustrated the intensity of the grip that Israel has on the British/US axis.

When it comes to a genocide, even two years on, for official Britain there is, it appears, nothing to see here. The ambassador's article was written in the hope of generating more trade between the two countries. It is what ambassadors do, but – in the midst of what he might diplomatically call a 'war', but that much of the world knows to be a genocide – it seems inappropriate. If Israel's indisputable savagery doesn't stop Britain marketing itself to its business community, should we really expect the UK to be concerned about Donald Trump's plans to redevelop the Gaza strip?

◆◆◆

The refuelling took about an hour; at one in the morning UK time, Air Force One headed towards the runway. The White House Pool noted that Donald Trump then concluded a gaggle, delaying departure by about fifteen minutes. Wheels up for Washington followed.

‘I saw [my brother 'Adel] wasting away, his body becoming emaciated, his bones protruding … I was the one who cared for 'Adel, and he was very attached to me. He slept next to me in the tent. At the end of his life, he could hardly speak because of his condition. But the night before he died, he called to me in a faint voice, as if he wanted to say goodbye. That night, I heard him groaning in pain, and I had no way to help him. I said to him: “Sleep, ya 'Adel. I’m right here with you.”’

Wafaa Madi
(5 August 2025)

FOUR

IT IS A GENOCIDE

Most US media have, in common with much of the established press in Europe, underperformed over the course of the genocide. The fourteen-minute gaggle on Air Force One as it prepared to take off for Washington on 13 October 2025 provided a clear illustration of why. It delayed the departure, but not because the short media interlude had become contentious. None of the press in the gaggle appeared interested in matters of substance.

Some questions concerned domestic issues. Those about the day's proceedings were inconsequential. Nobody asked about the fate of the Palestinians. Nobody questioned the appropriateness of a peace proposal which effectively shut them out. Nobody raised the inappropriateness of talking about Gaza's transformation into an economic nirvana when hundreds of thousands of Gazans were still living in famine conditions. None of the travelling White House press thought to ask a single question about Israel's responsibility for the destruction and the death. There was no probing of the language and imagery used by the president himself, who had chosen to speak of the genocide as a victory for Israel.

It was a dereliction of duty. The media representatives on Air Force One knew the IDF had acknowledged more than 80 per cent of those killed in Gaza were civilians, but none questioned the president about this. Donald Trump and his administration were fully aware of the facts when he chose to tell the Knesset that Israel had 'won'. They were aware of the facts when he said Gaza no longer mattered, that Benjamin Netanyahu was a great leader and that Israel stood to gain massively from his plans. The Gaza Strip he and his cohort talked of as a piece of real estate was 365 square kilometres of rubble covering the body parts and artefacts of its people.

That did not appear to matter to the journalists embedded with Team Trump on board Air Force One. Their questions on the day's events were: how was he feeling; had it been previous to reference a 'ceasefire'; would the 'peace' last if he weren't the US president; had he forewarned 'Bibi' that he was going to seek a pardon for him; what did he think of Bill Clinton giving him credit for 'ending' the 'war' in Gaza and of the Egyptian president's call for an independent Palestinian state? There was not one serious line of questioning of a president who'd spent an hour in the Knesset lauding Israel and its leaders two years into its genocide.

The essence of what President Trump had done was to tell Israel that America remained committed to its cause. It was a reaffirmation that it was placing no obstacle in the way of the Zionist ambition for a Greater Israel. The privileged members of the small media group travelling with him had the first chance to call him to account, to refuse his blandishments. Not one of them even tried. Hundreds of their Palestinian colleagues had been killed doing their job; none of them had the courage to do theirs. It reflects either individual failures or, more likely, editorial pressure, which a journalist follows for fear of losing their job.

It was an insight into how inept most Western media has been throughout this horror. In late summer 2025, there were National Union of Journalists protests in the UK and Ireland over the killing of five Al Jazeera journalists by the IDF that week. In 2025, 119 journalists were killed covering conflict around the world, fifty-six of them in Palestine.[1] International media was not allowed into Gaza, so most journalists killed by the IDF were locals. Some died because standard protections in conflict areas were absent; others were targeted. Their work – the words and pictures that they shared with the world in real time – threatened Israel and the nations that supported its genocide. That is why so many were killed. But slaughtering these brave men and women does not silence them. Their raw accounts, neither edited nor editorialised, will be critical to how, in time, the international bodies responsible will determine what occurred and to whom blame should attach.

There are different areas of international law that are relevant to the process that will inform that decision-making. We must trust that, despite the hostility of some powerful nations, international law will ultimately offer justice. All parties – states, institutions, individuals – must be held to account.

THE GENOCIDE CONVENTION

The Genocide Convention lists five acts, any of which constitutes genocide when committed with the deliberate intent of destroying 'in whole or in part, a national, ethnical, racial or religious group':[2]

> (a) Killing members of the group;
> (b) Causing serious bodily or mental harm to members of the group;
> (c) Deliberately inflicting on the group conditions of life calculated to bring about its physical destruction in whole or in part;
> (d) Imposing measures intended to prevent births within the group;
> (e) Forcibly transferring children of the group to another group.

It was adopted by the UN General Assembly in December 1948 and entered into force in January 1951. It is signed by 153 of the world's nations. The Convention emerged from the horror of the atrocities committed during the Second World War, most especially the Holocaust, in which about six million Jews perished. Interestingly, in light of Israel's settler-colonialism, the principal architect of the Convention, Polish-Jewish lawyer Raphael Lemkin, linked genocide with colonialism.

In October 2024, one year after the Hamas attack, Amos Goldberg, Professor of Jewish History at the Hebrew University of Jerusalem and renowned scholar of the Holocaust, wrote: 'Palestinian Gaza, as a geographical, political, cultural, and human entity no longer exists. Genocide is the deliberate destruction of a collective or part of it, not of all of its individual members – and that is what is happening in Gaza today … The result is undoubtedly genocidal'.[3]

The case against Israel was taken by South Africa to the ICJ in December 2023 and heard in January 2024. It sought preliminary measures in respect of a ruling that Israel was conducting a genocide in Gaza. The Court found the case plausible and ordered Israel to take all measures to prevent any further actions contrary to the Convention. It made no order for it to stop its military campaign, which, while it would likely have been ignored, was seen by some as diminishing its findings. The absence of this weakened how the Court's ruling of a plausible risk that Israel was committing a genocide was perceived.

The wording, that Israel was, in relation to Palestine, to 'take all reasonable measures within their power to prevent genocide' appears obtuse.[4] The most comprehensive means of doing so would have been for the Court to order Israel to end its military campaign. There were further orders made by the Court in March and May 2024. One said humanitarian aid should be allowed into Gaza at appropriate levels, the other that the Israeli offensive at the Rafah crossing into Egypt should be ended. Israel ignored the rulings. The Trump administration suspended all aid to South Africa because it had taken the case.

The Genocide Convention states that genocide is 'a crime under international law' and, using the language of the time, binds the signatories to the Convention as committed to liberating 'mankind from such an odious scourge'.[5] For such a straightforward document with powerful controls around sovereign behaviour, its use seems problematic. Israel is one of the nations party to the Convention, but, despite being bound to its provisions, it dismissed any notion of culpability.

Article 3 defines the crimes that can be punished under the Convention:

(a) Genocide;
(b) Conspiracy to commit genocide;
(c) Direct and public incitement to commit genocide;
(d) Attempt to commit genocide;
(e) Complicity in genocide.

What sets genocide apart is *dolus specialis* or 'specific intent'. This is the idea of it as the crime of crimes, because the perpetrator's purpose is to bring about the destruction of a particular people or protected group. To establish proof of a genocide is an immense task. South Africa knew the process would be torturous and take years, but also that preliminary findings could be valuable.

The ICJ's ruling in January 2024 energised those campaigning for Palestine, but the exact legal nature of the ruling – plausible case of violations of the Convention – isn't always referenced. The shorthand – that the ICJ had ruled that South Africa made a plausible case that Gazans were suffering a genocide – was enough for those campaigning for it to end. Israel's supporters argued that, as there was no absolute instruction to end its military actions, the Court believed it could continue. Global PR battle lines were drawn along traditional lines. The US and UK were most hostile to the findings.

The US had objected to South Africa's move from the outset. One of Joe Biden's National Security team, John Kirby, described it as 'meritless, counterproductive, completely without any basis in fact whatsoever'.[6] The swift response included a bill calling for a reassessment of US–South Africa relations. The US–South Africa Bilateral Relations Review Act claimed that South Africa had 'a history of siding with malign actors, including Hamas, a U.S. designated Foreign Terrorist Organization and a proxy of the Iranian regime'.[7] The political rush to support Israel was cross-party, AIPAC-backed and centred on antisemitism. Over 200 legislators on Capitol Hill signed a letter to Biden's secretary of state, Anthony Blinken, from the co-chairs of the House Task Force for Combating Antisemitism. The letter denounced the case as perpetrating 'false and dangerous allegations against the Jewish state'.[8] The signatories, almost 40 per cent of the membership of Congress, asked the government to help Israel 'as it responds to this scurrilous abuse of the International Court'.[9]

Britain, too, chose to dismiss the ICJ's findings. The UK political establishment closed ranks and much of its media followed suit. Britain's contempt for international law may have been less pronounced than that of the Americans, but it was evolving. Unlike Washington, Whitehall's rejection notes were always prefaced by claims to respect the ICJ and to welcome its pressing for the return of hostages or increased aid. Its hard line on the substantive points was generally wrapped in positivity on the softer issues. The camouflage was just that; it was as trenchant on what mattered. Even with the Labour government, foreign policy appeared increasingly unresponsive to the global rules-based order. 'Israel's actions in Gaza cannot be described as a genocide, which is why we thought South Africa's decision to bring the case was wrong and provocative.'[10]

Britain's abrogation of responsibility represents a mix of its standard approach of denial, the Zionist grip on its politics and the institutional racism which pervades most of the West. It may have shed many of its colonial undergarments, but the UK retains the robes of superiority and pomp of a previous time. The legal profession saw the ICJ's ruling differently. More than 600 lawyers, including three retired Supreme Court justices, along with legal academics signed a letter to the prime minister saying that all arms sales to Israel should stop.[11] The letter warned that the government would be in violation of international law if it continued to supply Israel with arms. Over a year later, a similar letter reaffirming the key points was sent to the new prime minister, Keir Starmer, a former DPP. It was more prescriptive. It opened with a firm declaration that if genocide had not occurred, there was, at a minimum, 'a serious risk of genocide occurring'.[12] It went beyond a warning about the implications of possible findings. The letter called for sanctions on Israeli ministers and accused Israel of an 'unparalleled assault on the United Nations'.[13] It had 800 signatories when it was published, with many more added since. Britain's most experienced lawyers were demanding that its government initiate proceedings for the suspension of Israel's membership of the UN.

In May 2025, Israel began the process of permanently moving the population of Gaza to small, designated areas as phase one of an attempt to transition them to other countries.[14] The forcible transfer of a population is illegal under International Humanitarian Law (IHL), which regulates the conduct of conflict and seeks to limit its inhumanity. Such a breach was never going to concern Israel's government, and the West again sat on its institutional hands. As well as this, the theft of land in the West Bank was increasing, marginalising its population. This conflicted with the fundamental rights of the Palestinians to self-determination, also protected under international law. Israel's contempt for international norms peaked, yet the international community remained relatively unperturbed.

The US and UK put Zionist ambitions ahead of meeting

their most fundamental responsibilities. In doing so, they enabled Israel and greatly undermined international law and the institutions there to uphold it. It will take years before there is a formal finding on any case brought before the ICJ. While 'mass killing' is not necessary for a finding of genocide to be made, this criterion is the one on which Israel's guilt seems most clear.

In September 2025, a UN Independent International Commission of Inquiry established that Israel had committed genocide under four of the five criteria set out in the Genocide Convention.[15] Tragically, the lengthy process involved means that a great number more Palestinians will have perished at Israel's hands before this can ever be formally recognised. The establishment of plausibility was as far as South Africa's case could go. It delivered that much.

International law moves slowly, but the ICJ's ruling on South Africa's case mattered. It was a critical if small step in registering the issue of accountability, something Israel has never had to consider in its decades of colonial abuse of Palestine. This source of hope for justice comes in the face of opposition from some of the world's more powerful nations. The Italian lawyer, Francesca Albanese, who was appointed UN special rapporteur on Palestine in 2022, has been fearless in her analysis of events since October 2023. Her 2024 report, *Anatomy of a Genocide*, released just five months into Israel's campaign, concluded that, 'the threshold indicating the commission of the following acts of genocide against Palestinians in Gaza has been met: killing members of the group; causing serious bodily or mental harm to groups' members; and deliberately inflicting on the group conditions of life calculated to bring about its physical destruction in whole or in part.'[16] Lawyers, and Albanese is an experienced one, concern themselves with evidence, not emotion. It is where Israel and its sponsors are most exposed.

THE FACTS: GAZA

Save the Children reported in autumn 2025 that at least 2 per cent of the children of Gaza have been killed, including 1,000 babies less than a year old.[17] Gaza's civilian infrastructure, including water and sanitation systems, was targeted, as Israel successfully engineered severe shortages of potable water, increasing the spread of disease from untreated sewage.[18] In 2026, the figures for all those killed in Gaza by the IDF remain in dispute, but only in terms of by how much they will breach 100,000.

One of Israel's more heinous acts has been the destruction of Gaza's healthcare system and the deliberate targeting of medical workers. This is a war crime. By October 2025, more than 1,700 medical professionals had been killed,[19] which included the massacre of fifteen medics and volunteers by the IDF in March 2025. The victims were buried in a mass grave. A number of reputable sources, including UN agencies, have reported on the targeting of the Gazan medical community. The IDF abducted hundreds of doctors, nurses and medical assistants, imprisoning them and torturing them and, in several cases, killing them. This focus on Gaza's medics began right at the start of Israel's campaign. A group of US medical volunteers wrote to Joe Biden and Kamala Harris about this in July 2025, but their appeal was ignored. Gaza's hospitals were targeted and destroyed.

Gaza's health system faced chronic problems well before October 2023, but, as Professor Nick Maynard of Oxford

University Hospital and other distinguished Western doctors who have volunteered there for many years attest, it was a functioning system. It met people's needs. Those same expert witnesses say Israel's bombardment deliberately devastated Gaza's capacity to care for its citizens. Some in Israel's medical community agreed. In July 2025, Physicians for Human Rights in Israel (PHRI) published a report highly critical of events. 'Over a 22-month period, Israel's actions have destroyed Gaza's healthcare infrastructure in a manner that is both calculated and systematic.'[20] By 2025, the healthcare system, that first place of refuge for a beleaguered people, for a place under a savage bombardment, was 'on its knees, barely able to function'.[21] In startling testimony to the UN in May 2025, American consultant, Dr Feroze Sidhwa, spoke of unspeakable horror he had witnessed over his two periods volunteering in hospitals in Khan Younis during the genocide. In March 2025, he spent five weeks there and said that he did not see or treat a single combatant in that time. 'My patients were six-year-olds with shrapnel in their hearts and bullets in their brains and pregnant women whose pelvises had been obliterated and foetuses cut in two while still in the womb.'[22] In testimony that received little or no attention outside the UN chamber, Sidhwa explained how he had witnessed a huge decline in people's welfare in the second of his two visits, a year apart. 'Let us not forget this is man-made catastrophe, it is entirely preventable; participating in it or not, allowing it to happen is a choice … preventing genocide means refusing to normalise these atrocities, it means refusing to demonise the Palestinians.'[23] In some respects, his most distressing comments were about those who had escaped physical harm: 'According to the War Child Alliance, nearly half of Gaza's children are suicidal.

They ask, why didn't I die with my sister, my mother, my father, not out of extremism but out of unbearable grief. I wonder if any member of this Council has ever met a five-year-old child who no longer wants to live, let alone know of a society where so many children feel this way? And what astonishes me is not that so many children in Gaza feel this way but that any cling to hope.'[24]

Israel's wanton destruction of the health system over the course of the genocide is almost impossible to comprehend. Healthcare professionals knew as they did their work that they were one of the groups targeted by the Israeli military operation. The Israeli aerial bombardment had directly attacked Gaza's thirty-six hospitals, resulting in none being able to function normally and only fourteen functioning at all. Around the time of Trump's day of celebration in the region, about 17,000 people were waiting for medical evacuation. UNRWA reported that the rate at which healthcare workers were being killed in Gaza was 75:100,000, compared to 0.8 in Ukraine, and 0.3 in both Sudan and Myanmar. The next highest figure globally is Lebanon, where Israel is also very 'active' militarily, at 7:100,000.[25]

The chronology of the attacks reveals a deliberate progression. It began with the bombing and forced evacuation of hospitals in northern Gaza. As the health system's collapse extended southward, displaced people overwhelmed the remaining facilities, which were then subjected to bombardment, siege and resource deprivation. According to the PHRI, 'Gaza's health system has been systematically dismantled – its hospitals rendered non-functional, medical evacuations blocked, and essential services like trauma care, surgery, dialysis and maternal health eliminated. The killing and detention of over 1,800 healthcare workers, including many senior specialists, has decimated Gaza's medical capacity and rendered recovery nearly impossible … PHRI concludes that these acts are not incidental to war, but rather part of a deliberate policy targeting Palestinians as a group.'[26]

Dr Ahmed Muhanna, a Gazan anaesthesiologist, was detained by the IDF in December 2023 at the Al-Awda hospital where he worked. He was imprisoned, without charge, for 665 days. When he was released, as part of the October 2025 ceasefire, he returned to a hospital and neighbourhood he barely recognised. Seventy-five of his hospital colleagues had been killed and the building was a shell with few staff and no equipment or medicines. In an interview with *The Guardian*, Dr Muhanna said, 'The deliberate military targeting of the healthcare system has been successful not only in destroying the infrastructure but also now depriving the people of medical care and increasing the mortality rates.'[27] He worries about his children, knowing there's nowhere for them to go: 'Gaza used to have life; restaurants, beaches. Now there is nothing left.'[28] As a medical professional, he also knows how fortunate he is that his children are still alive.

Child deaths in Gaza tell the story of Israel's brutality. Some Israeli ministers have called for them to be targeted, so perhaps the figures are not that surprising. Statistics from UNICEF show that to August 2025, 18,000 children had been killed, representing 28 a day, or the size of a typical classroom in the West being wiped out by Israel each and every day of its genocide. No conflict in the world has figures that are remotely similar.[29] Save the Children reported that 20,000 children had been killed by September 2025. Four thousand children had lost at least one limb. Most remarkably, health statisticians believe that if indirect causes (starvation or disease) were included,

Israel's genocide in Gaza over 2024–25 would represent one of the main causes of child mortality worldwide. The *Scandinavian Journal of Public Health* says that it is, calling it 'the leading cause of child mortality worldwide'.[30] Public health experts reference that report 'recognizing and coding genocide as a preventable cause of death' as being critical to the issue of accountability.[31]

These accounts, these statistics, reflect the impact of the massive number of explosives and other weaponry used by Israel in its onslaught on Gaza. It is where the guilt of the West is most powerfully manifest. A report by Special Rapporteur Albanese documented the quantities of arms involved: 'By September 2024, the United States had reportedly supplied 57,000 artillery shells, 36,000 rounds of cannon ammunition, 20,000 M4A1 rifles, 13,981 anti-tank missiles and 8,700 MK-82 500-pound bombs. By April 2025, Israel had 751 active sales [with the US] valued at $39.2 billion.'[32] The report was clear that the Biden and Trump administrations were equally involved.

The UK's commitment to Israel throughout was well known, despite the repeated attempts of Prime Minister Starmer to distance Britain from the genocide. Albanese saw the sleight of hand for what it was and called it out: 'The United Kingdom has also played a key role in military collaboration with Israel, despite internal opposition. From its bases in Cyprus, the United Kingdom has enabled a crucial United States supply line to Tel Aviv and flown more than 600 surveillance missions over Gaza throughout the genocide, sharing intelligence with Israel.'[33] The duplicity of some nations – and there were others – was remarkable. They continued to supply Israel with armaments and other forms of military support through the autumn of 2025, playing at diplomacy at the same time. Nations continued to facilitate the genocide right up to the Trump ceasefire initiative of 13 October, further illustrating the hold Israel has on many in the West. In the midst of their complicity, many feigned concern for Palestine.

France, initially a strong supporter of Israel, had altered its position by autumn 2024. One year on from the Hamas attack, President Macron said France was going to stop supplying arms: 'If one is calling for a ceasefire, coherence would be to not supply weapons of war.'[34] When Netanyahu responded in fury, Macron said France would remain a friend of Israel, but the value of its arms deliveries to Israel fell by 50 per cent in 2024,[35] and that trend downwards continued. However, the transfer of some military equipment did continue. In June 2025, port workers in Marseilles refused to load crates with parts being shipped to Israel. The government said the parts were for Israel's own, substantial armaments industry and for re-export. That month, it ordered the closure of five stands of Israeli arms manufacturers at the annual Paris Air Show. Signals, no matter how weak, mattered. Yet France is among the nations listed by Albanese as a 'third state' that breached its legal obligation to prevent genocide by maintaining military, economic and diplomatic support of Israel. She lists the provision of ports, the supply of parts and weapons, and that the French air force had cooperated with the IDF as reasons for its inclusion.

It will take years of investigation to establish each nation's complicity or otherwise, but France was, at that time, preparing to lead, with Saudi Arabia, the most meaningful peace effort since the genocide began. It co-chaired the New York Declaration of July 2025, which stated that the leaders and representatives gathered at the UN had 'agreed to take collective action to end the war [*sic*] in Gaza'.[36] Clause six of that Declaration committed the signatories to 'taking tangible, timebound, and irreversible steps for the peaceful settlement of the question of Palestine'.[37]

If France is found to have been speaking through both sides of its sovereign mouth, it won't be alone. Spain was a signatory to the New York Declaration and a nation hailed for its vocal opposition to Israel. Its prime minister, Pedro Sanchez, has been the most assertive European leader on the rights of Palestine and opposition to Israel, but there are some inconsistencies even in its position. Italy has been a big arms supplier, while its unions have been among the strongest in Europe in protesting the export of any military equipment. Ireland, which, with Spain, moved early to recognise Palestine's statehood, continued to trade and permit the use of its airspace after they'd signed the Declaration. There were more than sixty nations that, to different degrees, were identified in Albanese's report as part of the support cast behind Israel's genocide. The lack of courage, the absence of leadership, the refusal to put morality before money, betrayed a West where more than the size of its population is in decline.

◆◆◆

The brutality of Israel's pursuit of Greater Israel at the expense of the indigenous people of Palestine has always been there. In unleashing a genocide, its determination to wipe out Palestine is now beyond debate. The scale and nature of its destructiveness and the capacity of the West to sponsor its egregiously violent pursuit of that end is what international law must bring to account. Decades of complicity that go back to the very origins of the Zionist mission need to be unravelled.

The 1948 Nakba set the tone for how Israel has conducted itself since. Over the course of this genocide, Nakba II, it has forcibly displaced an estimated 90 per cent of the two million Palestinians in Gaza, destroying nearly every home and, in the process, making it ever more challenging to return. The experience has been the same for each generation of Palestinians, compounding the intergenerational trauma. In May 2025, MSF reported that 'nearly 70 percent of all structures in the [Gaza] Strip have been destroyed or damaged, along with 92 percent of all housing units'.[38] In March 2025, Prime Minister Netanyahu told a closed-door Likud parliamentary party meeting, 'Israel is "destroying more and more houses in Gaza to make it uninhabitable so Palestinians have nowhere to return"'.[39] This is consistent with the decades-old ambition to deny any basis on which Palestinians can claim to be refugees. The prosecution's case on genocide that experts continue to build will never be short of material.

What Netanyahu's government also focused on was having multiple ways in which the Palestinians might 'die'. This Israeli government is indifferent to how Palestinian lives end; the only thing of interest is the speed with which the job can be done. Among its crimes, it stands charged with weaponising hunger to starve the population to death. The evidence is overwhelming. In August 2025, the UN declared a Phase 5 famine, the highest tier, which means 'Starvation, death, destitution and extremely acute malnutrition levels are evident'.[40] At least 440 people had died of starvation and malnutrition, over 100 of them children and babies.[41] At that very moment, Israel restricted the delivery of supplies of baby formula to the point of preventing individual volunteer doctors and nurses from bringing it into Gaza.

Signs of this determination to use starvation as a weapon had been evident more than a year earlier. In April 2024, just six months into the genocide, the global NGO Oxfam reported that people in Gaza were surviving on an average of 245 calories a day. This was an early signal of how Israel had deliberately destroyed Gaza's agricultural infrastructure, which, with whatever degree of fragility, had allowed the Palestinians to feed themselves. That daily average of 245 calories was 11 per cent of the recommended minimum caloric requirement set by the Israeli government itself for Gaza for almost two decades. In its 2008 report, *Food Consumption in the Gaza Strip: Red Lines*, made public by the Israeli rights group Gisha, the Israeli government determined, considering factors like age and gender, that an average of 2,279 calories per person per day was required for survival in Gaza.[42]

In history, there have been many conflicts or wars where civilians have starved on account of the conditions of warfare or where it has been difficult to establish intent. There are such places in the world today where, in the midst of brutal violence, people are cut off from food and water, and the combatants use this to their advantage. This is not what occurred in Gaza. Starvation was a deliberate part of Israel's genocidal campaign, a siege tactic that goes back to the Middle Ages. Here too, the West stands complicit. In May 2024, USAID, an American aid agency, reported to the State Department that Israel was preventing critically needed aid from getting into Gaza, resulting in circumstances that could create a famine. Secretary of State Anthony Blinken ignored the advice. The Genocide Convention is clear that 'deliberately inflicting on the group [Palestinians] conditions of life calculated to bring about its physical destruction' would constitute genocide. Under international law, violations of *erga omnes* (towards all) norms carry responsibilities for third states to bring them to an end. Violations, by any and all, are considered to be offences against the international order with serious implications for all those found to have contributed to undermining the interests of the global community. This specifically refers to 'obligations of non-recognition and non-assistance'.[43]

The assessment of one of the world's foremost experts on famine, Alex de Waal, is almost as critical of the West as of Israel: '… there is no case since World War II of starvation that is being so minutely designed and controlled. This is preventable starvation. It is entirely man-made. And every stage of this has been predicted. And at every stage, action could have been taken, by Israel, by the international authorities, [the] international community, those who back Israel, to prevent what is happening now … And those steps have simply not been taken.'[44] De Waal goes further, claiming that the Israeli-induced famine goes beyond anywhere else, like Syria, Yemen, Ethiopia, or Sudan. '[T]here is no other case in modern history in which you have such minutely, precisely engineered starvation.'[45] Were more proof needed of Israel's deliberate intent to cleanse Gaza of Palestinians, it is in its utterly debased use of starvation as one means of getting the job done. It has wider intentions too; the task at hand involves more than the destruction of Gaza.

THE FACTS: THE WEST BANK

While Gaza and its people were being bombarded, the West Bank was being overrun by settlers like never before. In late autumn 2025, I contributed to a seminar on Gaza and the West

Bank. A senior Palestinian Authority official in Ramallah told us that, earlier in the day, two brothers in his village, aged ten and twelve, had been shot dead by settlers. The boys were out shepherding their family's sheep. 'Please remember that the genocide includes us too, includes what is happening here in Ramallah and right across the West Bank.'[46] UN Special Rapporteur Francesca Albanese would agree. Her reports focus on Gaza, but her mandate and reporting are in the wider context of the Occupied Territories and the obligations of UN member states towards all Palestinians. It is founded on the obligation to respect the Palestinian people's 'right to self-determination and freedom from apartheid and genocide'.[47]

The Gaza offensive was on a scale large enough to distract from Israel significantly increasing its activities in the West Bank in 2024 and 2025. This was directly through IDF strikes, but also through greater support for the settler movement's violence and accretion of land. The enormity of events in Gaza shielded the West Bank from global attention. It is critical to Greater Israel, so, as the international community focused on Gaza, Netanyahu's government created conditions for more of the West Bank to be stolen.

The UN reported that over the two years of the genocide, more than 1,000 Palestinians were killed by the IDF in the West Bank. Forty-one Israelis died, while settler attacks and illegal demolitions of properties displaced more than 10,000 Palestinians.[48] Israel's intent remains to colonise both the West Bank and Gaza. It is utterly predictable and it is again evidence of the world's acquiescence to the conduct of a state that trades in terror and has done for decades. One of its most admirable citizens, Gideon Levy, recently described what he has witnessed and reported on himself. 'What the settlers together with the army did in the last two years is unprecedented and irreversible. This is not the occupied, oppressed West Bank that you knew before, because it's much worse now … The whole West Bank looks now like a collection of concentration camps; there's no other way to describe it … In the same time the settlers saw the war in Gaza and now in Iran as a huge historical opportunity for them. They took over tens of thousands of acres all over the West Bank by force and they kicked out, they are kicking out, the population, the farmers, the shepherds, one community after another, after months and months of tyranny.'[49]

To better understand this process, it's important to examine the impact through the lens of those being displaced, specifically those whose land is being taken. In summer 2024, I saw this first hand with the Treish family, who live near Ramallah, where different generations have lost land. From the roof of his house, the family elder, Munif Treish showed me the road that cut through the illegally occupied land. It ran from Ramallah to Jerusalem, was newly built and cut the journey time in half but was for the exclusive use of the Jewish settlers or the IDF. We could see for many kilometres; the landscape was pockmarked with illegal settlements, some of them on the land of his family. Later we looked from the road; it was easy to see how the land that's stolen is always the best land: accessible and fertile. It was heavily fortified too. Once taken, it is almost impossible to recover. Munif Treish, in his seventies, was fighting in the courts for the return of land lost, and through his political activism, for land of his own and that of neighbours threatened with occupation by settlers.

The humiliation of the local people is as strong as it was when the first settlers came. In *Mapping My Return*, Abu Sitta offers a powerful insight into the long-term impact of this from the day Israel was formally declared in May 1948. His family home was destroyed and they were forced to flee. He was ten. Today, that land, stolen almost eighty years ago by Zionists, is divided between descendants of the original 'settlers' at a density of fifteen per square kilometre. Abu Sitta, writes, 'Those of my family, the least privileged, who still live in a refugee camp in Gaza, live at a density of five thousand persons per square kilometre. Yet they live only a few kilometres from their home.'[50]

The theft of land is not the only problem facing the West Bank. Its economy has been shattered. More than 100,000 of its residents had daily permits allowing them to cross into Israel to work. These were all revoked after 7 October 2023, so not only have those families been impacted, but the knock-on effect has been considerable. Palestinian Authority reports point to the already fragile economy reducing by 25 per cent in 2025. The Authority, itself one of the principal employers in the region, has cut salaries, threatening its own survival. Israel has not wasted the opportunity this presents. It has constructed hundreds of new barriers and security impediments to the movement of people. It has built more roads that are exclusively for the use of Israelis, while the IDF has actively supported the most aggressive and violent theft ever of land and homes by Zionist settlers.

Israel is committed to the annexation of all Palestine, so the scale of Zionist accretion of land in the West Bank over the course of the genocide is no coincidence. In the US, much was made of how Vice President J.D. Vance told reporters that the West Bank was off limits. 'The West Bank is not going to be annexed by Israel.'[51] Trump said the same, but it's a moot political point.

Israel has facilitated the accretion of West Bank land by settlers for decades, so it wasn't compelled to realise its objectives by any grand act of annexation. The overwhelming evidence shows that the seizure of West Bank land increased after 13 October 2025, in part because the IDF is providing more on-the-ground support for the settlers.

There were other ways that Israel strengthened this process. In 2024, it changed the law so that Palestinian land that had been taken was under civil supervision, which has the effect of making it 'de jure [legal] annexation'.[52] With this move, macho statements by the US vice president or others internationally were no more than political grandstanding. In the days after Vance's pronouncement, Israeli officials arrived in the village of Qalandiya, north of Jerusalem. They had eviction notices for the residents of two apartment buildings to 'vacate their homes and adjoining agricultural lands within 20 days'.[53] As evident, Israel would continue to steal more of the land of Palestine in the West Bank and elsewhere by any means it wished. Its default position was that of Herzl, who had always counselled that land be taken by stealth.

The rate of increase in the number of settlements has never been impacted by international disapproval. In July 2024, the ICJ ruled that Israel's actions amounted to 'annexation' and called for the evacuation of all settlers.[54] Israel's direct response was to announce the building of a large new settlement, Nahal Heletz, knowing it would have a direct impact on the lives of Palestinians in five nearby villages and towns. Immediately after the ICJ's ruling, Israel was reminding the international community of its complete autonomy. It cared nothing for what international courts or public opinion thought of its actions. Finance Minister

Bezalel Smotrich said the intention was to 'fight the dangerous idea of a Palestinian state, and establish facts on the ground'.[55] Nahal Heletz was the first new official settlement approved by Israel's government since 2017. In 2024, it also approved government grants for seventy outposts ('settlements' not legally 'authorised') without the standard process, and it declared *c*. 24,000 dunams (2,400 hectares) as state (Israeli) land. This was a formal recognition of what it was doing in the West Bank. It represented about half of all land declared as 'state land' since the Oslo Accords thirty years earlier.[56]

Israel's push towards colonising all of Palestine includes Lebanon, at least to the Litani river, and it continues to occupy the Golan Heights, on its border with Syria, moving to increase its holding after the fall of the al-Assad regime. Reflecting the Zionist ambition, a 2024 EU report noted, 'The nature of settlement advancement has also shifted qualitatively. Rather than merely increasing density within existing settlements, a greater proportion of plans now involve territorial expansion into new areas. In East Jerusalem, nearly half (48.4%) of all units advanced in 2024 were for new settlements or territorial expansions.'[57]

IDF-backed settler activities in the West Bank have become more violent. On 27 November 2025, two Palestinians in Jenin were filmed being ordered out of a warehouse and checked for weapons. They removed their shirts and placed their hands behind their heads to show they were unarmed. Then, as they were motioned to return to the building, they were both shot dead from a distance of one or two metres. Human Rights organisation Al Haq reported that the two men were not bearing weapons at the time. It amounted to an extrajudicial killing.[58] As such, it represents a clear breach of Article 6 of the International

Covenant on Civil and Political Rights and IHL. It was not an isolated event.

The UN and OCHA reported that settler violence markedly increased during the 2025 harvest season. In December 2025, hundreds of olive trees were destroyed, and in one village, Qaryut, the damage affected the critical harvest potential of twelve families. In January 2026, YNET, Israel's main news platform, reported that in a neighbouring village, settlers attacked Israeli citizens who had come to help the locals with the harvest. Earlier in the season, The Wall and Settlement Resistance Commission reported that the 'Israeli army and colonists have committed 259 attacks against olive harvesters since the season began in early October'.[59]

The number of Palestinians killed in the West Bank in 2023 and 2024 makes the assurances of US officials meaningless. There has been no let-up in settler violence since the Trump announcement in October 2025. The displacement of people and the levels of violence are at unprecedented levels. This Israeli government is as driven to colonise more and more of the West Bank as it is to control Gaza. Its determination to plunder Palestinian land in the West Bank was not going to stall, never mind end. Into February 2026, the state-backed aggression was intensifying. The headline of one article in *Haaretz* illustrated the backing the settler community was getting in its theft of Palestinian land: 'Israeli Settlers Shot Three Palestinians in the West Bank, as IDF Troops Looked On'.[60] Israel knows pronouncements from a US administration are just that; no action would be taken to back them up. Israel can do as it pleases in the West Bank, just as in Gaza.

THE FACTS: DETENTION

There are increasing numbers of Palestinians dying at the hands of Israel in detention. The prison conditions they endure contribute greatly to the risk of perishing at Israel's hands, and with that, the charge of genocide. The Genocide Convention is breached if torture, rape and other cruel, inhuman or degrading treatment or punishments are committed with the requisite intent. PHRI, one of the many admirable Israeli human rights organisations that do so much to keep the world informed, reported that at least ninety-eight Palestinians died in custody between 7 October 2023 and late 2025. This represents a disturbing increase. In the entire decade from 2013 to 2023, fewer than thirty Palestinians died while detained by the Israeli prison service. The report says these deaths are the result of 'a systemic denial of medical care and the torture of Palestinians in Israeli custody', which it claims, 'points to a deliberate Israeli policy of killing Palestinians in custody'.[61]

B'Tselem, HaMoked and Yesh Din are Israeli human rights NGOs, which, despite government harassment, have continued to report on Israel's oppression of the Palestinians. They've been tracking the abuse of prisoners and the unlawful detention of Palestinians for decades. Once Israel began the offensive in Gaza in October 2023, the situation for those already in the prison system became a great deal more difficult. In summer 2024, B'Tselem said that detainee statements it reviewed showed how the system had 'become an instrument for the widespread, systematic and arbitrary oppression of Palestinians through torture'.[62]

HaMoked published figures of the Israeli Prison Service showing that, in January 2026, Israel held a total of 9,243 'security' (political) prisoners in jails inside Israel. Only 1,293 of those have been sentenced; 3,328 were on remand, while 3,385 were what it calls 'administrative detainees', meaning people who are being held without trial. These internees include individuals who have been 'disappeared' and who can be and are held for indeterminate lengths of time. The other 1,237 are those who are described as unlawful combatants. HaMoked reports that all 'security' prisoners receive different treatment. 'The overwhelming majority of security inmates are Palestinians from the Occupied Territories. Holding prisoners and detainees from the OPT inside Israel is a violation of the Fourth Geneva Convention … and also violates basic human rights enshrined, inter alia, in Israeli law.'[63]

Israel is a terror state. It has inflicted a genocide on the people of Gaza for more than two years. The sustained assistance it has received in that pursuit has compromised the international community's use of international law. Israel has drawn many of the West's powers into its devastation of the Palestinians, knowing that the deeper their involvement, the more compromised they will be in the application of international law. Most have shown no interest in holding it to account.

The Israeli government of Netanyahu glories in the suffering it inflicts on the Palestinians, especially those it holds in prison. In early February 2026, National Security Minister Ben-Gvir visited a prison where some Hamas fighters were detained. He had a short video made of events, which he then posted on social media. Israeli human rights groups say the prisoners are held in very harsh conditions and their treatment breaches international law. They are shackled all day, routinely starved and, in contravention of the Geneva Convention, the Red Cross is not allowed to visit. The video showed blindfolded men being taken from their cells, their feet and hands cuffed. The minister instructs that they be thrown into a corner of the corridor, on top of each other, as he says they 'need to be executed, by hanging, by injection, in an electric chair: the important thing is to execute them'.[64] This same minister was then taking a bill through the Knesset to reinstate the death penalty for non-Jews.

COMPLICITY

The 1948 UN Convention on the Prevention and Punishment of the Crime of Genocide criminalises complicity in, attempts to commit and incitement of genocide. All member states are prohibited from engaging in genocide. They must also act to pursue the enforcement of the prohibition: 'Persons committing genocide or any of the other acts enumerated in article III shall be punished, whether they are constitutionally responsible rulers, public officials or private individuals.'[65]

The Convention's scope goes beyond the perpetrators, which means that, when it comes to Gaza, Western powers are in the frame. From what we know, other nations could face serious consequences for their active sponsorship of a genocide were Israel to be found guilty of this crime. Were that to be the outcome, a number of Western nations could, under the terms of the Genocide Convention, be charged with complicity. International law does not discriminate; it 'imposes a range of obligations on all States to respect, prevent and bring an end to violations whenever they occur'.[66]

This contributed to the strong opposition to the case South Africa brought. Third states know that encouraging the ICJ to pursue Israel creates the very real risk that the pursuers will, someday, come knocking on their own door. There are two distinct charges that could be brought against such states: complicity in and failure to prevent genocide. In terms of the second charge, the ICJ recognises that some states have a capacity to influence the perpetrator, but others do not, a de facto recognition of the world order within a legally tight charter.

Providing military support to Israel throughout its destruction of Gaza and killing of its citizens is a serious charge that could be levelled at some. It's difficult to see how, were charges brought against Israel, some Western powers would not automatically face the charge of complicity. Charges can be brought contemporaneously with a case against the perpetrator, so third states could find themselves being pursued at the same time as Israel. In March 2024, Nicaragua took a case against Germany on that very basis. While the ICJ found no compelling evidence, it's illustrative of the exposure of third states as set out comprehensively in Special Rapporteur Albanese's 2025 report.

Israel is unconcerned at what these different global agencies may think, including those mandated to fulfil various international conventions. Given that its actions have been supported by many of their signatories and by some of the world's most powerful nations, this is not surprising. Israel has never attempted to conceal its intent. The brazenness of its approach is influenced by a belief in the rightness of its cause, but also by the level of international support it has received. This is what makes the events from October 2023 to October 2025 unprecedented. In full public view, Israel set out to remove Palestine and its people from the map. It did so with brutality. It did so with considerable and completely disproportionate military power.

It did so without regard for age or gender. It did so with the utmost violence. It did so using starvation, which is one of the grounds for the ICC arrest warrants,[67] and it conducted its whole campaign with a total disregard for international law, even the rules of war. While there were occasional sovereign voices calling for restraint, the numbers who called for it to stop were few and, even then, the appeals lacked conviction. The two whose advice it would have been under pressure to heed, did the opposite.

America, at any point, under Biden or Trump, could have stopped the genocide. Instead, it arms-rolled Israel's genocidal endeavour. In the months before 13 October 2025, Trump warned Venezuela, Cuba, Colombia and Iran about their conduct, threatening serious consequences for non-compliance with his wishes. The threats were not idle. US actions that followed breached international law, cost lives and undermined any sense of a world order. We were told that what determined right from wrong was Trump's morality. Israel has always been immune. With President Trump's moral compass as the sole arbiter, it knew more than ever that it would have a free run at doing whatever it wished.

ACCOUNTABILITY

As President Trump was on his 20,000-kilometre round trip from Washington to Egypt via Israel to promote his deal, debate on whether it could end a 'genocide', a 'war' or a 'conflict' continued. A debate on how to describe what was going on, when millions of Gazans were still suffering, might have seemed academic. It wasn't. Defining the horror correctly matters a great deal.

Most academics around the world were of the view that it was a genocide, including some eminent Jewish scholars: 'What is happening in Gaza is not Auschwitz. However, it is of the same family – a crime of genocide … After the war is over, we will be forced to look at ourselves in the mirror. It will reflect back to us a society that committed this terrible act in Gaza – a genocide that will stain Jewish history from now on and forever.'[68]

What we know of Israel's relationship with Western powers is that it's unlikely to face consequences, even for conducting a genocide. The free pass it has always had is what allowed it to conduct itself as it has since October 2023. Robert Fisk was never slow to criticise Hamas or Hezbollah for attacks on Israel, especially if they harmed or threatened civilians. More than once, he condemned them for committing war crimes, but a consistent theme through his analysis was how Israel's response would nearly always be 'disproportionate'. Israel, and some among its leadership, need to be held to account for their actions, no matter the outcome of any protracted ceasefire/peace negotiations. So, too, the sponsors and enablers of the genocide, irrespective of whether or not they were subsequently involved in any potential resolution.

The Hamas attack on Israeli soil on 7 October was a callous and brutal guerrilla army exercise that left hundreds of Israeli civilians dead. It was a war crime. Yet there is evidence the Israeli authorities knew it was coming and had intelligence reports of both its nature and its likely location. It is not at all conspiratorial to question how Israel's prized intelligence and security operation did not prevent it. A report by the Institute for Defense Analyses showed that Israel's intelligence services 'had strategic and tactical warning that Hamas was planning a large-scale attack, and numerous junior analysts and border sentries raised the alarm on multiple occasions. Their warnings were ignored.'[69] Over the second year of the genocide, Israel's government resisted internal pressures to establish an independent inquiry until, in November 2025, Benjamin Netanyahu announced legislation for a political inquiry that he himself would chair. Opposition parties and relatives of those killed reacted furiously. The October Council, a group representing relatives of those killed, injured and kidnapped, said, 'The Israeli government continues to spit in the face of the bereaved families, freed hostages, the hostages' families ... and of all the citizens of Israel.'[70]

There is some evidence that Israel stood down some border guards, knowing there was an imminent threat of an attack. There is evidence that some of its citizens died because of the use of the Hannibal Directive. This controversial tactic allows soldiers to engage in heavy fire to block the escape of insurgents, even if there's a high probability of non-combatants being killed. In February 2025, former Minister of Defense Yoav Gallant acknowledged it had been used 'tactically' on the day of the attack.[71] None of this changes the brutality of the Hamas attack, but understanding what Israel knew and how it reacted is critical. The Hamas-led guerrilla force did what it did. While the IDF and the government's original claims of rape and beheadings were debunked, the scale of the attack was a huge shock to the people of Israel. But those who study or understand the history of Israel's oppression of Palestinians would have known an attack was inevitable and, given the intense levels of oppression, not without cause.

The Geneva Convention bestows the right to resist when 'peoples are fighting against colonial domination and alien occupation and against racist régimes in the exercise of their right of self-determination'.[72] It is important to consider why those responsible for the attack of 7 October 2023 felt compelled to meet violence with violence. While they must take responsibility for the nature of their response that included killing civilians, the Hamas attack cannot be profiled as a random, groundless act of terror. Israel's relentless oppression of the Palestinian people right up to that day was what caused Hamas to attack. When you oppress an indigenous population, humiliate them, incarcerate them and kill them as routinely as Israel has the Palestinians for more than seven decades, there can only ever be one outcome – 7 October 2023 was it.

Israel had, in that moment, a right to respond. It had been attacked, however understandable or justifiable Hamas's action may have been. Striking back would not, of itself, have been unreasonable. The nature and scale of that response are what's at issue. In this respect, Israel has 'form'. Towards the end of 2008, Hamas started an offensive on the city of Sderot, five kilometres from the border with Gaza on Israel's side. It fired rockets and mortars indiscriminately, causing eight civilian deaths. The UN and Amnesty International found that it had committed crimes against humanity. In that case, Israel's response, Operation Cast Lead, which killed at least 1,160 Palestinians, was described as a 'grotesque disproportion' by Robert Fisk, who also condemned the actions of Hamas.[73] It is how Israel does things; how it has always done things. The international community's refusal to ever hold it to account is what nurtured its right to continue. In this respect, the genocide is the fault of the West. This time, its violent oppression has been more sustained, more brutal, than over the course of the Nakba in 1948/49. Since October 2023, the culmination of war crime upon war crime, of crimes against humanity amounts to a genocide that the West has enabled, sponsored even.

THE ICC

The ICC's role is to prosecute cases against individuals whom it deems guilty of crimes against humanity or war crimes. In November 2024, it issued an arrest warrant for Prime Minister Benjamin Netanyahu and former Minister of Defense Yoav Gallant. The indictment served as a 'rap sheet' for the state of Israel. It has implications for those in the international community of nations that chose to support them. The alleged crimes include the intentional attack of a civilian population and 'the crimes against humanity of murder, persecution, and other inhumane acts'.[74] The ICC also issued a warrant for the arrest of three Hamas leaders. All of them – Yahya Sinwar, who led its military operations in Gaza, Ismail Haniyeh, its political leader, and Mohammed Diab Ibrahim Al-Masri, the commander of its armed forces – were killed by Israel.

The ICC is distinct from the ICJ, whose brief relates to monitoring the conduct of states and proceeding to take action against those it believes have violated the Genocide Convention. Unlike the ICJ, the ICC is an independent body with no direct affiliation to the UN, though its Security Council can and has referred some cases to it. Either court can initiate action or manage applications on behalf of member states. The ICC has 125 member states. Israel originally indicated its intention to join but never ratified membership and does not recognise its authority.

In 2000, it signed along with America, but both withdrew two years later.

Just weeks into his second term, Donald Trump signed an executive order imposing sanctions on the ICC. It was an Israel-oriented move. It was classic Trump; aggressive and intended to send a signal of just how tough and uncompromising he is. He claimed the ICC had abused its power by issuing 'baseless' warrants for the arrest of Gallant and Netanyahu. 'The ICC has no jurisdiction over the United States or Israel, as neither country is party to the Rome Statute [which established the ICC] or a member of the ICC. Neither country has ever recognized the ICC's jurisdiction, and both nations are thriving democracies with militaries that strictly adhere to the laws of war.'[75]

With overwhelming evidence that the arrest of Netanyahu and Gallant would be warranted by an international court that has the support of most of the world's nations, the likelihood of either putting himself at risk of arrest is unlikely. Technically, the 125 countries that are signatories to the Rome Statute are obliged, under the statute, to arrest them. A few have indicated that they would defy that duty. Politics dictates that those who would want to see the two Israelis, and others, in court, are unlikely to see justice by this means. It's noteworthy that the UK's Labour government, otherwise supine on Israel, announced that it would act on the warrant if any of those indicted were found in its jurisdiction.

THE UN

The ICJ's genocide ruling on third parties, or third states, is the focus of the UN's special rapporteur on Palestine, Francesca

Albanese. She's a reviled figure in Israel and with its closest allies. In *Gaza Genocide: A Collective Crime*, her fourth report since the genocide began, she broadens responsibility for events. Published weeks before Trump's day-long odyssey in the Middle East, she describes the Gaza genocide as 'a collective crime, sustained by the complicity of influential third States that have enabled longstanding systemic violations of international law by Israel'.[76] It is detailed and uncompromising in framing where responsibility rests.

Albanese is explicit in her criticism of more than just Israel. She refers throughout to it committing a genocide, but also probes the roles of others that 'maintain relations with Israel', or those that 'created the conditions for their complicity in ongoing Israeli crimes'.[77] She sets out the case against offending nations under four distinct but intersecting criteria: political, military, economic and the weaponising of aid. Those most culpable are the third states whose 'direct support, material aid, diplomatic protection and, in some cases, active participation' has facilitated what she terms 'this live-streamed atrocity'.[78] Albanese's report is robust and direct. It is unafraid to draw conclusions on the evidence her team has gathered. Drawing on that evidence, she paints a broad picture of complicity in a genocide the world has observed in real-time.

There have been many events in history where an oppressed people has been left to suffer, neglected by others who chose to look away. Europe's neglect of the Jewish people is one example. More recent history has witnessed double standards in the application of international law and experiences, where the remnants of colonialism have been allowed to obscure grave injustices being committed. There are also examples of where the international order moved, however slowly, against the unjust treatment of minorities and oppressive regimes. South Africa, which brought the case against Israel to the ICJ, is an example of how international law helped the indigenous people determine their future. It should resonate. Racism meant it took a long time for the white-dominated West to mobilise against the oppression of the South African blacks. That same condition is part of the indifference over Israel's oppression of the Arabs (Christian and Muslim) of Palestine. Racism has been an inhibitor to many Western countries taking action against Israel. Israel knows this and plays on it.

Much of the West shares a Judeo-Christian connection with Israel, while, to many, the Arab/Islamic world is alien. Israel claims those who support the Palestinians are motivated by antisemitism, marking these people as racist. Israel has so mastered this tactic that many are intimidated out of expressing a view. There are strong supporters of Palestine, some of whom are appalled by Israel's conduct, who know that to say so would be to leave themselves open to the charge of antisemitism. In parts of the West today, it's about as serious a charge as you can face. Many people choose not to risk it.

In the weeks after 7 October, the language used by leaders in the West and by many leading voices in Western media betrayed the bias. This has lessened over the two years of the genocide, but racial 'profiling' continues. Israelis taken on 7 October are 'hostages', while Palestinians detained without charge, often for years in appalling conditions, are 'prisoners'. It's hard to think of any place, any people, as abandoned to their fate in modern history as Palestine and its unfortunate children, women and men. Often young IDF soldiers are referred to as 'teenagers', particularly if they've been killed, whereas actual Palestinian minors are called 'young adults'. For much of the genocide, Hamas figures on the number of fatalities were presented as though they were unreliable, even though all recognised independent agencies regard them as accurate. In late January 2026, the IDF did too.

The West's neglect is not about resources or a lack of preparedness to act. It is about a lack of interest. Two of its most significant powers, Britain and America, have chosen to intervene and to shape outcomes in all sorts of places, many of them more remote than Palestine. They've invested vast sums and committed the lives of thousands of their soldiers in missions they've claimed are critical to justice and 'the rule of law'. Palestine has never qualified for that sort of commitment and most likely never will. Worse, when these two countries, and others, chose to intervene, it was to help the oppressor kill, maim and starve the oppressed.

Decades of neglect by these nations and others should be a source of shame. The original cause of Palestine's trouble is the carelessness of Britain planting the seed of Zionism in its midst. Nothing since, not even a genocide, will prompt the UK to acknowledge its responsibility to right such a grievous wrong. Moreover, the Middle East narrative is different to the more standard interventions of British and US foreign policy. Palestine is underdeveloped. Its people are Arab, mainly Muslim and have no connection with the West.

Some political pragmatists believe that continuing to support Israel as it approaches its eightieth birthday makes sense. The tragedy of some of its peoples' past, and its origins, its economic performance and its geographic position at the heart of the Middle East, close to Iran, mean the West will support it. These are considered reasonable grounds to ignore the excesses of its settler-colonialism. The genocide has, however, drawn a spotlight on Israel that's unprecedented in its history. It shines too on all those who stood by as it bullied Palestine for decades before unleashing its savagery on a largely defenceless people.

This is the backdrop of the charge of genocide. It is the backdrop to the special rapporteur's demand that 'complicity is confronted, responsibilities are met, and justice is upheld'.[79] She is right. By any historic measure, one of the more remarkable features of Israel's genocide is how so many actors, some of whom would claim to be among the world's great upholders of democratic principles and of human rights, knowingly supported its realisation.

Israel has its own highly developed armaments industry, and it had become a net exporter of arms before initiating the genocide.[80] However, without the military support of its Western allies, the genocide could not have been perpetrated. Under international law, those political leaders and other decision-makers who chose to provide that support have grave questions to answer. The list of those 'in the dock' might be a great deal longer than Benjamin Netanyahu and Yoav Gallant.

◆◆◆

The charge of genocide is not yet proven; lawyers even debate the precise meaning of the ICJ's ruling. For most observers, if Israel's savagery in Gaza and its continuing occupation of the West Bank don't constitute grounds for the charge, it's hard to see the value of the Genocide Convention. The war crimes charges may be more likely to 'stick' against Hamas commanders, as well as Netanyahu et al., but whatever the legalities, the imperative is that Israel be somehow held to account. It never has been before, but this time, as the perpetrator of one of the most egregious acts of oppression in modern times, serious consequences should follow. The complete lack of accountability is being challenged through the work of many agencies. Results matter. There should be consequences for more than Israel. Francesca Albanese's focus on the third states is entirely justified, most especially when it comes to the US. Without the active sponsorship of the US, the UK, and others, the genocide in Palestine could not have happened. It is to Albanese's rollcall of complicit – to whatever varying degrees – third states that attention must also turn.

◆◆◆

On 13 October 2025, before the president turned in for the night aboard Air Force One, the press gaggle he accommodated had raised barely a mumble about Gaza and its forlorn people. The toughest question was a nothing. The answer focused on Trump's favourite thing: money.

‘I heard from people that the aid trucks were going to pass through the a-Tahliyah area. I got dressed and ran out of the house to get there early. When I arrived, there were already huge crowds, but no trucks with flour. Just masses of people waiting for them. Suddenly, Israeli tanks started to fire at the people ... There were injuries and casualties. People went over to the wounded to try and help them, and then the army fired again. And again. The sight of the mutilated bodies was horrifying. Some were without hands and legs, others decapitated, some were shredded to bits.’

Muhammad Abu Mu'amar
(17 June 2025)

FIVE

CONSEQUENCES

President Trump and his team of advisers and friends slept on the trip from the southeast of England to Washington DC. It had been a remarkably busy day. It wasn't just the miles covered; it was the words spoken. In all, Trump had talked publicly for about two hours, never mind the huddles on airport runways and the gaggles with the members of the travelling press corps. So when the White House press pool's logout registered, Donald Trump had said all he was going to say about the Middle East that Monday. It was almost 14 October as the plane ascended and rose steeply over the English Channel. With a flight time of seven hours, it would be the day after Trump's genocide celebration when Air Force One landed at Joint Base Andrews, in Prince George's County, fifteen miles from the White House.

While Air Force One crossed the Atlantic, others were already reflecting on the insights 13 October 2025 gave us into what leadership by chaos might mean for the Middle East. What exactly was it that Team Trump had planned? What could the 'new dawn' he referred to in his speech in the Knesset mean for

Israel and its partners in genocide? What would it mean for the Palestinians, whose land and lives Israel's genocide targeted? What other consequences could there be, and who would benefit or suffer from their realisation? Was there a wider relevance to a world that, as Trump went on his peace-joyride on Monday 13 October, seemed more troubled than for decades? Was the case of Palestine one that could help rebalance it? As a new day dawned in the US, was it more likely it would become a touchstone for a wider Middle East conflagration?

Monday, 13 October 2025, marked an abandonment of all global norms, the same ones that had failed the Palestinians for decades. The idea of something less formulaic was, of itself, not problematic, but the change was cosmetic and wholly inappropriate. America's president wanted showbiz, with his standard fix of adulation. The day was emblematic of his first year as America's forty-seventh president. The whole day was offensive and betrayed the greater problem: in prioritising Israel's interests, the proposed 'solution' had exactly the same flaw as decades of failed attempts. In speaking as he did to Israel's Knesset, Donald Trump destroyed any idea that his plan was even-handed and would address the longstanding abandonment of Palestine. Whatever slim hopes they might have had, Palestinians who followed events in Jerusalem and Sharm el-Sheikh would have seen how far from a priority their cause was for this US president.

That day also suggested that the consequences for Israel, as President Trump talked of a 'win' that should be celebrated, may not be as they should be. Impunity was not at issue; that is a given. What Trump wanted to promote was the great opportunity that Israel's savagery had created. The depravity, the perversity of America's president proclaiming a 'victory' and highlighting the benefits that would flow can never be erased from history. Many tens of thousands of souls had perished, a people's land had been pulverised, much of its heritage obliterated, and Trump went to Jerusalem to pay tribute to his friend 'Bibi', who had led the foul campaign of slaughter.

In spite of all the razzmatazz, and what Trump and his team claimed to have achieved, he had not secured a ceasefire. It would quickly become clear that what was attained was no more than a reduced fire. Israel continued to maraud Palestine, just with less intensity. Into early 2026, though the frequency and levels were much less intense, attacks on Gaza continued and more innocent civilians perished at the hands of Israel and its sponsors. More than a hundred Palestinians were killed by Israel in the first ten days after the announcement. Hundreds more were injured. By March, more than 600 were dead and thousands injured since his claim of brokering peace. In the West Bank, violent theft of land continued with the number of fatal shootings increasing as Israel's security presence in the area grew. In February 2026, a Bedouin community in Mukhmas was burned off its land. Literally. *Haaretz* reported on a 'recent wave of Jewish terrorism in the West Bank. We see how in just a few minutes the attackers … set fire to a number of structures … At one burning structure, a man and a woman were prevented by the attackers from escaping the fire. When they managed to get out, they were beaten by the attackers.'[1]

Were Palestine's future to be determined by words of support, by statements of governments and global institutions and their leaders, its freedom and its welfare would not be in doubt. Those most responsible in Western politics, in business, in the media and other areas of influence, muttered into their institutional chests about how awful it all was, but, once again, they did no more. There were other pressing matters: Greenland, Venezuela, ongoing economic rows between the US and the rest, the horror of Russia's continuing campaign in Ukraine and, of course, Iran.

Even away from politics, Palestine's fate was reverting to where it normally rests, stowed away in some drawer in a cupboard full of all the world's hopeless cases. The institution that governs the world's most popular sport, the International Federation of Association Football (FIFA), led the way. On 5 December 2025, an organisation not known for its ethics awarded its inaugural 'Peace Prize' to Trump, who, in a cringe-making ceremony, accepted, saying about America, 'we saved millions and millions of lives'.[2] This abomination matters only because of football's extraordinary worldwide appeal.

For all the public protests around the world, as long as Palestine's fate is dependent on institutional courage its future will remain perilous. A unique blend of cowardliness, money and a fixation on economic considerations will determine Palestine's future. The events of 13 October 2025 proved this. 'The Trump Declaration for Enduring Peace and Prosperity' promised nothing more hopeful or positive for Palestine than any other initiative taken by America since 1948. Nothing in the almost 9,000 words he used to address the Knesset suggested this US administration believed Palestinian rights were being destroyed, their land occupied. To repeat a fundamental: the fact that the US president thought addressing the Knesset was even appropriate spoke volumes about his contempt for Palestine's cause. The words he chose, the sentiments he expressed and the commitments to Israel that he made only reinforced the continuing hopelessness of their situation.

Racism is another complicating factor for Palestine with the Trump presidency. Trump is a racist. His attacks on Barack Obama and his repeated claims about Mexicans, along with his disgusting reference to Haiti, El Salvador and, more generally, countries in Africa as 'shitholes' proves it.[3] As far back as 1973, his property company was sued by the Department of Justice for discriminating against African-American tenants. That didn't impact his emergence as a successful, if very highly leveraged, real estate developer. While being a racist bully may work in the business of New York real estate, it should be problematic for a twenty-first-century president of the US. Reaching high office, however, changed neither his views nor how he expresses them.

Trump's Islamophobia is marked. It's often expressed crudely. In 2015, it hit a new low when, at a campaign rally he announced a call on the government to impose 'a total and complete shutdown of Muslims entering the United States until our country's representatives can figure out what is going on'.[4] However, much of his racist bigotry is linked to wealth and possessions; he's really a classist-racist. The Arabs of the Gulf can be business associates, political allies and friends, but others, like the majority of Palestinians, would represent a threat, as much because of their lack of wealth as their ethnicity.

Trump's coarseness has never undermined his political ambitions. In 2016, he became America's forty-fifth president, despite a campaign littered with indiscretions and stories of many more. When he lost the contest for re-election, his conduct should have rendered him unelectable if he ever stood again. It didn't, he did, and he won. For over a decade, Donald Trump, the politician, has displayed all the same characteristics as Donald Trump the businessman, yet none of his boorishness, sexism, racism and often infantile behaviour has hurt him politically. He remains an Islamophobe; indeed, his populist attacks on refugees, which disproportionately affect Muslims, appeal to his nativist, anti-Islam electoral gene pool. All of this works in Israel's favour.

ISRAELI IMPUNITY

The greatest impediment, bar none, to a solution for Palestine is the impunity that Israel enjoys. It is the single greatest obstacle to peace and has been for decades. The absence of any consequences for doing what Israel has done, prohibits progress towards peace. With almost any other nation in the developed world, its conduct would, long ago, have had consequences. Jewish people were given land that was not theirs on which to establish the state of Israel. Warnings against that fateful decision in 1917, some by eminent Jewish figures and Jewish groups in the West, were ignored. Most of those who opposed the move believed, as Edwin Montagu argued in his memorandum to Balfour, that the establishment of a Jewish state would disenfranchise the Arab people and would fuel antisemitism. Each time in history that the international community had cause to prevent Israel from deepening its colonial hold on Palestine, the West went missing.

Two decades after the Balfour Declaration the growing number of Zionist immigrants was increasingly disruptive for the Palestinians. Settler expansion caused widespread displacement, with violence by both sides contributing to a hostile environment. The cause was the age-old issue of colonialism and the resistance of the indigenous people. In 1938, a decade before the foundation of Israel, Henryk Ehrlich, a leading figure in the Jewish Labour movement in Europe, wrote, 'The Zionists regard themselves as second-class citizens in Poland. Their aim is to be first-class citizens in Palestine and make the Arabs second-class citizens.'[5] It mattered little what brutality the settlers meted out to the Arabs, the Zionist mission allowed it.

Less than a century later, Ehrlich's observation seems prophetic. Even those Palestinians who became citizens of Israel and now represent 20 per cent of its population have a second-class experience in the apartheid state. They are discriminated against across every area of life, though their troubles are nothing to those of their fellow Palestinians in the Occupied Territories. The West is most liable for this, Britain especially so. It never followed through on one of the conditions attached to the Balfour Declaration – that the rights of the Palestinians would be respected. It never intended to. It was no more than the colonial fig leaf of one established power handing over an asset to an aspiring settler-colonialist.

Since its establishment in 1948, Israel has shown itself well-equipped for the colonial task. It always wanted more land than was offered by its original borders. For decades, it pursued that goal. The Holocaust gave the mission further momentum and dulled, understandably, any resistance in Europe, however slight, to the Zionist land-offensive. The horror of what happened compromised the capacity of many to question, as Montagu and Ehrlich had done, the rights of the Jews to take the land of the Palestinians.

Even today, the stain of the Holocaust inhibits many in the West from calling out twenty-first-century Israel for what it is. When it set out on its campaign after the Hamas attack on 7 October 2023, it knew the West would support it. What will have surprised its government was the unrestricted nature of that support. It shouldn't have. Impunity is a byword for how Western powers have treated Israel. The complete absence of consequences for past foul deeds morphed into permission to do whatever it liked. Israel took the latitude it was granted in October 2023 and conducted a genocide; as its intentions became clear, no effort was made to restrain it. As its slaughter ran into many tens of thousands, not one of its primary sponsors stepped in to shout stop. Well into year three, with another ceasefire shredded by the IDF, the word 'stop' isn't even whispered.

Trump's 13 October speech in the Knesset was a new low, even by the standards of his second administration. Its vanity and inappropriateness were at the higher end of his scale; the absence of political substance was as normal. The intention was clear. There could be a peaceful outcome, but only if the Palestinians reformed. They had to deradicalise and be prepared to live under a provisional administration overseen by a board of world leaders. Their security would be protected by an international force, and all they would have to do would be to submit to this regimen so that the redevelopment of the Gaza Strip could begin. Team Trump would do what it could to bring calm to Gaza; there was a decade of work ahead to clear it before real money could be generated. What better motivation to keep the peace? This was the deal.

Where do you begin to make sense of it being Palestine that must deradicalise? How do you credit the viciously oppressed being told that it is they who must commit to offering no threat to Israel, their oppressor? Were they to sign up to that, then, but only then, could Palestinians hope for a 'return' to the basics of life and opportunities for work.

Impunity breeds impunity. Israel has never had any incentive to engage morally. The Netanyahu government is the most corrupt and bloodthirsty manifestation of what has gone before, and none of the brutal behaviour has ever been challenged. This time the scale of the horror is different. In the early 2020s, Western governments have failed the Palestinians as never before. Global institutions, there to protect the interests of the underdog, of the oppressed, have failed, as they tend to do. This time the failures are more glaring and so exposed that it is hard to see how some can recover. Underpinned by the international rule of law, they face uncertain futures when those laws themselves are being so widely ignored. The genocide that has played out since autumn 2023 is as much down to a chronic malaise across third states and global bodies as it is to the ruthless colonialism of Israel's thirty-seventh government.

Israel's impunity is intact. As long as it is, Palestine's cause is hopeless. The focus of the West's current peace plan is deradicalising the Palestinians. So, an impoverished, homeless and frightened Arab people needs to be detoxified, not the sovereign state that has conducted a genocide against it. It's the Arabs who need taming, not the Zionists. Trump never mentioned the Palestinians on his day of celebration, but he did a few months later. At the annual economic and political forum in Davos, Switzerland, he staged the inauguration of the Board of Peace, which he said would help oversee the reconstruction of Gaza. There were words for the Palestinians, or Hamas at least. 'They were born with rifles in their hands ... But they have to give up their weapons, and if they don't do that, it's going to be the end of them.'[6]

That was it. Israel carried no fault. To this well-informed audience of global political, institutional and corporate leaders, there was not a single word of admonition for Israel. Still, they listened, applauded and gave credence to his account. The deathly silence of indifference to the obliteration of Palestine extended to most of the other speakers. British Foreign Secretary Yvette Cooper said the UK would not join the Board but was otherwise supportive of the reconstruction plan. President Macron, who had already said France would not participate in Trump's initiative, asked that the rule of law should prevail. Chancellor Merz said Germany would join the Board of Peace, while stressing that Trump's plan must meet humanitarian needs. At no time was there any criticism of Israel. Today's political leaders did what generations before them have done: they left Israel alone. It's called impunity by default.

What the West either does not want to admit or does not believe is that, without the threat of serious repercussions, Israel will never make peace with the Palestinians. Its leaders are even more afraid to acknowledge that they are intimidated by Israel; afraid to act against it. Fear is a factor domestically too. Israeli society has been passive over the years of the genocide. The peace cohort so prevalent for so long seems to have evaporated in parallel with the loss of support for the Labor Party. In the 1990s, its leadership – Yitzhak Rabin, Shimon Peres and Ehud Barak – committed Labor to the two-state solution. However, Labor never recovered from the loss of Rabin in 1995.

There's a symbolism about the loss of principle or morality in Israeli public life since Rabin's assassination. Just weeks earlier, his car had been vandalised by Itamar Ben-Gvir, now Minister for National Security in Netanyahu's Cabinet. Ben-Gvir, a thug in the guise of a Cabinet minister, said at the time, 'We got to his car and we'll get to him, too.'[7] Ben-Gvir consistently derides the idea that there's any such thing as a Palestinian. He regularly talks of how he sets out to worsen the conditions of Palestinian detainees. In the Knesset, he wears a suit pin of a noose, signifying his support for the 2026 legislation which restored the death penalty, targeted at Palestinians.

When that bill passed on 30 March 2026, some government ministers and members of the Knesset were seen celebrating the outcome, including Ben-Gvir, who held a bottle of champagne aloft. The legislation he sponsored meant the brutal regime in Israel can now execute Palestinians. During the vote for the bill, Prime Minister Netanyahu sat in silence on the government benches, but he made a point of attending to cast his vote in favour. This means a Palestinian can be sentenced to death by a simple majority in a military court. The law has no means of appeal; once convicted the prisoner's fate is sealed. This vote, in the parliament of a state claiming to be a democracy, means execution is the possible fate of its 9,600 Palestinian prisoners, at least half of whom are being held without charge.

The grip of the centre-right to far-right parties on power and influence in Israel has tightened over the past two decades. It is manifest not just in increasingly aggressive settlement of land in the West Bank and more deliberately provocative acts at disputed holy sites, but also in the increasingly apartheid approach toward the 20 per cent of Israeli citizens who are Palestinian Arabs. Pew research found that 24 per cent of all Jewish Israelis and 89 per cent of those who describe themselves as ultra-Orthodox say that Jewish law should take precedence over democratic principles.[8] More recent data from The Israel Democracy Institute shows those identifying as politically right-wing grew from 46 per cent in 2019 to 62 per cent in 2022. In 1995, the year of Rabin's assassination, 29 per cent identified as right-wing. Recently, of those aged 18–34, 64 to 73 per cent said they were right-wing.[9]

Zionists haven't spent all their energy and resources on the Greater Israel project and on incursions into the land of others, whether in Golan, in Lebanon or in the support of settlers in the West Bank. Young Israelis are being radicalised by an education system and societal norms that are increasingly racist. There's a clear focus on indoctrinating future generations. In *Catastrophe: Nakba II*, I wrote, 'When young minds are being educated in a system where the supremacy of the students' ethnicity is being promoted and where issues like citizenship, democracy and human rights are not discussed, never mind taught, there can be only one outcome.'[10] The evidence from polling of the younger cohorts in Israeli society illustrates the success of that state effort.

The consequences are immense. In the summer of 2025, approaching two years on from the start of the genocide, Israeli public opinion started to firm around the need to end it. When those polled were given reasons to end it, only 2 per cent of the Jews chose 'ceasing harm to the residents of Gaza' as their reason. The same poll showed that 11 per cent more Jewish Israelis thought the Palestinians had no right to an independent state (72) than twelve months previously (61).[11]

Israeli society will not shift; there is no political movement, no public groundswell that is even questioning what is being done in their name. There have been protests, but the great majority of them were about the return of the hostages. Whereas in the 1980s and 1990s there would have been a quite sizeable peace movement concerned with the welfare of those under attack, that's hardly been in evidence during Israel's genocide.

There is no internal group of any size asking of Israelis: what are we doing, how can we behave in this manner?

There are, of course, people in Israel who feel this, who desperately want the slaughter being carried out in their name to be over. There are academics and thought leaders, there are prominent journalists and writers, there are extraordinary human rights organisations, but there is no coherent substantial movement that is protesting for it to end. Absent that, and with the portents as bad as they are, any solution has to come from outside. That has to start with a collective decision by Western nations, whose murderous hands are all over the dead, wounded and those still lost under Gaza's rubble, ending all support of Israel. That starts by refusing it the standard impunity that has marked almost every one of its attacks on the people of Palestine since before the state of Israel was founded in 1948.

With no left-wing movement of substance, no peace-based political grouping of scale, Israel's politics is dominated, with only a sliver of liberalism in evidence, by a far-right to centre-right political class. This is not just Israel's problem. As many parts of the West shift toward more isolationist politics, especially the two nations on whom its future relies, the right in Israel could find even more support forthcoming. Its dominant political class sees this as Israel's opportunity. The parties that control the Knesset in 2026 know that with Trump in power, there is zero chance of Israel being called to account. Those parties, in government and in opposition, who cheered his every word on 13 October 2025 and whose leaders lauded him in their remarks, know he is as bound to them as they are to him. Trump is a convicted felon. His conviction on thirty-four counts of falsifying records relating to the payment of money to a porn star came just six months before he was elected president for the second time. It's highly unlikely that this president would contact Benjamin Netanyahu, himself facing corruption charges, to say that the US has to call time on its relationship with Israel. That has been beyond every president for eighty years. It is, most certainly, not a job for Donald J. Trump.

The New York Declaration of July 2025 had offered a flicker of hope in this respect from the UN, enough to sound alarm bells loudly in Israel. It was a spur for some Western powers to acknowledge the state of Palestine, and in the midst of the gloom, it generated some momentum behind the Palestinian cause. The oppressed had been recognised by the ICJ, and political action had led to the Declaration, which established Palestine's right to self-determination. Its terms included nine provisions under the heading 'Empowering a sovereign and economically viable State of Palestine'. Its focus was a two-state solution, based on the 'recognized borders on the basis of the 1967 lines, including with regard to Jerusalem'.[12] It went further, saying that Israel must make a definitive commitment to this and immediately 'halt all settlement, land grabs and annexation activities in the Occupied Palestinian Territory, including East Jerusalem'.[13]

Its language was unusually stark, saying in Clause 23 that Israel must 'renounce any annexation project or settlement policy, and put an end to settlers' violence, including by implementing UN Security Council Resolution 904 and enacting legislation to punish and deter violent settlers and their illegal actions'.[14] As the prospects of such action and of Israel bringing the activities of settlers in the West Bank under control were nil, there was little to be lost by using such direct language. The Declaration noted that full admission of Palestine to the UN was imperative, with full regional integration then realisable. An additional cause for optimism, according to France, which has the largest Arab population in Europe, was offered by the Palestinians' commitment to work together through the Beijing Declaration.

The Trump plan was engineered to find a different outcome based on an entirely different premise. It saw the Palestinians as the obstacle to finding peace. Trump had long talked of Gaza's real estate potential, and in his limited diplomasphere, Palestinians are Islamic warmongers. In his world and among the growing far-right in the West, their very existence is threatening. It is based on this kind of narrative that Israel offers itself as a counter to the threat of Islamism. The speedy move to shut out the New York Declaration of summer 2025 massively reduced any risk of Israel being called to account for its deeds.

The seriousness of the New York Declaration and the considerable global support it garnered was its Achilles heel. Netanyahu's vision of a redeveloped Gaza was critical to his goal of reshaping the region to suit only Israel's interests. The economic corridor, without Palestine, that he has presented to the UN more than once depended on it. His political career depended on it and, quite possibly, even staying out of jail did too. So, Israel used its quasi-Western characteristics and the threat of Islamism to play to the instincts of Trump and his base. Trump, who sees himself as a political leader beyond the confines of America, projects his influence on a broader canvas, on populist leaders like Viktor Orbán in Hungary, Marine Le Pen in France and Nigel Farage in the UK. Trump revels in the attention these and other ultra-conservative figures offer. They, in return, use his trademark to endorse their own plans. There are many shared 'values' across these political parties, public movements and individuals, but the one that unites them all is Islamophobia.

Israel is key to this. It is an ethnocracy, and Islamophobia connects ethno-nationalists across the world, enabling apartheid and even genocide. With Islamophobia in their arsenal, most right-wing, even centre-right, groups in the West can mobilise support or at least dull opposition to their success. This is relevant to Palestine's continuing struggle to assert itself with the institutional West. Professor of Social Theory and Decolonial Thought Salman Sayyid says that while Trump didn't invent Islamophobia, the genocide in Gaza means 'observers need to recognize that neither the United States nor the European Union can be considered reliable defenders of human and civil rights'.[15] An irrational view of Islam has festered, largely unchallenged, for generations, resulting in Western complicity in a genocide being broadcast live on phones and laptops.

A just peace was never the focus of Donald Trump's 2025 plan. Other US presidents have initiated attempts that were prejudiced towards Israel, were naive and had no real chance of success. Most were ill-conceived, but none had such malintent from the start. None approached their task with such indifference to the oppressed. Trump's proposal had all the characteristics of a commercial plan. It used business language, and its terms were structured accordingly. The purpose was to allow sovereign entities and select corporations to create untold wealth that could pump economic growth in Gaza. This would enrich everyone except Palestine.

There were no promises for the Palestinians, no reason for hope that was not conditional on their changed behaviour. Monday, 13 October 2025 was about managing Palestinian expectations. Life's basics were on offer, but even that was conditional on a commitment to deradicalise, which meant more than Hamas decommissioning. It required Gazans to subjugate themselves to being governed by an international board and policed by a security force of soldiers from neighbouring Arab countries. Details were scarce. More than two years into a genocide that had slaughtered many tens of thousands and destroyed what infrastructure they had, Palestinians were still at the mercy of Israel and the US. As the US legislature moved on, consumed by the risk of war with Iran and the neurosis over Greenland, not one country in the West had the courage to call out Trump's plan for the private equity investment play that it really was or to force a change in the Middle East agenda.

THE ARAB STATES

It is not social or political romanticism to suggest that the New York Declaration, which would have forced a much more serious process on Israel, was in part fuelled by public mobilisation against Israel across many Western countries. Public opinion has been a more important consideration than many realise. In the West, despite the über-managed control of the story by the establishment media, the public was accessing material that shaped their outrage. The consistency and strength of public demonstrations had a direct bearing on some governments moving to recognise Palestine. Such pressure is there to stay and may well emerge as even more critical in the future.

As the genocide continued, public demonstrations also became more of a feature in the Arab states, many of which are autocracies. The Arab Spring uprisings in 2011 were a marker. Jordan, Morocco, Iraq and Yemen have all experienced hundreds of thousands of demonstrators taking to the streets to protest Israel's genocide. Displaying a full understanding of the genocidal axis, protests and vigils were regularly held at Israeli and US embassies. Informed by the global online access to Israel's brutality, public opinion was fiercely pro-Palestine. In such states, public protests are discouraged generally, but these had to be allowed and they built a momentum that exerted more pressure on Arab leaders to act.

Just four months into the genocide, the respected Arab Center for Research and Policy Studies published findings of an opinion poll taken of 8,000 people across sixteen different Arab nations. It showed that only 5 per cent thought the Hamas attack was illegitimate, 92 per cent expressed solidarity with the Palestinians and 94 per cent held a negative view of America's support of Israel. Arguably, the most significant finding was that 92 per cent of those polled said the cause of Palestine is an issue for all Arabs. That finding had increased from 76 per cent in 2022, with some national increases on that question particularly noteworthy: Egypt from 75 per cent in 2022 to 95 per cent in 2024, and Saudi Arabia from 69 per cent to 95 per cent.[16] Palestine, always an issue for people across the Arab world, had now become more so. That remained constant throughout 2025. Polling continued to show declining support for America as its role in the genocide became ever more apparent and widely commented upon.

Autocratic Arab leaders live by control. Citizens taking to the streets to support fellow Arabs and denounce Israel represented a challenge, but they couldn't be seen to stop the protests. Instead, they needed to be seen to work with the US towards bringing an end to Israel's barbarism. Trump's plan offered that chance; it could give the appearance of bringing the West to a point where, at the very least, the bloodshed would end. The Board of Peace would establish a means by which the Palestinians could be policed and, over a period of time, deradicalised. Trump was clear that, as what he called 'the mess' was being removed and the rebuilding of Gaza commenced, the mindset of the people could be changed. Inherent to his plan is the idea that outside forces will decide whether or not the Palestinians are worthy of determining their own future. This Israel can just about swallow.

Saudi Arabia had co-sponsored the New York Declaration with France in July 2025. It would involve a meaningful engagement with the Palestinians to help them recover, rebuild and govern Gaza as they saw fit. Then everything changed. In November, Saudi Arabia's Crown Prince, Mohammed bin Salman, visited Washington, the first such visit to the US since Trump was last president. The occasion was a conference focused on greater economic co-operation. Separately, the two men discussed Gaza and the Trump peace plan. It was widely reported that bin Salman told Trump that Saudi Arabia would only want a normalised relationship with Israel if there was a credible pathway to Palestinian statehood, something Netanyahu had again ruled out just days earlier. However, there were no public comments or briefings about the situation in Palestine.

Instead, Saudi Arabia made massive economic commitments to the US. Documentation marking the event included comments by bin Salman about how the 'partnership with the US will grow at an unprecedented pace in the coming years'.[17] Some of the financial commitments were eye-watering. A massive package of agreements totalling more than $575 billion was confirmed, but this was outdone by the Crown Prince's pledge to increase Saudi investment plans in the US to $1 trillion. The scale of these commitments meant that Saudi Arabia was unlikely to baulk at supporting Trump's plan rather than the New York Declaration, even knowing Israel's intention of continuing its subjugation of Palestine. Trump's plan would help to facilitate that outcome, but Saudi Arabia still committed to it. These machinations also occurred against the backdrop of Saudi Arabia's unprecedented investment in the fund managed by Jared Kushner.

TRUMP'S BOARDS

Over the months that followed, as Trump sought to broaden his status as a peace negotiator, more evidence of his and his administration's commitment to Israel emerged. In mid-January 2026 the make-up of the boards and the structure for managing Gaza emerged through a series of social media posts and White House press releases. These were structured so America's and Israel's interests remained protected.

Trump claimed phase two of his Gaza peace plan could advance because the ceasefire had held. It had not. In the three months since 13 October 2025, at least 463 people had been killed by Israel in Gaza. Israel had also maintained strict controls on food and other forms of aid, despite the continuing famine conditions. Most of the population of Gaza was living in tents with little protection from the elements. Children were reported to be dying of malnutrition and hypothermia. On the first day of the new year, Israel had revoked the licences of thirty-seven international NGOs, including the globally respected

MSF, ActionAid and the International Rescue Committee.[18] This was not a new move on Israel's part. In summer 2025, the only agency it had allowed to distribute food was the one it established with the US. It was a rogue agency; the IDF carried out numerous massacres of people queuing for food. Now, amidst a faux ceasefire with starving people living in appalling conditions, it once again shut down many of the more reliable sources of assistance. Brutality was stacked upon brutality. The usual condemnation followed, with the EU describing it as a move that would block humanitarian aid. UN Human Rights Commissioner Volker Türk said the move was outrageous and made 'an already intolerable situation even worse for the people of Gaza'.[19] Words can't save Palestine.

Trump's Board of Peace was to oversee the 'ceasefire' and the proposed reconstruction of Gaza. There were different tiers. There would be a Gaza Executive Board, which would approach the business of the 'ceasefire' and the enormous challenge of rebuilding the Gaza Strip. This founding Executive Board had no Palestinians on it. Former UK Prime Minister Tony Blair was the only non-American citizen. Its composition highlighted the emphasis on business. In addition to Trump as chair, three others were from his inner circle: Secretary of State Marco Rubio, Middle East Special Envoy Steve Whitkoff and Jared Kushner. The others were Marc Rowan, CEO of a large private equity fund in New York, Ajay Banga, president of the World Bank, Robert Gabriel, a business associate of Trump, and Stephen Miller, his political henchman. Blair, Kushner, Witkoff and Rowan were also nominated to a separate board, also, rather confusingly, called the Gaza Executive Board, led by former UN Middle East envoy and Bulgarian politician Nickolay Mladenov. Its other members included the Turkish foreign minister, a Qatari diplomat, a UAE minister and a director of Egypt's secret service.

The third tier, a Palestinian technocratic committee, would evaluate people's needs, the provision of services and on-the-ground management. These individuals would be chosen by the Gaza Executive Board, vetted and then appointed. The formal announcement also referenced two special advisers to lead 'day-to-day strategy and operations' and translate the board's 'mandate and diplomatic priorities into disciplined execution'.[20] They were Aryeh Lightstone, a US rabbi and political adviser, and Josh Gruenbaum, a prominent private equity executive and member of the US Federal Task Force on Antisemitism. These appointments are critical to delivery of the plan on a day-to-day basis, yet Lightstone and Gruenbaum's appointments barely raised any comment.

Israel's political leadership was unimpressed by this mid-January flurry of announcements by the White House. Benjamin Netanyahu dislikes having to challenge US presidents, most especially Donald Trump. But he also dislikes being blindsided, as he claimed he was by the announcements. Israel objected to the involvement of political figures from Turkey and Qatar in Trump's boards. It went further, saying that the White House announcement 'was not coordinated with Israel and contradicts its policy'.[21] Within hours, Israeli government ministers became more trenchant in their criticisms. Finance Minister Bezalel Smotrich, one of three ministers of the Religious Zionist party, criticised Netanyahu, warning that, 'The countries [Turkey, Qatar, UAE] that inspired Hamas cannot be the ones that replace it.'[22] The ultra-right in the coalition was making its presence felt.

Netanyahu desperately needed to hold on to power until the elections scheduled for October 2026. Retaining the support of Religious Zionism and the Otzma Yehudit party meant allowing no cracks to appear. That skirmish showed fissures were there, but also that Israel's sense of its own impunity was intact.

THE UNITED NATIONS

The UN itself is threatened by events well into the third year of the genocide. In an address given in January 2026 marking the eightieth anniversary of its first major meeting, Secretary General António Guterres warned of 'powerful forces lining up to undermine global cooperation'.[23] As he talked of global arms spending reaching record levels of $2.7 trillion, the ravages of climate destruction and algorithms providing 'authoritarians with powerful tools of control',[24] the forty-seventh president of the US could hardly have been far from his thoughts.

Yet only months earlier, even though it was clear from Trump's first term that the UN was in his line of fire, the organisation sanctioned America's deliberately pro-Israel, overtly political and dangerous peace plan. Thirteen of the fifteen members of the Security Council supported the US motion; Russia and China abstained, but even they chose not to veto it. The vote, taken a month after Trump's 13 October tour of celebration, gave the added weight of international recognition to his plan. By implication, the UN endorsed what he'd said both at the Knesset and in Sharm el-Sheikh. This was done without giving what was proposed due consideration; before the details had emerged such as they were. It's hard to understand why UN members took the decision, which would only benefit Israel, the US and a myriad of private interests. It disadvantaged the cause of Palestine – irreparably if it is implemented as planned.

The commentary of President Trump on Monday 13 October had ridiculed any notion of a world order based on international law. He had lavished praise on the coloniser; mocked the oppressed. And it was clear to all that Trump had colonial ambitions of his own. These included not only taking sovereign territory wherever he could and overthrowing (as many of his predecessors had done) elected leaders of other nations, but also undermining those global institutions supposed to maintain law and order.

Credibility issues have long plagued the UN, perhaps on no issue more than the Middle East. In the deliberations on UN Resolution 2803 of 17 November 2025, insufficient attention was paid to the fact that, by definition, Trump's Board of Peace would operate outside international law. Its charter establishes that the board chairman has the right to veto any proposal. As it was clear that the role of board chair is Trump's for life, a private individual could potentially determine outcomes on matters of global sovereignty. Dr Gershon Baskin, an Israeli peace activist warned, 'Trump has this complex that he's going to save the world – it's not by chance the charter of the new Board of Peace mentions him specifically as the chair, not the president of the United States. It's Donald J Trump.'[25] And while events in the Middle East may have prompted the creation of the Board of Peace, its full documentation revealed a wider intent – to oversee the resolution of conflicts elsewhere in the world. In a barely camouflaged challenge to the UN, the board's charter said it would provide 'a more nimble and effective international peace-building body'.[26]

Secretary General Guterres highlighted the UN's impotence in his anniversary speech.[27] It had, effectively, ceded responsibility for how Gazans were to be governed. The UN's autonomy and strength, not always in evidence, were perhaps never as absent as in the autumn of 2025 and early 2026. With the fate of Palestine at stake, it largely withdrew to the sidelines and allowed Israel, America and Trump to determine the outcome. Its relevance has rarely been so undermined.

In mid-January, as the board and executive structure for Gaza was outlined, the White House issued invitations to sixty nations to join its overarching Board of Peace. Israel's genocide was being used by Trump to shake up the world order and place the US's interests ahead of all others. Each selected country received a letter of invitation and a copy of the board's charter. The details, with offers of three-year terms for those who accepted, or life if they invested $1 billion, pointed to a new, US-controlled global organisation. As part of Resolution 2803 the UN had ceded financial autonomy to the Trump board. This meant placing responsibility for the *c.* $80 billion budget for rebuilding Gaza under the control of his Gaza Executive Board.

The Board of Peace is a ruse. Gaza's horror, for which the US bears great responsibility, was a base on which Trump wanted to establish an agency to oversee all global conflicts. The UN's decision to sanction the plan, handing responsibility for finding a peaceful resolution between Israel and Palestine to a US-managed entity, was catastrophic for Palestine. The UN backed Trump's plan in full knowledge that America was the principal sponsor of Israel's genocide. It knew Trump and Netanyahu had for long talked of the real estate potential of the Gaza Strip. It knew Trump's plan made no reference to reparation or accountability for the genocide.

The UN is often accused of being too bureaucratic, but on this occasion, it fell foul of a Trump manoeuvre. Trump leveraged the scale of the crisis in Palestine and his alignment of Middle East and Western states to offer a way to resolve one of the most intractable diplomatic issues globally. The UN took the bait. The outline of Trump's plan reads to some experts 'less like a pathway to justice than a return to colonial trusteeship'.[28] It is. Others say that 'the UN has found itself a victim of a classic bait-and-switch, thinking it was buying one thing, but getting quite another'.[29] It has. UN sanction of the plan also carried implications for other global institutions and their capacity to undertake their work. One of the most critical in circumstances of prolonged conflict is that of the ICJ in determining where fault lies and what consequences should follow.

REPARATION

In an Advisory Opinion of July 2024, the ICJ found that Israel's continued presence in Palestine was unlawful and demanded it end its occupation. It defined the territory in question as the West Bank, East Jerusalem and Gaza. It also ordered that it cease new settlements and that full reparations would be due on damages caused by the occupation. The ruling had been sought by the UN General Assembly in December 2022. Israel ignored it completely.

Under international statutes, the ICJ alone has the authority to set the levels and terms by which reparation must be made. There is recent precedent. In 2022, the Court found against Uganda and instructed that it pay $325 million in damages for crimes it committed in the Congo. Uganda reacted negatively to the findings but, recognising the importance of the ICJ, 'complied with the reparation judgment' and paid the first instalment on time as decreed by the Court.[30]

There are few certainties around conflict and post-conflict determinations, but the evidence that Gaza has been obliterated is compelling. Moral and financial accountability need to be established. This is critical when a state is found to have broken international law and oppressed a people. As each case is judged on its own merits and the demands of a legal entity like the ICJ are necessarily demanding, it seems reasonable to suggest that the burden of reparations on Gaza would fall on Israel and perhaps also its main sponsors. What is certain is that there is, at least, a case for Israel to answer.

Reparation payments are particularly important when the level of destruction involved is as huge as that in Gaza. The aggressor's identity is known. The international community is acutely aware of this and should resist any move to divert attention from the Court's task of holding Israel to account. It remains to be seen if nations that supported Israel could also be considered liable. When British Foreign Secretary Yvette Cooper appeared on *Channel 4 News* just before Christmas 2025 about moves to give Russian assets that had been frozen in 2024 to Ukraine, she was asked if the decision would not amount to theft. Her answer was: 'This is the principle that Russia should pay for the damage that they have done … We now believe that those assets should be mobilised to support Ukraine in the face of this aggression and war.'[31] It begged a question about Gaza, Israel and its allies in the West. It wasn't asked. Western money, arms and its indifference allowed Israel to conduct its genocide. Many awkward questions may yet arise.

The UN's decision to support the Trump plan may end up proving to be an act of self-harm. To neuter the ICJ, as the UN's decision on Resolution 2803 did, represented another step that makes it a great deal more difficult to hold Israel accountable. It damaged the potential of the ICJ to pursue Israel on reparations. This is evident in Trump's allocation of $10 billion by the US towards the rebuilding programme, and his demand that nations joining his Board of Peace contribute $2 billion each to the same purpose. That the US should be involved in the reparation payments, given its egregious sponsorship of the genocide, is not in question, but there is an international process by which such matters are managed. The ICJ is where these decisions should be taking place, not the Board of Peace. By allowing this, the UN has effectively compromised any potential for the ICJ to force Israel and its sponsors to make reparations.

THIRD STATES AND INDIVIDUALS

The ICJ ruling of July 2024 also referenced third-party obligations, which included refraining from providing aid or any form of assistance that could help maintain the situation. Many states in the West fell foul of this particular provision and continued to do so, even after the Court's decision was adopted by the UN General Assembly on 18 September 2024.[32]

UN Special Rapporteur Francesca Albanese's autumn 2025 report focused on the role of third states in Israel's genocide in Gaza. The crime of genocide is so egregious that international law pursues not just the primary perpetrator but those states that facilitate it. One hundred and ninety-three sovereign nations are members of the UN. In order to assert its importance, to reinforce the centrality of its mission, any members found to have assisted Israel should be prosecuted. To do otherwise would greatly undermine international law.

When Albanese refers to the genocide, she terms it 'a collective crime, sustained by the complicity of influential third States that have enabled long-standing systematic violations of international law by Israel'.[33] She references about sixty, though different degrees of culpability apply. In the case of the US, such a claim would be hard to challenge.

As with the UK, America's ties to Israel go well back in time. Since 1967, when it expanded its territories through occupation, Israel has received substantial US military aid that has underpinned decades of mutual defence and economic interests. Under US statutes, Israel enjoys preferential access and terms for military assistance. It alone has permission (though Taiwan and Ukraine have benefited from this on an interim basis recently) to use the financial military aid America provides to purchase Israeli-manufactured military equipment. Albanese's report sets out, in detail, the extent to which those basic commitments of aid and arms have increased since the genocide began. The figures, running to tens of billions of dollars in arms and ammunition, are alarming, as is the deliberate suppression of information by both the Biden and Trump administrations.

It was not the idle or loose commitment of an ailing president when Joe Biden promised 'unprecedented' support for Israel in October 2023. It was his righteous Zionism. And there's been no let-up in this support, even as the evidence of a genocide became clear. In 2024, testimony from US volunteer medics on the deliberate destruction of Gaza's medical capacity was ignored by Biden and Blinken. US NGOs wasted their time pleading for the arms sales to stop, while, in July 2024, Congress roared itself hoarse in support of the genocide conductor, Benjamin Netanyahu. Year two, with Trump and Marco Rubio in charge, changed nothing.

Other Western nations were compromised, as were some of the Arab states that attended Trump's signing ceremony in Sharm el-Sheikh on 13 October 2025. Israel's almost twenty-year blockade of Gaza wouldn't have had anything like the same impact on the people if Egypt hadn't followed suit, closing the Rafah crossing in 2007. Albanese's report cites this as contributing to the deliberate weaponising of aid distribution by Israel, making Egypt complicit. Turkey suspended all trade with Israel during the genocide. In contrast the UAE, Morocco, Egypt and Jordan all increased trade with Israel significantly over the period. Five EU countries did so too: Germany by a staggering $836 million, and Denmark, Italy, Greece and Poland all by *c.* $100 million.[34]

Germany is one of the two biggest offenders in the West after the US when it comes to supporting Israel's actions, the other being the UK. Germany has been the second-largest arms exporter to Israel. Francesca Albanese's report records how, 'In addition to suspending ethical and legal assessments of the Israeli occupation, from October 2023 to July 2025, Germany issued individual export licences worth €489 million – 15 per cent of all licences to Israel in 22 years. This does not include any arms transferred under collective licences or on a Government-to-Government basis. Although the Chancellor of Germany, Friedrich Merz, temporarily suspended future export approvals in August 2025, €2.46 million in exports were approved a month later.'[35] That the amount was so small was not the point.

Albanese believed that Germany was aligning itself with Israel by maintaining economic ties; the sleight of hand involved between Merz's statement and the approval a month later was marked.

Some politicians and others in public life justify this support because of the Holocaust, over which a national sense of shame still prevails eighty years later. Israel plays on this expertly. Yet many Holocaust survivors and children of survivors have spoken of their anger at Israel's conduct and objected to the idea that the Jewish state can use one horror to justify another. One, Rene Lichtman, said, 'I think Israel is a fascist state today. What else would you call it? Can you imagine dying in a way where the building falls on you? That's the way the death occurs in those places, day after day. It is almost like torture … So, the Warsaw Ghetto uprising seemed to me like a parallel to what Hamas was doing. And they were very conscious, they were going to die in the Warsaw Ghetto and they were going to take some with them. The Warsaw Ghetto fighters were these young people, they were idealistic, they were all socialists, they were all on the left. The Jewish world has forgotten that. [The Hamas fighters,] their grandparents originally came from the Nakba of 1948.'[36]

Albanese's report also highlights the role of the UK. She describes the government's support as 'key', acknowledging that it was in spite of strong levels of public opposition. What receives most attention is the active involvement through the provision of critical military intelligence. The use of its RAF bases in Cyprus is described in her report as enabling 'a crucial United States supply line to Tel Aviv'.[37] She reports that more than 600 surveillance missions were flown over Gaza by RAF operators, often coinciding with military action taken by the IDF. The most damning line in her account on Britain is that the information her team has accessed suggests its 'detailed knowledge and cooperation in the destruction of Gaza'.[38]

Under international law, all states have an obligation to prevent genocide. This would suggest either that there is no basis for considering Israel's conduct to be a genocide or that only South Africa and the sixteen countries that supported its case in the ICJ may not be open to the charge of complicity. The great majority of Western nations did not back South Africa. The absence of that backing would, under the Genocide Convention, have serious implications if a case of genocide were successfully prosecuted. For corporations too – given the huge levels of trade different nations are doing with Israel, it is inevitable that many global corporations are also responsible for sustaining Israel's economy and, therefore, its capacity to conduct this genocide. In one of her reports, *From Economy of Occupation to Economy of Genocide*, the special rapporteur highlights why large businesses are exposed. 'While political leaders and governments shirk their obligations, far too many corporate entities have profited from Israel's economy of illegal occupation, apartheid and now genocide.'[39] Albanese is clear about the greater complexities in dealing with corporations, but she is equally clear that, unless there's proof they refused to be complicit, they must be held to account.

There is another, however unlikely, strand that prosecutors could pursue on this genocide once it's so determined legally. After the Second World War, when the full scale of the horrors committed by the Nazis was no longer in doubt and many of the main figures had been held accountable, the Allies made the decision to pursue only those in leadership positions who were responsible for war crimes. A number of civilians disagreed and chose to cast the net further. Individuals such as Simon Wiesenthal, Tuvia Friedman, Elizabeth Holtzman, Beate and Serge Klarsfeld became recognised 'Nazi hunters'. These individuals saw their task as doing the necessary research to build a case that would allow their governments to pursue second- and third-tier Nazi war criminals. This directly resulted in the trials at Auschwitz and the trial against the SS death squads, the Einsatzgruppen. It was at the Einsatzgruppen trials in 1947/48, which saw twenty-four men found guilty, that the word 'genocide' was used for the first time in a legal setting. The individuals who pursued war criminals collaborated with NGOs that had embarked on the same mission. It was the World Jewish Congress that exposed the Nazi connections of two-time UN Secretary General Kurt Waldheim.

In a world of social media, a tech-enabled world where even those with little to their name and who are under bombardment from a colonising neighbour are armed with smartphones, facts are more easily accessed and verified. Bad things are harder to hide, no matter where they occur or who is responsible. When Francesca Albanese warns that the abomination of Gaza requires some form of moral renewal, she's not talking only of the accountability of nations and corporations. She's talking about individuals too.

Those individuals may not just be those who were in positions of leadership or influence. Members of the IDF who posted, as many have, videos of themselves desecrating the homes of Palestinians or wearing personal items in some moronic ritual, have left evidence of their deeds. There is plenty of evidence on social media of individuals, who would claim to be soldiers at war, departing dramatically from the rules under which war is conducted. Some IDF members who served in Gaza have dual citizenship. Declassified UK revealed that over 6,000 French, 4,000 German and 2,000 UK citizens served.[40] *The Ditch* reported that seventy-five Irish citizens also did so.[41]

The world will watch how this plays out. The priority is that all those who were directly involved or complicit in providing support or cover for the state of Israel are brought to justice. The special rapporteur lists a dozen steps that must be taken, a number of which are particularly relevant to this account:

- Recognising Palestinian self-determination;
- Israel dismantles its occupation;
- Securing reparations, including the full reconstruction and return of refugees;
- Full cooperation with the ICC and ICJ;
- Suspension of Israel from the UN under Article 6 of its Charter;
- Suspension of all military, trade and diplomatic relations with Israel;
- Investigation and prosecution of all officials, corporations and individuals involved or facilitating genocide or other grave breaches of international law.[42]

It falls to America to lead this turnaround. Only the US and the UK can change the narrative they helped to compose. It is only these two nations that can tell Israel that it must live within the 1967 borders and respect the right of the Palestinian people to establish their own homeland. As Israel's largest trading partners, the EU, the US and the UK must, by economic, political and security initiatives, force Israel to abandon its hatred. It is these parties and Israel's neighbouring Arab states that must establish for the people of Israel that it's about the deradicalisation of their state, nothing more. Without such an approach, backed up by the ultimate threat of intervention, if necessary, Israel will continue to do as it has always done. Past history shows us that if the genocide of the mid-2020s fails to achieve the Zionist objective and is followed by a period of relative quiet, that objective will only have been postponed, not halted.

This is why the events of Monday, 13 October 2025 matter. It is why the players – the countries and their high-ranking figures – who took part in the pageant need scrutiny. It is why we need to reflect on the choreography of that one day: who spoke, what they said and how they were received. We need to ask, against a backdrop of a lengthy list of failed Middle East peace initiatives that put Israel's interests first, how Trump's initiative ever gained traction. How could someone who has never given thought to the needs and rights of the people of Palestine be considered at all seriously? Most importantly, we should examine that day for what it says about the West and its institutions.

This calls for leadership. That search also starts with the US. It needs a leader who will ignore the Zionist/evangelical lobby, the Zionist funds, the history and the Islamophobes. The US has never failed that test more clearly than over Israel's genocide, but it remains the only country that can change the narrative and hold Israel to account. It has to be the US that tells Israel that the days of its impunity are over. It is only the US that could credibly say that there is an armada on its way to the Gulf, and it's not Iran that they are concerned about on this occasion. It really is that serious. Only through an intervention of that nature, one Israel and the world may think impossible, can the cycle of Zionist hatred be brought to an end.

In twenty-two years' time Israel will celebrate its centenary. The current custodians of its status need to understand that without a seismic change in its approach, it will not happen; certainly not as they would envisage it. We know the history. We know that, in simple terms, the US has continually led the work of reconciliation, ceasefires and peace-planning, and has always put the needs of Israel first by making utterly unreasonable demands of Palestine. These demands are unachievable for good reason: they allow the cycle to continue. Palestine cannot do what is demanded of it knowing that episode after episode of the diplomatic soap opera sees Israel seize more land. These processes run one into the other, the prolonged diplomatic dance providing cover for Israel to move, however slowly, towards the ultimate goal of taking control of all Palestine. This should be part of the assessment needed to force the West's hand. Interregnums suit Israel. It will always engage in peace half-measures that distract world attention.

WHO WANTS PEACE?

Israel benefits from the Trump plan, not the oppressed, colonised Palestine. Everywhere in it there are stipulations about what the Palestinians or what Hamas must do. It's not about emphasis; it's about multiple demands being made of the oppressed and none of the oppressor. We know it is Israel that needs to be deradicalised. There's evidence that Israel, a majority of its people, as well as most of its institutions need to reform their mindset.

This could start with a basic understanding of the history and an appreciation that they can have a good life without that being dependent on denying others that same ambition.

Palestine's governance needs reform if the people are to live in peace, but these reforms have to be worked out by the Palestinian people, not imposed by outsiders. It's also important that there is equal pressure on Israel to address the flaws inherent in its governance, starting with the apartheid nature of some of its laws that discriminate against more than 20 per cent of its population who are not Jewish. The Palestinian movement has many factions, but a government to serve the people could emerge if it was ever given the chance. That allegation is a convenient, if fabricated, reason for not giving autonomy to Palestine. The 2024 Beijing Declaration proved it false when the fourteen recognised factions came together and pledged to recognise the Palestinian Authority as the sole legitimate representative of the Palestinian people.

This move towards a unified Palestinian movement frightened Israel. Division in Palestine increased the prospect of more wars, and more wars serve the interests of Zionism. Israel had paid hundreds of millions to Hamas, through Qatar, in order to destabilise the region and to ensure the fractures would remain. Unity of Palestinian factions and political movements is an enormous risk to Israel. The success of the Zionist plan for a Greater Israel depends on feeding the divisions. A unified, coherent Palestine, politically, would greatly undermine the potential for Israel to realise its ambition to have boundaries extending to include Gaza, the West Bank and East Jerusalem. While Israel did not want any plan that could curb its colonialism, Trump's was dramatically more palatable than that sponsored by France and Saudi Arabia. The latter's momentum needed to be stopped. Trump's Comprehensive Plan to End the Gaza Conflict met that need. It was not perfect, but if some form of peace initiative was going to be imposed, one that kept the Palestinians in their place was preferable. That way more violence, more conflict was guaranteed. That appealed to Israel.

Trump's proposal did carry some risk for Israel. Lurking in the details was a dimension that could also lead to cohesion across Palestine's factions. It related to one individual. The agreement for the return of all remaining hostages, alive and dead, was that Israel would release 2,000 detainees, most of them Gazans who had been held after 7 October 2023. The prisoner Hamas and all the Palestinians most wanted released was Marwan Barghouti. Barghouti personifies the threat that Israel fears: the replacement of a diffuse Palestinian representation with a unifying figure to lead the group that had started to emerge from the Beijing initiative. He has long been considered the one person who could unite the Palestinians and lead them towards nationhood. Israel was aware of this, so, instead of agreeing to his release, knowing what a formidable opponent he would be, they made it a non-negotiable condition that he would not be included. There were some reports that Trump tried to persuade Netanyahu, but to no avail. On 9 October, Israel announced that he and three other accomplished and high-profile Palestinian figures would not be released.

The need for Palestine to have international counsel in resolving its own internal differences is not questioned. While the right people could assist the Palestinians in moving towards self-determination, this has to be done by the Palestinians for the Palestinians. Whatever terms they are to meet in order to progress towards that end cannot be set by or influenced by the nation that's oppressed them for decades. Or by Israel's proxy, the US.

What has really been proposed by Trump is the submission of Palestine to the wishes of the oppressor, or the US as its main ally. What's perverse is not that this 'deal' is being organised and co-ordinated by America, whose interest is protecting the welfare of Israel. That's the norm. The perversity is that its president is promoting a plan that does more than prioritise Israel's interests; it clearly has the potential to enrich him and his family.

Israel's impunity is the foundation stone on which this travesty can be built. More than two years into its genocide, it has faced no consequences for its egregious behaviour. It has been stealing land for decades, slowly colonising more and more of it, with nothing but the odd whimper from the West. It has imprisoned hundreds of thousands of Palestinians, most without cause or trial, torturing many who are incarcerated in shocking conditions. It has been destroying the agricultural land of Gaza for decades to reduce the Palestinians' capacity to feed themselves. It has maintained a blockade that controls what gets in and out. This impunity has now extended to conducting a genocide. Israel has used an estimated 200,000 tonnes of explosives to bomb Gaza into 60 billion tonnes of rubble. It has slaughtered many tens of thousands of Palestinians and there have been no repercussions. Absent accountability, there's absolutely no incentive for Israel to change. The New York Declaration in July 2025 offered hope of that; Trump's plan does not. It halts progress toward a balanced approach in a rush to put economic potential before the welfare of the Palestinians.

Maybe America's decades-long indifference to Palestine is no more pronounced now than it ever was, but is just more evident, more visible, more tangible. The skyscrapers and Riviera-esque seafront envisaged by Team Trump is one of those rare occasions when US foreign policy is laid bare. It is perhaps the only positive of a Trump presidency: the absence of any pretence.

◆◆◆

Sent:	**Reports:**
October 14, 2025 *02:24 EDT*	**WH Travel Pool Note #42** AF1 wheels down at 2:24am
October 14, 2025 *02:37 EDT*	**WH Travel Pool Note #43: arrival and goodnight** POTUS deplaned at 2:35am at JBA. He waved to press. He did not gaggle. That's all from me! Thanks for bearing with me for this whirlwind! Handing off to in-town pool. Goodnight![43]

In the black of night, after his triumphant day, Trump arrived back in America. As he headed to the White House in the early hours of 14 October, he did so having spent the previous day showing the world how hopelessly compromised it was by the US's relationship with Israel. Other states too, but, more than any, it is the US that dictates how nations and global institutions must be observant of Israel's needs. It is not new. It is not just a Trump failing. It is not a flaw only within the Republican party. The Democrats have abandoned Palestine for generations and did so again with Biden, Harris and Blinken in charge. Israel's money, strategic location and the influence of the Zionist lobby means Palestine is friendless in American politics. That is true across the West; the few friends it has carry little weight globally.

Monday, 13 October 2025 was as grotesque a display of colonial power as any military intervention of modern times. It was colonial America and its pro-Israel allies establishing their priorities, none of which included any concern for the rule of law, for international norms or for human rights. Its position was presented, as is normal, by the president of the United States. This particular president is outside the norm, however, so the position was set out more starkly than usual, entirely absent any political niceties. It was, in part, his coarseness, that made the day remarkable. The commitment to the destruction of Palestine was on full display; words cannot save Palestine, but they could contribute to its demise.

ENDNOTES

A Note to Readers

1 All opening quotations in chapters are taken from 'Voices from Gaza': www.btselem.org/voices_from_gaza.

Introduction

1 Israel (ISR) Exports, Imports and Trade Partners, 10 February 2026: www.tradingeconomics.com.

2 'Patrick's Day: Government authorised US military plane to land at Shannon – used to deliver munitions to Israel', *The Ditch*, 17 March 2026.

One Victory Party

1 Address of President Donald Trump to Israel's Knesset, 13 October 2025.

2 euronews.com, 'Hamas crackdown in Gaza leaves dozens dead amid power struggle', 13 October 2025: www.euronews.com/2025/10/13/hamas-crackdown-in-gaza-leaves-32-dead-amid-power-struggle.

3 Laura Doan, 'Trump says he's ended 6 or 7 wars. Here's what the record shows', 2 September 2025: cbsnews.com/news/trump-ended-6-or-7-wars-what-record-shows.

4 'Pool reports by Dasha Burns, *Politico*', *The American Presidency Project*, 13 October 2025: www.presidency.ucsb.edu/documents/pool-reports-october-13-2025.

5 Ibid.

6 Facebook, US State Department, 30 October 2025.

7 X (Twitter), Donald J. Trump, 29 December 2014.

8 Yuval Abraham, 'Israeli army database suggests at least 83% of Gaza dead were civilians', *+972*, 21 August 2025: www.972mag.com/israeli-intelligence-database-83-percent-civilians-militants/.

9 Jon Henley, 'Public support for Israel in Western Europe at lowest ever', *The Guardian*, 3 June 2025.

10 'Israel's First Lady of Human Rights: A Conversation with Shulamit Aloni', *Democracy Now!* 14 August 2002: www.democracynow.org/2002/8/14/israels_first_lady_of_human_rights.

11 The Jerusalem Declaration on Antisemitism was convened in the Van Leer Institute, Jerusalem, March 2021. For the full text see: https://jerusalemdeclaration.org/.

12 Liam Stack, 'Mamdani Revokes Executive Orders that Adams Signed to Support Israel', *The New York Times*, 2 January 2026.

13 'Pool reports by Dasha Burns, *Politico*', 13 October 2025.

14 'President Donald J. Trump's Plan to end the Gaza Conflict', White House press release, 29 September 2025: www.presidency.ucsb.edu/documents/white-house-press-release-president-donald-j-trumps-comprehensive-plan-end-the-gaza.

15 'James Armand de Rothschild (1878–1957)', Ramat Hanadiv: www.ramat-hanadiv.org.il/en/rothschilds-legacy/the-rothschild-legacy/the-house-of-rothschild/james-armand-de-rothschild1878-1957/.

16 'The Full Story of the Knesset Building', The Knesset: https://main.knesset.gov.il/en/about/pages/building/knessetbuildingstory.aspx.

17 Ibid.

18 Remarks of Knesset Speaker Amir Ohana, 'President Trump Delivers Remarks to the Knesset', C-SPAN, 13 October 2025.

19 Ibid.

20 Ben Farmer, 'IDF is the most moral army in the world, says Netanyahu', *The Telegraph*, 28 December 2023: www.telegraph.co.uk/world-news/2023/12/28/idf-most-moral-army-in-the-world-says-netanyahu/.

21 Remarks of Knesset Speaker Amir Ohana, 'President Trump Delivers Remarks to the Knesset', C-SPAN, 13 October 2025.

22 Knesset address of Prime Minister Netanyahu on visit of Donald Trump, 'President Trump Delivers Remarks to the Knesset', C-SPAN, 13 October 2025.

23 Ibid.

24 J. Diamond, 'Donald Trump tries to prove his Israel bona fides', CNN, 21 March 2016.

25 Private recording of Benjamin Netanyahu in 2001.

26 James Zogby, 'Netanyahu Playing Us for Fools', *Huffington Post*, 31 May 2014 (updated 31 July 2014): www.huffpost.com/entry/netanyahu-playing-us-for_b_5423717.

27 Knesset address of Prime Minister Netanyahu on visit of Donald Trump, 'President Trump Delivers Remarks to the Knesset', C-SPAN, 13 October 2025.

28 Ibid.

29 Ibid.

30 'Clearing most of Gaza's rubble is possible in seven years under right conditions', UNDP: www.undp.org/stories/clearing-most-rubble-gaza-strip-possible-seven-years-under-right-conditions.

31 'Interview with Mohammed bin Abdulrahman Al Thani, PM of Qatar', CNN, 10 September 2025.

32 Knesset address of Prime Minister Netanyahu on visit of Donald Trump, 'President Trump Delivers Remarks to the Knesset', C-SPAN, 13 October 2025.

33 Ibid.

34 'Letters to the Editor', *Irish Examiner*, 5 December 2025.

35 Laura Fletcher and Henry Manning, 'Israeli President condemns motion to rename Dublin park', *RTÉ News*, 30 November 2025.

36 Netta Ahituv, 'An Artillery Shell Signed by Israel's President Could Have Hit a Child in Gaza', *Haaretz*, 3 January 2023.

37 Law for Palestine, 'Database of Israeli Incitement to Genocide', 15 January 2024: https://law4palestine.org/wp-content/uploads/2024/02/Database-of-Israeli-Incitement-to-Genocide-including-after-ICJ-order-27th-February-2024-.pdf.

38 'Interview Israeli President Isaac Herzog', MSNBC, 5 December 2023.

39 Address of US President Donald Trump, 'President Trump Delivers Remarks to the Knesset', C-SPAN, 13 October 2025.

40 Yair Lapid address, 'President Trump Delivers Remarks to the Knesset', C-SPAN, 13 October 2025.

41 Ibid.

42 Ibid.

43 Ibid.

44 Address of US President Donald Trump, 'President Trump Delivers Remarks to the Knesset' C-SPAN, 13 October 2025.

45 Ibid.

46 Islamic Republic News Agency, 16 September 2001: http://www.irna.com/en/hphoto/010916000000.ehp.shtml.

47 Address to the UN General Assembly, 9 November 2001: http://www.president.ir/cronicnews/1380/8008/800818/80018.htm#b3.

48 James Dobbins, 'Negotiating with Iran: Reflections from Personal Experience', *The Washington Quarterly*, *33*(1), 2010: www.tandfonline.com/doi/full/10.1080/01636600903424833#d1e145.

49 'President Delivers State of the Union Address', The White House, 29 January 2002: https://georgewbush-whitehouse.archives.gov/news/releases/2002/01/20020129-11.html.

50 Condoleezza Rice, *No Higher Honor: A Memoir of My Years in Washington* (Crown Publishers, 2011).

51 Address of US President Donald Trump, 'President Trump Delivers Remarks to the Knesset', C-SPAN, 13 October 2025.

52 Ibid.

53 Ibid.

54 Ibid.

55 Ibid.

56 'President Donald J. Trump's Comprehensive Plan to End the Gaza Conflict',

White House press release, 29 September 2025: www.presidency.ucsb.edu/documents/white-house-press-release-president-donald-j-trumps-comprehensive-plan-end-the-gaza.

57 Address of US President Donald Trump, 'President Trump Delivers Remarks to the Knesset', C-SPAN, 13 October 2025.

58 Ibid.

59 Ibid.

60 Ibid.

61 Ibid.

62 Norman Finkelstein, Chris Hedges, 'Deconstructing Trump's Gaza "Peace" Plan', 15 January 2026: https://braveneweurope.com/norman-finkelstein-chris-hedges-deconstructing-trumps-gaza-peace-plan.

63 Address of US President Donald Trump, 'President Trump Delivers Remarks to the Knesset', C-SPAN, 13 October 2025.

64 Ibid.

65 Norman Finkelstein, 'The Jewish Supremacist State', *Mondoweiss*, 15 January 2021: https://mondoweiss.net/2021/01/the-jewish-supremacist-state-a-comment-on-btselems-apartheid-regime-designation-for-israel/.

66 Quoted in Noam Chomsky, *Fateful Triangle: The United States, Israel & The Palestinians* (London, 1999).

67 '*JPS* Responds to CAMERA's Call for Accuracy: Ben-Gurion and the Arab Transfer', *Journal of Palestine Studies*, 41(2) (Winter 2012), pp. 245–50.

Two All the World is Israel's Stage

1 Rishabh Sharma, 'Opinion: How America's War Support Strategies Differ for Ukraine and Israel', *India Today*, 4 October 2024.

2 '"People Regret What They Said to Me", Michael Wolff Tells NPR About Trump Book', NPR, 5 January 2018: www.npr.org/2018/01/05/575916244/as-fire-and-fury-goes-on-sale-trump-attacks-keep-coming.

3 Jim VandeHei and Mike Allen, 'Reality Bites: Trump's Wake-Up Call', Axios, 18 January 2017: www.axios.com/2017/12/15/reality-bites-trumps-wake-up-call-1513299979.

4 'Oslo Accords Timeline: 20 Years of Failed US-led Peace Talks', Institute for Middle East Understanding, 13 September 2013: https://imeu.org/resources/resources/oslo-accords-timeline-20-years-of-failed-us-led-peace-talks/239.

5 'Pool reports by Dasha Burns, *Politico*', *The American Presidency Project*, 13 October 2025: www.presidency.ucsb.edu/documents/pool-reports-october-13-2025.

6 Ibid.

7 'Speech: Donald Trump Delivers Remarks at the Peace Ceremony in Egypt – October 13, 2025', *Roll Call*: https://rollcall.com/factbase/trump/transcript/donald-trump-speech-israel-gaza-peace-event-egypt-october-13-2025/.

8 Charlayne Hunter-Gault, 'Meeting with Mandela', PBS, 22 June 1990.

9 'Speech: Donald Trump Delivers Remarks at the Peace Ceremony in Egypt – October 13, 2025', *Roll Call.*

10 News agencies and Brian Osgood, 'World leaders gather in Egypt for signing of Gaza ceasefire deal', *Al Jazeera Live*, 13 October 2025: www.aljazeera.com/news/2025/10/13/world-leaders-gather-in-egypt-for-signing-of-gaza-ceasefire-deal.

11 'Global Leaders Meet in Egypt's Sharm el-Sheikh to Solidify Gaza Ceasefire and Peace Plan', Qatar News Agency, 13 October 2025.

12 Remarks of Prime Minister Shehbaz at peace ceremony, 'Speech: Donald Trump Delivers Remarks at the Peace Ceremony in Egypt – October 13, 2025', *Roll Call*: https://rollcall.com/factbase/trump/transcript/donald-trump-speech-israel-gaza-peace-event-egypt-october-13-2025/.

13 'Speech: Donald Trump Delivers Remarks at the Peace Ceremony in Egypt – October 13, 2025', *Roll Call.*

14 Ibid.

15 Ibid.

16 'U.S. Military Aid and Arms Transfers to Israel, October 2023–September 2025', The Watson School of International and Public Affairs, Brown University, 7 October 2025: https://costsofwar.watson.brown.edu/paper/AidToIsrael.

17 Fintan Drury, *Catastrophe: Nakba II* (Dublin, 2025), pp. 231–3.

18 Daniel Araya, 'America's Global Dominance is Ending: What Comes Next?', Centre for International Governance Innovation, 5 October 2022: www.cigionline.org/articles/americas-global-dominance-is-ending-what-comes-next/.

19 Robert Fisk, *Night of Power: The Betrayal of the Middle East* (London, 2024), p. 269.

20 Nelofer Pazira-Fisk, 'Reflections from "Truth to Power": The Legacy of Robert Fisk', *Belfast Telegraph*, 2 August 2025.

21 'Speech: Donald Trump Delivers Remarks at the Peace Ceremony in Egypt – October 13, 2025', *Roll Call.*

22 Ibid.

23 Ibid.

24 'Gaza crossings: movement of people and goods', OCHA: www.ochaopt.org/data/crossings.

25 Emanuel Fabian and Jacob Magid, 'Katz calls for confining all Gazans in "humanitarian city" built over Rafah's ruins', 7 July 2025: www.timesofisrael.com/katz-calls-for-confining-all-gazans-in-humanitarian-city-built-over-rafahs-ruins/.

26 Dahlia Scheindlin, 'A Grim Poll Showed Most Jewish Israelis Support Expelling Gazans. It's Brutal – and It's True', *Haaretz*, 3 June 2025: www.haaretz.com/israel-news/2025-06-03/ty-article/.premium/a-grim-poll-shows-most-

jewish-israelis-support-expelling-gazans-its-brutal-and-true/00000197-3640-d9f1-abb7-7e742b300000.

27 'Speech: Donald Trump Delivers Remarks at the Peace Ceremony in Egypt – October 13, 2025', *Roll Call*.

28 '"Conquer, crush, win": Israel's Ben-Gvir calls for return to war in Gaza', Al Jazeera, 20 October 2025: www.aljazeera.com/video/newsfeed/2025/10/20/conquer-crush-win-israels-ben-gvir-calls-for-return-to-war-in-gaza#flips-6383377569112:0.

29 'New York Declaration on the Peaceful Settlement of the Question of Palestine and the Implementation of the Two-State solution – UN High-Level International Conference', United Nations, 29 July 2025 [hereafter New York Declaration], Clause 2: www.un.org/unispal/document/un-high-level-international-conference-new-york-declaration-29jul2025/.

30 New York Declaration, Clause 9.

31 'Netanyahu's Response to the New York Declaration: Five Principles for Ending the War', British Palestine Project substack, 8 August 2025: https://britainpalestineproject.substack.com/p/netanyahus-response-to-the-new-york.

32 AFP, 'US calls recognition of Palestinian state by allies "performative"', *Times of Israel*, 22 September 2025: www.timesofisrael.com/liveblog_entry/us-calls-recognition-of-palestinian-state-by-allies-performative/.

33 Reuters and TOI staff, 'World Summit to meet on two-state solution; 6 more nations set to recognize Palestine', *Times of Israel*, 22 September 2025.

34 Beatrice Farhat, 'The Beijing Declaration; China brokers Hamas-Fatah unity deal; What we know', Al-Monitor, 23 July 2024: www.al-monitor.com/originals/2024/07/beijing-declaration-china-brokers-hamas-Fatah-unity-deal-what-we-know.

35 'How Saudi-France diplomatic initiative moved Palestine closer to statehood', *Arab News*, 14 September 2025: https://arab.news/mybb3.

36 Ibid.

37 Ibid.

38 New York Declaration, 29 July 2025, Clause 2.

39 Charles H. Johnson and Frederic Wehrey, 'How the Flaws of Trump's Gaza Deal Prevent an Enduring Peace', *Emissary*, 14 November 2025: https://carnegieendowment.org/emissary/2025/11/trump-gaza-deal-fatal-flaws-prevent-peace.

40 Jack Hunter, '1,000 US Pastors Travel to Train as "Ambassadors" for Israel', *Responsible Statecraft*, 15 December 2025: https://responsiblestatecraft.org/israel-christians-gaza/.

41 Jaisal Noor, 'Why faith leaders are standing up to the largest pro-Israel Christian lobby', Waging Nonviolence, 4 July 2025: https://wagingnonviolence.org/2025/07/why-faith-leaders-are-standing-up-to-the-largest-pro-israel-christian-lobby/.

42 Ibid.

43 'Speech: Donald Trump Delivers Remarks at the Peace Ceremony in Egypt – October 13, 2025', *Roll Call*.

44 Ibid.

45 United Nations Security Council, 'Resolution 2803', 2025: https://docs.un.org/en/s/res/2803(2025).

46 Tony Xun, 'UN expert condemns Security Council Resolution on Gaza endorsing US-led peace plan', JURISTnews, 22 November 2025: www.jurist.org/news/2025/11/un-expert-condemns-security-council-resolution-on-gaza-endorsing-us-led-peace-plan/.

47 Steve Holland, 'Jared Kushner investment firm Affinity raises $3 billion in committed funding', Reuters, 23 December 2021: www.reuters.com/markets/deals/jared-kushner-investment-firm-affinity-raises-3-billion-committed-funding-2021-12-23/.

48 D. Kirkpatrick and K. Kelly, 'Before Giving Billions to Jared Kushner, Saudi Investment Fund Had Big Doubts', *The New York Times*, 10 April 2022: www.nytimes.com/2022/04/10/us/jared-kushner-saudi-investment-fund.html.

49 Ibid.

50 Mohamed Bazzi, 'Jared Kushner is back – and so are big questions about his financial ties', *The Guardian*, 29 October 2025: www.theguardian.com/commentisfree/2025/oct/29/jared-kushner-financial-ties-trump.

51 'World Jewish Congress president urges global fight against surging antisemitism', *The Jerusalem Post*, 11 December 2025: www.jpost.com/conferences/article-880055.

52 'Ronald Lauder praises Trump as "man of incredible insight and intelligence"', *Jewish Telegraphic Agency*, 8 January 2018: www.jta.org/2018/01/08/united-states/ronald-lauder-praises-trump-as-man-of-incredible-insight-and-intelligence.

53 Joseph Massad, 'Why Arab normalisation with Israel means more colonisation', *Middle East Eye*, 26 December 2025: www.middleeasteye.net/opinion/why-arab-normalisation-israel-means-more-colonisation.

54 @AmbDennisRoss, X (formerly Twitter), 2.56, 14 February 2019.

55 'EA Announces Agreement to be Acquired by PIF, Silver Lake, and Affinity Partners for $55 Billion', Electronic Arts press announcement, 29 September 2025: http://ir.ea.com/press-releases/press-release-details/2025/EA-Announces-Agreement-to-be-Acquired-by-PIF-Silver-Lake-and-Affinity-Partners-for-55-Billion/default.aspx.

56 Benjamin Netanyahu, Address to UN General Assembly, 22 September 2023: www.gov.il/en/pages/event-un220923.

57 Ibid.

58 Aron Heller and Matthew Lee, 'Trump Peace Plan delights Israelis, enrages Palestinians', Associated Press, 29 January 2020: https://apnews.com/article/donald-trump-ap-top-news-international-news-jerusalem-politics-f7d36b9023309ce4b1e423b02abf52c6.

59 'Grave concern about US plan to resolve Israel-Palestine organisation conflict', *The Guardian*, 27 February 2020: www.theguardian.com/world/2020/feb/27/grave-concern-about-us-plan-to-resolve-israel-palestine-conflict.

60 'Peace to Prosperity: A Vision to Improve the Lives of the Palestinian and Israeli People', White House National Archives, January 2020: https://trumpwhitehouse.archives.gov/wp-content/uploads/2020/01/Peace-to-Prosperity-0120.pdf.

61 'Trump Middle East plan: Palestinians reject "conspiracy"', BBC, 29 January 2020: www.bbc.com/news/world-middle-east-51292865.

62 'Trump Doubles Down on Gaza Plan, says Palestinians could be "happy"', Al Jazeera, 6 February 2025: www.aljazeera.com/news/2025/2/6/us-officials-walk-back-elements-of-trumps-gaza-takeover-plan.

63 Office of the High Commissioner for Human Rights, press release, 17 October 2025.

64 Dasha Burns, Felicia Schwartz, Nahal Toosi and Paul McLeary, 'Trump has promised peace for Gaza. Private documents paint a grim picture', *Politico*, 11 November 2025: www.politico.com/news/2025/11/11/trump-peace-gaza-documents-00642466.

65 Avi Scharf and Jonathan Lis, 'Netanyahu's 2024 Diary Reveals Close Ties with Republican Lawmakers, Phone Call with UAE Leader', *Haaretz*, 21 November 2025: www.haaretz.com/israel-news/2025-11-21/ty-article/.premium/netanyahu-diary-reveals-close-ties-with-republican-lawmakers-secret-call-with-uae-leader/0000019a-a275-dd6e-a5fa-fbf5d4bc0000.

66 Owen Bowcott, 'I wouldn't have taken his word for anything', *The Guardian*, 14 March 2007: www.theguardian.com/politics/2007/mar/14/northernireland.devolution1.

67 'In full: Laura Kuenssberg interview with Sir John Chilcot', BBC, 6 July 2017: www.bbc.com/news/av/uk-politics-40516908.

68 Burns et al., 'Trump has promised peace for Gaza. Private documents paint a grim picture'.

69 Amichai Stein, 'First int'l force to be deployed to Gaza in early 2026, US official tells "Post"', *Jerusalem Post*, 19 November 2025: www.jpost.com/middle-east/article-874515.

70 Burns et al., 'Trump has promised peace for Gaza. Private documents paint a grim picture'.

71 'A Dual Crisis – Palestinian Public Opinion Amidst Occupation and a Leadership Vacuum', PCPSR press release: Public Opinion Poll No (96), 28 October 2025: www.pcpsr.org/en/node/1000.

72 Ibid.

73 Norman Finkelstein, 'Israel is committing a holocaust in Gaza', *Today's Zaman*, 19 January 2009.

74 Gideon Levy, 'Everyone in This Country Has Gone Insane' *Haaretz*, 5 March 2026.

75 'Full Text: Prime Minister Benjamin Netanyahu's 2023 UN General

Assembly Speech', *Haaretz*, 22 September 2023: www.haaretz.com/israel-news/2023-09-22/ty-article/full-text-benjamin-netanyahus-2023-un-general-assembly-speech/0000018a-bd3c-d490-adca-fdff21270000.

76 Ibid.

77 Ibid.

78 Ibid.

79 Ibid.

Three Nurturing a Genocide

1 'Speech: Donald Trump Delivers Remarks at the Peace Ceremony in Egypt – October 13, 2025', *Roll Call*: https://rollcall.com/factbase/trump/transcript/donald-trump-speech-israel-gaza-peace-event-egypt-october-13-2025/.

2 Ibid.

3 Edwin Montagu, 'The Anti-Semitism of the Present Government', 23 August 1917: https://britainpalestineproject.org/edwin-montagu-and-zionism-1917/.

4 Ibid.

5 Tobias Holcman, 'Smotrich, Sa'ar approve NIS 2.35 billion in hasbara budget for campaigns, influencers in 2026', *The Jerusalem Post*, 6 December 2025: www.jpost.com/israel-news/politics-and-diplomacy/article-879369.

6 Arthur Koestler, *Promise and Fulfilment: Palestine 1917–1949* (Ramage Press, 2011), p. 197.

7 Janine Roberts, 'The Influence of Israel in Westminster', *The Palestine Chronicle*, 24 May 2008: www.palestinechronicle.com/the-influence-of-israel-in-westminster/.

8 Peter Beaumont, '"Fatal Flaws": analysts cast doubts on Tony Blair's plan for future of Gaza', *The Guardian*, 15 September 2025: www.theguardian.com/world/2025/sep/30/fatal-flaws-analysts-cast-doubt-on-tony-blair-plan-for-future-of-gaza.

9 Conor Burns MP, personal account of comments made by Margaret Thatcher, 11 April 2008.

10 Imran Mulla, 'The Six British PM's Who Have Restricted Arms Sales to Israel', *Middle East Eye*, 2 September 2024: www.middleeasteye.net/news/british-prime-ministers-who-have-restricted-arms-sales-israel.

11 Peter Oborne, *Complicit: Britain's Role in the Destruction of Gaza* (New York, 2025), p. 159.

12 Ibid., p. 160.

13 Jehuda Reinharz, 'Zionism in the USA on the Eve of the Balfour Declaration', *Studies in Zionism*, vol. 9, no 2 (1918).

14 Edwin Montagu, 'The Anti-Semitism of the Present Government', 23 August 1917.

15 Yuval Noah Harari, 'Only Generosity Can Secure Peace between Israelis and Palestinians', *Financial Times*, 8 November 2025.

16 E.L. Woodward and Rohan Butler, *Documents on British Foreign Policy, 1919–1929* (London, 1952).

17 Ibid.

18 *La Palestine*, special English edition, 25 March 1925.

19 Ibid.

20 'Statistics of Jews: (A) Jewish Population: Palestine', *American Jewish Year Book*, pp. 601–2: www.jewishdatabank.org/api/download/?studyId=910&mediaId=bjdb%5C1946_Statistics_of_Jews_World_and_US_Jewish_Population_(AJYB%2C_1946-1947).pdf.

21 Kenneth W. Stein, 'Zionist Land Acquisition: a core element in establishing Israel', Emory University, n.d.: https://ismi.emory.edu/documents/Zionist%20Land%20Aquisition.pdf.

22 Captain Chisholm Dunbar Brunton, 'Zionist Colonisation', *La Palestine*, 25 March 1925.

23 Ursula Von der Leyen, 'X EU in Israel, A special message from President of the EU Commission', statement on the 75th anniversary of the foundation of Israel, 26 April 2023.

24 'Address to AIPAC Policy Conference, Kamala Harris 2017', Black Agenda Report, 14 August 2024: https://blackagendareport.com/speech-address-aipac-policy-conference-kamala-harris-2017.

25 'Keir Starmer's Speech to LFI's Annual Lunch 2021', LFI, 16 November 2021: www.lfi.org.uk/keir-starmers-speech-to-lfis-annual-lunch-2021/.

26 Ahmad Amara, 'Israel's Perpetual "State of Emergency"', Meezaan Organization for Human Rights, March 2016.

27 Rashid Khalidi, *The Hundred Years' War on Palestine: A History of Settler Colonial Conquest and Resistance* (London, 2020), p. 70.

28 John F. Kennedy, letter to his father, 1939, Kennedy Family Archive.

29 Memorandum of meeting President Kennedy and French Foreign Minister, 25 May 1963, John F. Kennedy Presidential Library and Museum.

30 Philip Weiss, 'When a U.S. President Demanded Inspections of a Nuclear Facility in the Middle East (and Failed)', *Mondoweiss*, 27 July 2015: https://mondoweiss.net/2015/07/president-inspections-facility/.

31 'Remarks of Senator John F. Kennedy at the Convention of the Zionist Organization of America, New York City, August 26, 1960', John F. Kennedy Presidential Library and Museum: www.jfklibrary.org/archives/other-resources/john-f-kennedy-speeches/new-york-ny-19600826.

32 Ibid.

33 'The DOJ Orders the American Zionist Council (AZC) to Register as a Foreign Agent', 21 November 1962, The Israel Lobby Archive – Institute for Research: Middle Eastern Policy: http://israellobby.org/FARA/default.asp.

34 *HaBoker*, 21 November 1963, archive in association with Tel Aviv University: www.nli.org.il.

35 Shay Hazkani, 'Catastrophic Thinking: Did Ben-Gurion Try to Rewrite

History?', *Haaretz*, 16 May 2013: www.haaretz.com/2013-05-16/ty-article/.premium/ben-gurion-grasped-the-nakbas-importance/0000017f-e12d-d38f-a57f-e77fcfdd0000.

36 'US Stand Angers Israel', *The New York Times*, 21 November 1963.

37 '1967: Conférence de presse de Charles de Gaulle "L'Etat d'Israël"', INA Politique, 27 November 1967: www.youtube.com/watch?v=25hAYHwboFk.

38 UN Resolution 32/5, 28 October 1977: https://jewishvirtuallibrary.org/un-general-assembly-resolution-32-5-october-1977.

39 'Admission of Israel to membership in the United Nations', UN General Assembly, 3rd Ses: 1948–49, Paris: https://digitallibrary.un.org/record/210373?ln=en.

40 UN General Assembly debate on Resolution 273, 11 May 1949: https://unispal.un.org/pdfs/AAC24SR47.pdf.

41 UN Security Council, 'Resolution 242 (1967) / [adopted by the Security Council at its 1382nd meeting], of 22 November 1967', UN Digital Library: https://digitallibrary.un.org/record/90717?ln=en&v=pdf.

42 Ronan Mainprize, 'How LBJ forged the US-Israel alliance', Engelsberg Ideas, 22 January 2024: https://engelsbergideas.com/notebook/how-lbj-forged-the-us-israel-alliance/.

43 'Unwilling and Unable: Israel's Whitewashed Investigations of the Great March of Return Protests', B'Tselem, December 2021: www.btselem.org/publications/202112_unwilling_and_unable.

44 'Statement of ICC Prosecutor Bensouda Regarding the Worsening Situation in Gaza', United Nations, 8 April 2018: www.un.org/unispal/document/statement-of-icc-prosecutor-bensouda-regarding-the-worsening-situation-in-gaza/.

45 Human Rights Council, *Report of Detailed Findings of the Independent International Commission of Inquiry on the Protests in Occupied Palestinian Territory*, March 2019: www.ohchr.org/sites/default/files/HRBodies/HRC/RegularSessions/Session40/Documents/A_HRC_40_74_CRP2.pdf.

46 'Snipers Speak', *Hamakor*, 25 May 2021.

47 Ibid.

48 'In Conversation with Prime Minister Netanyahu', Policy Exchange, 7 June 2018: https://policyexchange.org.uk/wp-content/uploads/2018/06/Transcript-of-Shawcross-Netanyahu-Dialogue.pdf.

49 'Snipers Speak', *Hamakor*, 25 May 2021.

50 UN OCHA, 'Two years on: people injured and traumatised during the "Great March of Return" are still struggling', 6 April 2020: www.ochaopt.org/content/two-years-people-injured-and-traumatized-during-great-march-return-are-still-struggling.

51 Colm Kelpie, 'Ballymurphy Inquest: Coroner finds 10 victims were innocent', BBC, 11 May 2021: www.bbc.com/news/uk-northern-ireland-56986784.

52 The Rt Hon The Lord Saville of Newdigate (Chairman), The Hon William Hoyt OC, The Hon John Toohey AC, *Principal Conclusions and Overall Assessment*

of the Bloody Sunday Inquiry, 15 June 2010: https://assets.publishing.service.gov.uk/media/5a7580c6e5274a1242c9ed33/0030.pdf.

53 Alfred M. Lilienthal, 'The Kennedys and I: JFK's Bold Words on the Middle East Conflict', *Washington Report on Middle East Affairs*, October/November 1999: www.wrmea.org/jfk-assassination/the-kennedys-and-i-jfks-bold-words-on-the-middle-east-conflict.html#.

54 Peter Baker, 'In Unforgiving Terms, Biden Condemns "Evil" and "Abhorrent" attack on Israel', *The New York Times*, 10 October 2023.

55 Jeff Mordock, 'Biden warns Israelis not to be consumed by rage', *The Washington Times*, 18 October 2023: washingtontimes.com/news/2023/oct/18/biden-warns-israelis-not-be-consumed-rage.

56 Bethany Dawson, 'Rishi Sunak tells Israeli PM Benjamin Netanyahu: 'We want you to win', *Politico*, 18 October 2023: www.politico.eu/article/rishi-sunak-uk-to-visit-israel-amidst-increasing-conflict/.

57 'PM Netanyahu and British Prime Minister Rishi Sunak Issue Statements', Ministry of Foreign Affairs, 19 October 2023: www.gov.il/en/pages/pm-netanyahu-and-british-prime-minister-rishi-sunak-issue-statements-19-oct-2023.

58 Fintan Drury, *Catastrophe: Nakba II* (Dublin, 2025), p. 143.

59 Marc Owen Jones, interviewed in 'October 7', *Al Jazeera Investigations*, 20 March 2024.

60 Noah Keate, 'Netanyahu is wrong about UK arms embargo, says Starmer', *Politico*, 25 September 2024: http://politico.eu/article/uk-keir-starmer-ben jamin-netanyahu-israel-arms-embargo-export-license/.

61 Aysu Bicer, 'FACTBOX – How British arms and intelligence fueled Israel's Gaza genocide', Anadolu Ajansi, 2 July 2025: www.aa.com.tr/en/europe/factbox-how-british-arms-and-intelligence-fueled-israel-s-gaza-genocide/3620091.

62 Francesca Albanese, *Report of the Special Rapporteur on the Situation of Human Rights in the Palestinian Territories Occupied since 1967*, 20 October 2025: www.un.org/unispal/wp-content/uploads/2025/10/n2527993.pdf.

63 Iain Overton, 'Did Britain fly at least 623 spy flights over Gaza? AOAV's data suggests so', AOAV, 22 October 2025: https://aoav.org.uk/2025/did-britain-fly-at-least-623-spy-flights-over-gaza-aoavs-data-suggests-so/.

64 AOAV, 'The UK Royal Surveillance Flights over the Occupied Palestinian Territory Examined', n.d., https://aoav.org.uk/wp-content/uploads/2025/04/The-UK-Royal-Air-Forces-surveillance-flights-over-the-Occupied-Palestinian-Territory-examined.pdf.

65 Iain Overton, 'US flew spy flights for UK months before MoD admitted it', Declassified UK, 12 August 2025: www.declassifieduk.org/us-flew-spy-flights-for-uk-months-before-mod-admitted-it.

66 'PM's address to British troops in RAF Akrotiri, Cyprus: 10 December 2024': www.gov.uk/government/speeches/pms-address-to-british-troops-in-raf-akrotiri-cyprus-10-december-2024.

67 Overton, 'Did Britain fly at least 623 spy flights over Gaza? AOAV's data suggests so'.

68 Oborne, *Complicit*, p. 165.

69 Statement by Yvette Cooper, House of Commons, 23 June 2025: https://questions-statements.parliament.uk/written-statements/detail/2025-06-23/hcws729.

70 Prime Minister Rishi Sunak, letter to CFI, *Informed*, 7 September 2023.

71 Simon Walters, HM Ambassador to Israel, 7 September 2023 (CFI Informed 2023/2024).

72 'British Ambassador to Israel, Simon Walters: "If you build in Britain, we will back you"', CTech, 21 December 2025: www.calcalistech.com/ctechnews/article/hklbgzrq11l.

Four It is a Genocide

1 'IFJ Releases final 2025 list of 128 journalists and media workers killed', IFJ, 31 December 2025: www.ifj.org/media-centre/news/detail/category/impunity-2025/article/ifj-releases-final-2025-list-of-128-journalists-and-media-workers-killed.

2 United Nations, 'Convention on the Prevention and Punishment of the Crime of Genocide', 9 December 1948: www.ohchr.org/en/instruments-mechanisms/instruments/convention-prevention-and-punishment-crime-genocide.

3 Amos Goldberg, 'The Problematic Return of Intent', *Journal of Genocide Research*, 28(1), pp. 169–178, 15 October 2024: www.tandfonline.com/doi/full/10.1080/14623528.2024.2413175.

4 International Court of Justice, 'Order of 26 January 2024': www.icj-cij.org/node/203447.

5 United Nations, 'Convention on the Prevention and Punishment of the Crime of Genocide'.

6 Agence France-Presse, 'Top UN Court to Hear Genocide Case Against Israel', VOA, 3 January 2024: www.voanews.com/a/un-top-court-to-hear-genocide-case-against-israel-next-week/7425367.html.

7 H.R.2633 – U.S.–South Africa Bilateral Relations Review Act of 2025, 4 March 2025: www.congress.gov/bill/119th-congress/house-bill/2633/text.

8 For the full text of the letter see: https://chrissmith.house.gov/uploadedfiles/smith_manning_letter_to_sec._blinken_re._south_africa_claims_against_israel_at_ijc_1.23.24.pdf.

9 'Smith, Manning lead letter denouncing South Africa's grossly unfounded genocide accusation against Israel', press release, 23 January 2024: https://chrissmith.house.gov/news/documentsingle.aspx?DocumentID=411833.

10 Foreign Commonwealth and Development Office, 'International Court of Justice Interim Ruling on South Africa vs Israel: FCDO statement', press release, 27 January 2024: www.gov.uk/government/news/statement-on-the-interim-icj-ruling-in-south-africa-vs-israel.

11 'UK Judges' and Lawyers' Open Letter Concerning Gaza – April 2024', 3 April 2024: https://lawyersletter.uk/april2024letter/.

12 'UK Judges' and Lawyers' Open Letter Concerning the Occupied Palestinian Territory – May 2025', 26 May 2025: https://lawyersletter.uk/wp-content/uploads/2026/01/Gaza-letter-24-May-12.20PDF.pdf.

13 Ibid.

14 'Israel approves plan for Gaza "conquest" and mass displacement', TheCradle.co, 5 May 2025: https://thecradle.co/articles/israel-approves-plan-for-gaza-conquest-and-mass-displacement.

15 'Israel Has Committed Genocide in the Gaza Strip, UN Commission Finds', OHCHR press release, 16 September 2025: www.ohchr.org/en/press-releases/2025/09/israel-has-committed-genocide-gaza-strip-un-commission-finds.

16 UN Special Rapporteur Francesca Albanese, 'Anatomy of a Genocide', 25 March 2024: www.un.org/unispal/document/anatomy-of-a-genocide-report-of-the-special-rapporteur-on-the-situation-of-human-rights-in-the-palestinian-territory-occupied-since-1967-to-human-rights-council-advance-unedited-version-a-hrc-55/.

17 'Gaza: 20,000 children killed in 23 months of war – more than one child killed every hour', *Save the Children News*, 6 September 2025: www.savethechildren.net/news/gaza-20000-children-killed-23-months-war-more-one-child-killed-every-hour.

18 Elis Gjevori, 'Gaza's water turns poisonous as Israel's genocide leaves toxic aftermath', Al Jazeera, 8 November 2025: www.aljazeera.com/news/2025/11/8/gazas-water-turns-deadly-as-israels-genocide-leaves-toxic-aftermath.

19 'Gaza's maternal and newborn health system decimated, UN warns', *UN News*, 11 December 2025: https://news.un.org/en/story/2025/12/1166569.

20 Physicians for Human Rights, *Destruction of Conditions of Life: A Health Analysis of the Gaza Genocide*, July 2025: www.phr.org.il/wp-content/uploads/2025/07/Genocide-in-Gaza-PHRI-English.pdf.

21 Professor Nick Maynard, One Health for Palestine Webinar, 13 November 2025.

22 Testimony of Dr Feroze Shidhwa to United Nations Security Council, 28 May 2025.

23 Ibid.

24 Ibid.

25 Ibid.

26 Physicians for Human Rights, *Destruction of Conditions of Life: A Health Analysis of the Gaza Genocide*, July 2025.

27 Hoda Osman and Annie Kelly, 'No staff, no equipment, no medicine: a doctor on returning to Gaza after 665 days in an Israeli prison', *The Guardian*, 12 January 2026: www.theguardian.com/global-development/2026/jan/12/no-staff-no-equipment-no-medicine-a-doctor-on-returning-to-gaza-after-665-days-in-an-israeli-prison.

28 Ibid.
29 'More than 18,000 children have been killed in Gaza over the last 22 months', UNICEF on X, 4 August 2025; Nick Maynard, One Health for Palestine Webinar, 13 November 2025.
30 Reuben Granich, Somja Gupta, Victoria Rose, 'Childhood Mortality during Gaza Genocide in 2024: A Comparative Analysis with Global Disease Burden', *Scandinavian Journal of Public Health*, 10 November 2025: https://journals.sagepub.com/doi/10.1177/14034948251389044.
31 Ibid.
32 Francesca Albanese, *Report of the Special Rapporteur on the Situation of Human Rights in the Palestinian Territories Occupied since 1967*, 20 October 2025: www.un.org/unispal/wp-content/uploads/2025/10/n2527993.pdf.
33 Ibid.
34 'How top arms exporters have responded to the war in Gaza: 2025 update', SIPRI, 3 October 2025: www.sipri.org/commentary/topical-backgrounder/2025/how-top-arms-exporters-have-responded-war-gaza-2025-update.
35 Ibid.
36 New York Declaration, 29 July 2025: www.un.org/unispal/document/un-high-level-international-conference-new-york-declaration-29jul2025/.
37 Ibid.
38 'Destruction of homes leaves Palestinians unable to safely return to Rafah', MSF, 28 January 2025: www.doctorswithoutborders.org/latest/destruction-homes-leaves-palestinians-unable-safely-return-rafah.
39 'PM said to tell MKs: Israel destroying homes in Gaza so Palestinians have nowhere else to go but outside the Strip', *The Times of Israel*, 13 May 2025: www.timesofisrael.com/liveblog_entry/pm-said-to-tell-mks-israel-destroying-homes-in-gaza-so-palestinians-have-nowhere-else-to-go-but-outside-the-strip/.
40 IPC, 'Fact Sheet: The IPC Famine', August 2025: www.un.org/unispal/wp-content/uploads/2025/08/IPC_Famine_Factsheet.pdf.
41 Jack Khoury and Yaniv Kubovich, 'Gaza Officials Say 75 Palestinians Killed by IDF Fire, Four Died of Malnutrition in Past Day', *Haaretz*, 21 September 2025: www.haaretz.com/israel-news/2025-09-21/ty-article/.premium/gaza-officials-say-75-killed-by-idf-fire-four-died-of-malnutrition-in-past-day/00000199-6d9e-d27b-affd-7f9eab5d0000.
42 Ministry of Defense Coordination of Government Activities in the Territories, 'Food Consumption in the Gaza Strip – Red Lines', 1 January 2008: www.gisha.org/UserFiles/File/publications/redlines/red-lines-presentation-eng.pdf.
43 Eugenio Carli, 'Obligations Erga Omnes, Norms of Jus Cogens and Legal Consequences for "Other States" in the ICJ Palestine Advisory Opinion', EJIL, Talk! Blog of European Journal of International Law, 26 August 2024:

www.ejiltalk.org/obligations-erga-omnes-norms-of-jus-cogens-and-legal-consequences-for-other-states-in-the-icj-palestine-advisory-opinion/.

44 Interview with Alex de Waal, Middle East Eye, 21 July 2025: www.instagram.com/reel/DMYjHyQsOJ0/.

45 Mathilda Mallinson and Sondos Asem, 'Children will die quickly amid "genocidal starvation" in Gaza, warns top famine expert', Middle East Eye, 23 July 2025: www.middleeasteye.net/news/children-will-die-quickly-amid-genocidal-starvation-gaza-warns-top-famine-expert-alex-de-waal.

46 Mahmoud Fatafta, Ministry of Agriculture, Ramallah, *One Health for Palestine*, webinar, 15 November 2025.

47 Albanese, *Report of the Special Rapporteur on the Situation of Human Rights in the Palestinian Territories Occupied since 1967.*

48 'Humanitarian Situation Update #330 | West Bank', OCHA, 9 October 2025: www.ochaopt.org/content/humanitarian-situation-update-330-west-bank.

49 'Israeli Journalist Gideon Levy: Israel Will Not Stop Wars & Occupation Until U.S. Pulls Support', *Democracy Now!*, 13 March 2026: www.democracynow.org/2026/3/13/gideon_levy_israel.

50 Salman Abu Sitta, *Mapping My Return: A Palestinian Memoir* (Cairo, 2017).

51 Yolande Knell and David Gritten, 'Vance and Rubio criticise Israeli parliament's vote on West Bank annexation', *BBC News*, 23 October 2025: www.bbc.com/news/articles/cn8xvj108z9o.

52 Yesh Din, 'Urgent Appeal to Defense Minister: Immediately Cancel the Order Transferring CA Powers to Political Entities, Which Constitutes De Jure Annexation', 8 July 2024: https://s3.eu-west-1.amazonaws.com/files.yesh-din.org/Updates+to+the+International+Community/Diploupdate_080724.pdf.

53 'Evacuation Orders for Dozens of Palestinians to Make Way for Jerusalem Waste Facility Outside the Separation Barrier', PEACENOW, 12 November 2025: https://peacenow.org.il/en/%D9%8Eqalandiya-confiscation.

54 Barak Ravid, 'ICJ rules Israel has illegally annexed large parts of Palestinian territory', Axios, 19 July 2024: www.axios.com/2024/07/19/icj-rules-israeli-settlements-illegal-annexation.

55 'Land allocation approved for first new West Bank settlement to be built since 2017', *The Times of Israel*, 15 August 2024: www.timesofisrael.com/land-allocation-approved-for-first-new-west-bank-settlement-to-be-built-since-2017/.

56 EU, Office of EU Rep UNRWA, *2024 Report on Israeli settlements in the occupied West Bank, including East Jerusalem*, 14 August 2025: www.eeas.europa.eu/sites/default/files/2025/documents/Report%20on%20Israeli%20Settlements%20in%20the%20occupied%20West%20Bank%20including%20East%20Jerusalem%20%28Reporting%20period%20January%20-%20December%202024%29.pdf.

57 Ibid.

58 'Extrajudicial Killing of Unarmed Palestinians in Jenin, Inhuman Acts of

Apartheid', Al Haq Advocacy Report 27062, 2 December 2025: www.alhaq.org/advocacy/27062.html.

59 'Israeli colonists cut down hundreds of ancient olive trees near Nablus', WAFA, 29 October 2025: https://english.wafa.ps/Pages/Details/163881.

60 Matan Golan, 'Israeli Settlers Shot Three Palestinians in the West Bank, as IDF Troops Looked On', *Haaretz*, 24 February 2026: www.haaretz.com/israel-news/2026-02-24/ty-article-magazine/.premium/palestinians-soldiers-looked-on-as-settlers-shot-three-killed-teen/0000019c-8c49-d930-ad9f-fcfdfffc0000.

61 'Death Sentence for Palestinians in Custody – New Report and Testimonies', Physicians for Human Rights – Israel, 16 November 2025: www.phr.org.il/en/palestinian-deaths-behind-bars-eng/.

62 B'Tselem, 'Welcome to Hell: The Israeli Prison System as a Network of Torture Camps', August 2024: www.btselem.org/sites/default/files/publications/202408_welcome_to_hell_summary_eng.pdf.

63 '9,243 "Security" Inmates Are Held in Prisons Inside Israel', HaMoked, n.d.: https://hamoked.org/prisoners-charts.php.

64 Editorial, 'Ben-Gvir's Prison Spectacle Shows the Government's Descent into Lawless Brutality', *Haaretz*, 16 February 2026: www.haaretz.com/opinion/editorial/2026-02-16/ty-article-opinion/ben-gvirs-prison-spectacle-shows-the-governments-descent-into-lawless-brutality/0000019c-6314-de36-a19f-ef9f32330000.

65 UN Convention on the Prevention and Punishment of the Crime of Genocide 1948, 9 December 1948: www.un.org/en/genocideprevention/documents/atrocity-crimes/Doc.1_Convention%20on%20the%20Prevention%20and%20Punishment%20of%20the%20Crime%20of%20Genocide.pdf.

66 Francesca Albanese, *'Gaza Genocide: a collective crime' – Report of the Special Rapporteur on the Situation of Human Rights in the Palestinian Territories Occupied since 1967*, United Nations report no A/80/492, 20 October 2025: www.ohchr.org/en/documents/country-reports/a80492-gaza-genocide-collective-crime-report-special-rapporteur-situation.

67 ECCHR, 'Q&A on Arrest Warrants issued by the ICC against Netanyahu and Gallant', April 2025: www.ecchr.eu/fileadmin/Q_As/ECCHR_QA_arrest_warrant_ICC_Netanjahu_Gallant_042025.pdf.

68 Daniel Blatman and Amos Goldberg, 'There's no Auschwitz in Gaza. But It's Still Genocide', *Haaretz*, 30 January 2025: www.haaretz.com/israel-news/2025-01-30/ty-article-magazine/.highlight/theres-no-auschwitz-in-gaza-but-its-still-genocide/00000194-b8af-dee1-a5dc-fcff384b0000.

69 Larry Hanauer and Michael P. Connell, *Political Priorities, Poor Intelligence Tradecraft and the Suppression of Dissenting Views: Why Israel Failed to Warn of Hamas's October 7 Attack*, Institute for Defense Analyses, September 2024, p. v: www.ida.org/-/media/feature/publications/p/po/political-priorities-poor-

intelligence-tradecraft-and-the-suppression-of-dissenting-views/3002823.ashx.

70 Simon Speakman Cordall, 'Netanyahu finally announces October 7 inquiry: Why are Israelis furious?', Al Jazeera, 20 December 2025: www.aljazeera.com/news/2025/12/20/netanyahu-finally-announces-october-7-inquiry-why-are-israelis-furious.

71 Asa Winstanley, 'Army was ordered to kill Israelis on 7 October, defense minister confirms', *The Electronic Intifada*, 7 February 2025: https://electronicintifada.net/blogs/asa-winstanley/army-was-ordered-kill-israelis-7-october-defense-minister-confirms.

72 'Palestinians and the Right to Resist', Canadians for Justice and Peace in the Middle East, Factsheet 236, August 2023: www.cjpme.org/fs_236.

73 Robert Fisk, *Night of Power: The Betrayal of the Middle East* (London, 2024), p. 268.

74 United Nations, 'ICC issues warrants of arrest for Benjamin Netanyahu and Yoav Gallant', UN News, 21 November 2024: https://news.un.org/en/story/2024/11/1157286.

75 Donald Trump, 'Imposing Sanctions on the International Criminal Court', The White House, 6 February 2025: www.whitehouse.gov/presidential-actions/2025/02/imposing-sanctions-on-the-international-criminal-court/.

76 Francesca Albanese, *'Gaza genocide: a collective crime'*.

77 Ibid.

78 Ibid.

79 Ibid.

80 Terrence Guay, 'Where do Israel and Hamas Get their Weapons?', The Conversation, 23 January 2024: https://theconversation.com/where-do-israel-and-hamas-get-their-weapons-220762.

Five Consequences

1 Yarden Michaeli and Matan Golan, 'In four minutes, Israeli settlers descended from the hills and burned down an entire West Bank Bedouin community', *Haaretz*, 5 February 2026: www.haaretz.com/israel-news/security-aviation/2026-02-05/ty-article-magazine/.premium/watch-israeli-settlers-burn-down-a-bedouin-community-in-four-minutes/0000019c-1e11-d6ab-a7df-bf7d083b0000.

2 'President Donald J. Trump awarded "FIFA Peace Prize – Football Unites the World"', *INSIDE FIFA*, 6 December 2025: https://inside.fifa.com/campaigns/football-unites-the-world/news/president-trump-peace-prize-football-unites-the-world.

3 Eugene Kiely, 'Trump Confirms His Disparaging Remark About "Shithole Countries" at Immigration Meeting', Factcheck.org, 11 December 2025: www.factcheck.org/2025/12/trump-confirms-his-disparaging-remark-about-shithole-countries-at-immigration-meeting/.

4 Jessica Taylor, 'Trump Calls for "Total and Complete Shutdown of Muslims Entering" US', NPR, 7 December 2015: www.npr.org/2015/12/07/458836388/trump-calls-for-total-and-complete-shutdown-of-muslims-entering-u-s.
5 Molly Crabapple, 'The War on Memory: Learning from the Jewish Labor Bund', *The Funambulist*, Issue 57, 17 December 2024: https://thefunambulist.net/magazine/the-night/the-war-on-memory-learning-from-the-jewish-labor-bund.
6 Aaron Boxerman, 'U.S. Lays Out a Glittering Plan for Gaza, Including Skyscrapers', *The New York Times*, 22 January 2026: www.nytimes.com/2026/01/22/world/middleeast/us-gaza-peace-trump-kushner-davos.html.
7 Judy Maltz, 'The Lawyer for Jewish Terrorists Who Started Out by Stealing Rabin's Car Emblem', *Haaretz*, 4 January 2016: www.haaretz.com/israel-news/2016-01-04/ty-article/.premium/jewish-terrorisms-star-lawyer/0000017f-eda1-da6f-a77f-fdaff1f00000.
8 'Israel's Religiously Divided Society', Pew Research Centre, 8 March 2016: www.pewresearch.org/religion/2016/03/08/israels-religiously-divided-society/.
9 Prof. Tamar Hermann, Dr Or Anabi, Yaron Kaplan, Inna Orly Sapozhnikova, '20th Edition of the Israeli Democracy Index', The Israel Democracy Institute press release, 15 January 2023: https://en.idi.org.il/articles/47344.
10 Drury, *Catastrophe: Nakba II*, p. 129.
11 'Two Years since Oct. 7: Majority of Israelis say time has come to end the war', The Israel Democracy Institute, 30 September 2025: https://en.idi.org.il/articles/61845.
12 New York Declaration, Clause 19, 29 July 2025: www.un.org/unispal/document/un-high-level-international-conference-new-york-declaration-29jul2025/.
13 New York Declaration, Clause 23.
14 Ibid.
15 Salman Sayyid, 'Trump did not start Islamophobia, but he will make it clear', Anadolu Agency, 15 March 2025: www.aa.com.tr/en/opinion/opinion-trump-did-not-start-islamophobia-but-he-will-make-it-clear/3510461.
16 'Arab Public Opinion Poll about the Israeli War on Gaza', Arab Center for Research and Policy Studies, 10 January 2024: https://arabindex.dohainstitute.org/EN/Pages/APOIsWarOnGaza.aspx.
17 Hala Saghbini, 'Saudi Crown Prince's Washington Trip Signals Future-Focused Strategic Shift', Asharq Al-Awsat, 20 November 2025: https://english.aawsat.com/business/5211019-saudi-crown-prince%E2%80%99s-washington-trip-signals-future-focused-strategic-shift.
18 'Israel bans life-saving international NGOs from operating in Palestine in a catastrophic move to deepen the humanitarian crisis', ICJP, 5 January 2026: www.icjpalestine.com/2026/01/05/israel-bans-life-saving-international-

ngos-from-operating-in-palestine-in-a-catastrophic-move-to-deepen-the-humanitarian-crisis/.

19 Daniel Johnson, 'Another Child Dies in Extreme Conditions in Gaza: UNICEF', *UN News*, 31 December 2025: https://news.un.org/en/story/2025/12/1166686.

20 The White House, 'Statement on President Trump Comprehensive Plan to End the Gaza Conflict', 16 January 2026: www.whitehouse.gov/briefings-statements/2026/01/statement-on-president-trumps-comprehensive-plan-to-end-the-gaza-conflict/.

21 Jacob Magid, Lazar Berman and Nava Freiberg, 'Netanyahu fumes at Gaza oversight panel makeup as Trump invites Erdogan to peace board', *The Times of Israel*, 17 January 2025: www.timesofisrael.com/israel-fumes-at-gaza-oversight-panel-makeup-as-trump-invites-erdogan-to-peace-board/.

22 Lorenzo Tondo, 'Israel far-right ministers reject US-backed postwar Gaza panel', *The Guardian*, 18 January 2026: www.theguardian.com/world/2026/jan/18/israel-far-right-ministers-reject-us-backed-postwar-gaza-panel.

23 Mark Townsend, 'Guterres Warns of "Powerful Forces" Undermining "global cooperation"', *The Guardian*, 17 January 2026: www.theguardian.com/world/2026/jan/17/antonio-guterres-warns-forces-undermining-global-cooperation-un-80th-anniversary-secretary-general-multilateralism-international-law.

24 Ibid.

25 Bridget Rollason, 'Why Could Donald Trump's Board of Peace Be a Threat to the United Nations?', *ABC News*, 20 January 2026: www.abc.net.au/news/2026-01-20/what-is-donald-trump-s-board-of-peace/106247750.

26 John Irish and Andreas Rinke, 'World Leaders Show Caution on Trump's Broader "Board of Peace" Amid Fears for UN', Reuters, 19 January 2026: www.reuters.com/world/europe/world-leaders-show-caution-trumps-broader-board-peace-amid-fears-un-2026-01-18/.

27 'FULL SPEECH: UN Secretary-General António Guterres' Powerful 80th Anniversary Address | AC1E', DWS News: www.youtube.com/watch?v=qjgykUu1z7c.

28 Ola El-Taliawi, 'Trump's Peace Plan for Gaza: The Good, the Bad, and the Unknown', *The Cairo Review of Global Affairs*, fall 2025: www.thecairoreview.com/essays/trumps-peace-plan-for-gaza-the-good-the-bad-and-the-unknown/.

29 Julian Borger, 'Trump's Board of Peace is an Imperial Court Completely Unlike What Was Proposed', *The Guardian*, 20 January 2026: www.theguardian.com/us-news/2026/jan/20/trumps-board-of-peace-is-an-imperial-court-completely-unlike-what-was-proposed.

30 'The ICJ's First Determination of War Reparations: Practical Challenges and Legal Solutions', Questions of International Law, 29 September 2022: www.qil-qdi.org/the-icjs-first-determination-of-war-reparations-practical-challenges-and-legal-solutions/.

31 Krishnan Guru-Murthy, 'Russia "Should Pay" for Damage to Ukraine – Foreign Secretary', *Channel 4 News* interview with UK Foreign Secretary Yvette Cooper, 17 December 2025: www.channel4.com/news/russia-should-pay-for-damage-to-ukraine-foreign-secretary.

32 Resolution ES-10/24, UN General Assembly, 18 September 2024: https://docs.un.org/en/A/RES/ES-10/24.

33 Francesca Albanese, *Report of the Special Rapporteur on the Situation of Human Rights in the Palestinian Territories Occupied since 1967*, 20 October 2025: www.un.org/unispal/wp-content/uploads/2025/10/n2527993.pdf.

34 Ibid.

35 Ibid.

36 Jerry White, Zac Corrigan and Usman Khan, 'Holocaust Survivor Rene Lichtman "Israel Is Committing War Crimes in Gaza. We've Got to Fight Back"', World Socialist Web Site, 23 January 2024: www.wsws.org/en/articles/2024/01/24/fwpx-j24.html.

37 Albanese, *Report of the Special Rapporteur on the Situation of Human Rights in the Palestinian Territories Occupied since 1967.*

38 Ibid.

39 Francesca Albanese, *From Economy of Occupation to Economy of Genocide*, July 2025: www.un.org/unispal/document/a-hrc-59-23-from-economy-of-occupation-to-economy-of-genocide-report-special-rapporteur-francesca-albanese-palestine-2025/.

40 John McEvoy and Alex Morris, 'Over 2,000 Britons Served for IDF in Gaza Genocide', Declassified UK, 11 February 2026: www.declassifieduk.org/over-2000-britons-served-for-israel-amid-gaza-genocide/.

41 'Seventy-five Irish citizens served in IDF during Gaza genocide', *The Ditch*, 12 February 2026: www.ontheditch.com/seventy-five-irish-citizens/.

42 Albanese, *Report of the Special Rapporteur on the Situation of Human Rights in the Palestinian Territories Occupied since 1967.*

43 'Pool reports by Dasha Burns, *Politico*', *The American Presidency Project*, 13 October 2025: www.presidency.ucsb.edu/documents/pool-reports-october-13-2025.

BIBLIOGRAPHY

Articles

Crabapple, M., 'The War on Memory: Learning from the Jewish Labor Bund', *The Funambulist*, Iss. 57 (17 December 2024)

Dobbins, J., 'Negotiating with Iran: Reflections from Personal Experience', *The Washington Quarterly*, 33(1) (2010)

El-Taliawi, O., 'Trump's Peace Plan for Gaza: The Good, the Bad and the Unknown', *The Cairo Review of Global Affairs*, Fall 2025

Goldberg, A., 'The Problematic Return of Intent', *Journal of Genocide Studies*, Vol. 28, Iss. 1 (15 October 2024)

Granich, R., Gupta, S., and Rose, V., 'Childhood Mortality during Gaza Genocide in 2024: A comparative analysis with global disease burden', *Scandinavian Journal of Public Health*, online edition, 10 November 2025

Reinharz, J., 'Zionism in the US on the eve of the Balfour Declaration', *Studies in Zionism*, Vol. 9, No. 2 (1918)

'Statistics of Jews: (A) Jewish Population: Palestine', *American Jewish Year Book*, pp. 601–2

Books

Abu-Sitta, S., *Mapping My Return: A Palestinian Memoir* (American University in Cairo Press, 2017)

Baer, M.D., *Children of Abraham, The Story of Muslim-Jewish Relations* (Profile Books, 2026)

Drury, F., *Catastrophe: Nakba II* (Merrion Press, 2025)

Fisk, R., *Night of Power: The Betrayal of the Middle East* (4th Estate, 2024)

Herzl, T., *The Jewish State*, trans. S. D'Avigdor (originally published as *Der Judenstaat*, 1896, translation published 1946)

Khalidi, R., *The 100 Years War on Palestine: A History of Settler Colonial Conquest and Resistance* (Profile Books, 2020)

Koestler, A., *Promise and Fulfilment: Palestine 1917–1949* (Ramage Press, 2011)

Malm, A., *The Destruction of Palestine is the Destruction of the Earth* (Verso, 2024)

Oborne, P., *Complicit: Britain's Role in the Destruction of Gaza* (OR Books, 2025)

Pappé, I., *Israel on the Brink: Eight Steps for a Better Future* (One World Publishing, 2025)

Rice, C., *No Higher Honor: A Memoir of My Years in Washington* (Crown Publishers, 2011)

Shedehah, R., *What Does Israel Fear from Palestine?* (Profile Books, 2025)

Stein, K.W., 'Zionist Land Acquisition: A Core Element in Establishing Israel', in Michael J. Cohen (ed.), *The British Mandate in Palestine: A Centenary Volume, 1920–2020* (Routledge, 2020)

Straw, J., *The English Job: Understanding Iran and Why it Distrusts Britain* (Biteback Publishing, 2020)

Woodward, E., and Butler, R., *Documents on British Foreign Policy, 1919–1929* (Her Majesty's Stationery Office, 1952)

News Sources (online, print and TV)

AFP, 'US calls recognition of Palestinian state by allies performative', *Times of Israel*, 22 September 2025

Agence France-Presse, 'Top UN Court to Hear Genocide Case Against Israel', *VOA*, 3 January 2024

Ahituv, N., 'An Artillery shell signed by Israel's President could have hit a child in Gaza', *Haaretz*, 3 January 2023

Baker, P., 'In unforgiving terms, Biden condemns "Evil" and "Abhorrent" attack on Israel', *The New York Times*, 10 October 2023

Barak, R., 'ICJ rules Israel has illegally annexed large parts of Palestinian territory', *Axios*, 19 July 2024

Bazzi, M., 'Jared Kushner is back and so are big questions about his financial ties', *The Guardian*, 29 October 2025

Beaumont, P., 'Fatal Flaws – analysts cast doubts on Tony Blair's plan for the future of Gaza', *The Guardian*, 15 September 2025

Bicer, A., 'FACTBOX – How British arms and intelligence fueled Israel's Gaza genocide' *Andalou Anjasi*, 2 July 2025

Blatman D., and Goldberg, A., 'There's no Auschwitz in Gaza but it's still Genocide', *Haaretz*, 30 January 2025

Borger, J., 'Trump's Board of Peace is an Imperial Court Completely Unlike What was Proposed', *The Guardian*, 20 January 2026

Bowcott, O., 'I wouldn't have taken his word for anything', *The Guardian*, 14 March 2007

Boxerman, A., 'US lays out a Glittering Plan for Gaza Including Skyscrapers', *The New York Times*, 22 January 2026

Brezar, A., 'Hamas crackdown in Gaza leaves dozens dead amid power struggle', *Euronews*, 13 October 2025

Brunton, C.D., 'Zionist Colonisation', *La Palestine*, 25 March 1925

Burns, D., Schwartz, F., Toosi, N., and McLeary, P., 'Trump has promised peace for Gaza: private documents paint a grim picture', *Politico*, 11 November 2025

'Conquer, Crush, Win – Israel's Ben-Gvir calls for return to war in Gaza', *Al Jazeera*, 20 October 2025

Dawson, B., 'Rishi Sunak tells Israeli PM Benjamin Netanyahu: "We Want You to Win"', *Politico*, 18 October 2023

Diamond, J., 'Donald Trump tries to prove his Israel bona fides', *CNN*, 21 March 2016

Doan, L., 'Trump Says He's Ended 6 or 7 Wars. Here's what the record shows', *CBS News*, 2 September 2025

Fabian, E., and Magid, J., 'Katz calls for confining all Gazans in "humanitarian city" built over Rafah's ruins', *Times of Israel*, 7 July 2025

Farhat, B., 'The Beijing Declaration; China brokers Hamas-Fatah unity deal; What we know', *Al-Monitor*, 23 July 2024

Farmer, B., 'IDF is the most moral army in the world, says Netanyahu', *The Telegraph*, 28 December 2025

Finkelstein, N., 'Israel is committing a Holocaust in Gaza', *Today's Zaman*, 19 January 2009

Finkelstein, N., 'The Jewish Supremacist State', *Mondoweiss*, 15 January 2021

Finkelstein, N., and Hedges, C., 'Deconstructing Trump's Gaza 'Peace' Plan', *Brave New Europe*, 15 January 2026

Fletcher, L., and Manning, H., 'Israeli President condemns motion to rename Dublin park', *RTÉ News*, 30 November 2025

'Gaza: 20,000 children killed in 23 months of war – more than one child killed every hour', *Save the Children News*, 6 September 2025

'Gaza's maternal and newborn health system decimated, UN warns', *UN News*, 5 December 2025

Gjevori, E., 'Gaza's water turns poisonous as Israel's genocide leaves toxic aftermath,' *Al Jazeera*, 8 November 2025

'Global Leaders Meet in Egypt's Sharm el-Sheikh to Solidify Gaza Ceasefire and Peace Plan', *Qatar News Agency*, 13 October 2025

Golan, M., 'Israeli settlers shot three Palestinians in the West Bank as IDF Troops Looked On', *Haaretz*, 24 February 2026

'Grave concern about US plan to resolve Israel–Palestine organisation conflict', *The Guardian*, 27 February 2020

Guay, T., 'Where do Israel and Hamas Get Their Weapons?', *The Conversation*, 23 January 2024

Guru-Murthy, K., 'Russia "Should Pay" for Damage to Ukraine – Foreign Secretary', *Channel 4 News*, 17 December 2025

Haaretz Editorial, 'Ben-Gvir's Prison Spectacle Shows the Government's Descent into Lawless Brutality', *Haaretz*, 16 February 2026

Harari, Y.N., 'Only Generosity Can Secure Peace between Israelis and Palestinians', *Financial Times*, 8 November 2025

Hazkani, S., 'Catastrophic Thinking – Did Ben-Gurion Try to Rewrite History?', *Haaretz* 16 May 2013

Heller, A., and Lee, M., 'Trump Peace Plan delights Israeli's, enrages Palestinians', *Associated Press*, 29 January 2020

Holcman T., 'Smotrich, Sa'ar approve NIS2.35 billion in hasbara budget for campaigns, influencers in 2026', *Jerusalem Post*, 6 December 2025

Holland, S., 'Jared Kushner investment firm Affinity raises $3billion in committed funding', *Reuters*, 23 December 2021

Hunter, J., '1,000 US Pastors Travel to Train as "Ambassadors" for Israel', *Responsible Statecraft*, 15 December 2025

Hunter-Gault, C., 'Meeting with Mandela', PBS, 22 June 1990

'IFJ Releases final 2025 list of 128 journalists and media workers killed', *IFJ*, 31 December 2025

'In full: Laura Kuenssberg interview with Sir John Chilcot', BBC, 6 July 2017

'In Conversation with Prime Minister Netanyahu', *Policy Exchange*, 7 June 2018

'Interview with Israeli President Isaac Herzog', MSNBC, 5 December 2023

'Interview with Mohammed bin Abdulrahman Al Thani, PM of Qatar', CNN, 10 September 2025

'Interview with Yoav Gallant', Channel 13 News, 6 February 2026

'Irish air staff assist US bomber on way to Iran', *The Ditch*, 14 March 2026

Irish, J., and Brinke, A., 'World Leaders Show Caution on Trump's Broader "Board of Peace" Amid Fears for the UN', *Reuters*, 19 January 2026

'Israel approves plan for Gaza "conquest" and mass displacement', *TheCradle.co*, 5 May 2025

Johnson, D., 'Another Child Dies in Extreme Conditions in Gaza: UNICEF', *UN News*, 31 December 2025

Kelpie, C., 'Ballymurphy Inquest: Coroner finds 10 victims were innocent', *BBC News*, 11 May 2021

Khoury, J., and Kubovich, Y., 'Gaza Officials say 75 Palestinians Killed by IDF Fire; Four Died of Malnutrition in Past Day', *Haaretz*, 21 September 2025

Kiely, E., 'Trump Confirms His Disparaging Remark About "Shithole Countries" at Immigration Meeting', *Factcheck.org*, 11 December 2025

Kirkpatrick, D., and Kelly K., 'Before giving billions to Jared Kushner, Saudi investment fund had big doubts', *The New York Times*, 10 April 2022

Knell, Y., and Gritten, D., 'Vance and Rubio criticise Israeli parliament's vote on West Bank annexation', *BBC News*, 23 October 2025

'Letters to the Editor', *Irish Examiner*, 5 December 2025

Lilienthal, A. M., 'The Kennedys and I – JFK's bold words on the Middle East Challenge', *Washington Report on Middle East Affairs*, October/November 1999

Magid, Berman and Friedman, 'Netanyahu fumes at Gaza oversight panel makeup as Trump invites Erdogan to peace board', *Times of Israel*, 17 January 2026

Mallinson M., and Sondos, A., 'Children will die quickly amid genocidal starvation in Gaza warns top famine expert', *Middle East Eye*, 23 July 2025

Maltz, J., 'The Lawyer for Jewish Terrorists Who Started Out by Stealing Rabin's Car Emblem', *Haaretz*, 4 January 2016

Massad, J., 'Why Arab normalisation with Israel means more colonisation', *Middle East Eye*, 26 December 2025

McEvoy, J., and Morris, A., 'Over 2,000 Britons Served for IDF in Gaza Genocide', *Declassified UK*, 11 February 2026

'Miriam Adelson: Who is the Israeli billionaire backing Trump?', *Middle East Eye*, 19 November 2024Mordock, J., 'Biden warns Israelis not to be consumed by rage', *The Washington Times*, 18 October 2023

Mulla, I., 'The Six British PMs Who Have Restricted Arms Sales to Israel', *Middle East Eye*, 2 September 2024

Noor, J., 'Why faith leaders are standing up to the largest pro-Israel Christian lobby', *Waging Nonviolence*, 4 July 2025

Osman, H., and Kelly, A., 'No staff, no equipment, no medicine, a doctor on returning to Gaza after 665 days in an Israeli prison', *The Guardian*, 12 January 2026

Overton, I., 'US flew spy flights for the UK months before the MOD admitted it', *Declassified UK*, 13 August 2025

Pazira-Fisk, N., 'Reflections from Truth to Power: the Legacy of Robert Fisk', *Belfast Telegraph*, 2 August 2025

'"People Regret What They Said to Me", Michael Wolff tells NPR about Trump book', NPR, 5 January 2018

'PM said to tell MKs: Israel destroying homes in Gaza so Palestinians have nowhere else to go but outside the Strip', *The Times of Israel*, 13 May 2025

'President Trump Delivers Remarks to the Knesset', C-SPAN, 13 October 2025

Reuters and TOI staff, 'World Summit to meet on two-state solution; 6 more nations set to recognise Palestine', *Times of Israel*, 22 September 2025

Roberts, J., 'The Influence of Israel in Westminster', *The Palestine Chronicle*, 24 May 2008

Rollason, B., 'Why Could Donald Trump's Board of Peace be a Threat to the United Nations', *ABC News*, 20 January 2026

'Ronald Lauder praises Trump as "man of incredible insight and intelligence"', *Jewish Telegraphic Agency*, 8 January 2018

Saghbini, H., 'Saudi Crown Prince's Washington Trip Signals Future-Focused Policy Shift', *Asharq Al-Awsat*, 20 November 2025

Sayyd, S., 'Trump did not start Islamophobia but he will make it clear', *Anadolu Agency*, 15 March 2025

Scharf, A., and Lis, J., 'Netanyahu's 2024 Diary Reveals Close Ties with Republican Lawmakers, Phone Call with UAE Leader', *Haaretz*, 21 November 2025

Scheindlin, D., 'A Grim Poll Showed Most Jewish Israelis Support Expelling Gazans. It's Brutal – and It's True', *Haaretz*, 3 June 2025

'Seventy-five Irish citizens served in IDF during Gaza genocide', *The Ditch*, 12 February 2026

Sharma, R., 'How America's War Support Strategies Differ for Ukraine and Israel', *India Today*, 4 October 2024

Sharon, J., 'Land allocation approved for first new West Bank settlement to be built since 2017', *Times of Israel*, 15 August 2024.

'Snipers Speak', *Hamakor*, 25 May 2021

Speakman Cordall, S., 'Netanyahu finally announces October 7 inquiry: Why are Israelis furious?', *Al Jazeera*, 20 December 2025

Stack, R., 'Mandani Revokes Executive Orders that Adams Signed to Support Israel', *The New York Times*, 2 January 2026

Stein, A., 'First In'l force to be deployed to Gaza in early 2026, US official tells Post', *Jerusalem Post*, 19 November 2025

Taylor, J., 'Trump Calls for Total and Complete Shutdown of Muslims Entering US', NPR, 7 December 2015

Tondo, L., 'Israel far-right ministers reject US-backed postwar Gaza panel', *The Guardian*, 18 January 2026

Townsend, M., 'Guterres Warns of "Powerful Forces" Undermining "global cooperation"', *The Guardian*, 17 January 2026

'Trump Middle East plan: Palestinians reject "conspiracy"', *BBC News*, 29 January 2020

'Trump Doubles Down on Gaza Plan, Says Palestinians Could be "happy"', *Al Jazeera*, 6 February 2025

'US Stand Angers Israel', *The New York Times*, 21 November 1963

VandHei, J., and Allen, M., 'Reality Bites, Trump's Wake-Up Call', *Axios*, 18 January 2017

Walters, S., 'British Ambassador to Israel, Simon Walters: "If you build in Britain, we will back you"', *CTech*, 21 December 2025

Weiss, P., 'When a US President Demanded Inspections of a Nuclear Facility in the Middle East (and failed)' *Mondoweiss*, 27 July 2015

White, J., Corrigan, Z., and Khan, U., 'Holocaust Survivor Rene Lichtman "Israel Is Committing War Crimes in Gaza. We've Got to Fight Back"', *World Socialist Web Site*, 23 January 2024

'World leaders gather in Egypt for signing of Gaza ceasefire deal', *Al Jazeera Live*, 13 October 2025

'World Jewish Congress President urges fight against surging antisemitism', *The Jerusalem Post*, 11 December 2025

Xun, T., 'UN expert condemns Security Council Resolution on Gaza endorsing US-led peace plan', *Jurist News*, November 2025

Yarden, M, and Golan, M., 'In four minutes, Israeli settlers descended from the hills and burned down an entire West Bank Bedouin community', *Haaretz*, 5 February 2026

Zakaria, Sherouk, 'How Saudi-France diplomatic initiative moved Palestine closer to statehood', *Arab News*, 14 September 2025

Zogby, J., 'Netanyahu Playing Us for Fools', *Huffington Post*, 31 May 2014 (updated 31 July 2014)

Online Sources

Antonio Guterres, 'FULL SPEECH: UN Secretary-General António Guterres' Powerful 80th Anniversary Address | AC1E': www.youtube.com/watch?v=qjgykUu1z7c

Arab Center for Research and Policy Studies, 'Arab Public Opinion Poll about the Israeli War on Gaza', 10 January 2024: www.arabindex.dohainstitute.org/En/Pages/APOIsWarOnGaza.aspx

Brivati, Brian,'Netanyahu's Response to the New York Declaration: Five Principles for Ending the War', *British Palestine Project substack*, 8 August 2025: https://britainpalestineproject.substack.com/p/netanyahus-response-to-the-new-york

Carli, E., 'Obligations Erga Omnes, Norms of Jus Cogens and Legal Consequences for "Other States" in the ICJ Palestine Advisory Opinion', EJIL: Talk! Blog of European Journal of International Law, 26 August 2024: www.ejiltalk.org/obligations-erga-omnes-norms-of-jus-cogens-and-legal-consequences-for-other-states-in-the-icj-palestine-advisory-opinion/

Congress.gov, 'H.R. 2633 – U.S.-South Africa Bilateral Relations Review Act of 2025': www.congress.gov/bill/119th-congress/house-bill/2633/text

Foreign Commonwealth and Development Office, 'International Court of Justice interim ruling on South Africa vs Israel: FCDO statement', www.gov.uk/government/news/statement-on-the-interim-icj-ruling-in-south-africa-vs-israel

Gov.uk, 'PM's address to British troops in RAF Akrotiri, Cyprus: 10 December 2024': www.gov.uk/government/speeches/pms-address-to-british-troops-in-raf-akrotiri-cyprus-10-december-2024

HaMoked, '9,446 Security Inmates are Held in Prisons Inside Israel': www.hamoked.org/prisoners-charts.php

Hanadiv, R., 'James Armand de Rothschild (1878–1957)', www.ramat-hanadiv.org.il/en/rothschilds-legacy/the-rothschild-legacy/the-house-of-rothschild/james-armand-de-rothschild1878-1957/

Hermann, T., et al., '20th Edition of the Israeli Democracy Index' 15 January 2023: www.en.idi.org.il/articles/47344

House of Commons, 'Statement by Yvette Cooper', 23 June 2025: https://questions-statements.parliament.uk/written-statements/detail/2025-06-23/hcws729.

INA Politique, '1967: Conférence de presse de Charles de Gaulle "L'Etat d'Israël"', 27 November 1967: www.youtube.com/watch?v=25hAYHwboFk

Instagram, 'Interview with Alex de Waal', *Middle East Eye*: www.instagram.com/reel/DMYjHyQsOJ0/

Instagram, 'Who is Miriam Adelson?', www.instagram.com/reel/DQb6fBdkzPN

The Israel Lobby Archive – Institute for Research: Middle Eastern Policy, 'The DOJ Orders the American Zionist Council (AZC) to Register as a Foreign Agent', http://israellobby.org/FARA/default.asp

IPC, 'Fact Sheet: The IPC Famine', August 2025, www.un.org/unispal/wp-content/uploads/2025/08/IPC_Famine_Factsheet.pdf

'Israel (ISR) Exports, Imports and Trade Partners', 10 February 2026: https://oecworld

Johnson, C., and Wehrey, F., 'How the Flaws of Trump's Gaza Deal Prevent an Enduring Peace, Emmisary', Carnegie Institute, November 2025: https://carnegieendowment.org/emissary/2025/11/trump-gaza-deal-fatal-flaws-prevent-peace

Mainprize, R., 'How LBJ forged the US-Israel alliance', Englesberg Ideas, 22 January 2024 www.englesbergideas.com

Médecins Sans Frontières, 'Destruction of homes leaves Palestinians unable to safely return to Rafah', 28 January 2025: www.doctorswithoutborders.org/latest/destruction-homes-leaves-palestinians-unable-safely-return-rafah

Ministry of Foreign Affairs, 'PM Netanyahu and British Prime Minister Rishi Sunak Issue Statements', 19 October 2023: www.gov.il/en/pages/pm-netanyahu-and-british-prime-minister-rishi-sunak-issue-statements-19-oct-2023

OCHA, 'Gaza Crossings: movement of people and goods': www.ochaopt.org/data/crossings

OCHA, 'Humanitarian Situation Update #330/West Bank', 9 October 2025: www.ochaopt.org/content/humanitarian-situation-update-330-west-bank

OCHA, 'Two Years On: people injured and traumatised during the Great March of Return are still struggling', 6 April 2020: www.ochaopt.org/content/two-years-people-injured-and-traumatized-during-great-march-return-are-still-struggling

PEACENOW, 'Evacuation Orders for Dozens of Palestinians to Make Way for Jerusalem Waste Facility Outside the Separation Barrier', 12 November 2025: https://peacenow.org.il/en/%D9%8Eqalandiya-confiscation

Pew Research Centre, 'Israel's Religiously Divided Society', 8 March 2016 www.pewresearch.org/religion/2016/03/08/israel's-religiously-divided-society

Physicians for Human Rights, 'Destruction of Conditions of Life: A Health Analysis of the Gaza Genocide', July 2025: www.phr.org.il/wp-content/uploads/2025/07/Genocide-in-Gaza-PHRI-English.pdf

Physicians for Human Rights – Israel, 'Death Sentence for Palestinians in Custody – New Report and Testimonies', 16 November 2025: www.phr.org.il/en/palestinian-deaths-behind-bars-eng/

'President Donald J. Trump awarded "FIFA Peace Prize – Football Unites the World"', *INSIDE FIFA*, 6 December 2025: https://inside.fifa.com/campaigns/football-unites-the-world/news/president-trump-peace-prize-football-unites-the-world

Questions of International Law, 'The ICJ's First Determination of War Reparations: Practical Challenges and Legal Solutions', 29 September 2022: www.qil-qdi.org/the-icjs-first-determination-of-war-reparations-practical-challenges-and-legal-solutions/

Roll Call, 'Speech: Donald Trump Delivers Remarks at the Peace Ceremony in Egypt – October 13, 2025': https://rollcall.com/factbase/trump/transcript/donald-trump-speech-israel-gaza-peace-event-egypt-october-13-2025/

Stockholm International Peace Research Institute, 'How top arms exporters have responded to the war in Gaza: 2025 update', 3 October 2025: www.sipri.org/commentary/topical-backgrounder/2025/how-top-arms-exporters-have-responded-war-gaza-2025-update

The American Presidency Project, 'White House Press Release – President Donald J. Trump's Comprehensive Plan to End the Gaza Conflict', September 2025: www.presidency.ucsb.edu/documents/white-house-press-release-president-donald-j-trumps-comprehensive-plan-end-the-gaza

The American Presidency Project, 'Pool reports by Dasha Burns, *Politico*', 13 October 2025: www.presidency.ucsb.edu/documents/pool-reports-october-13-2025.

'The Full Story of the Knesset Building': main.knesset.gov.il

The Rt Hon The Lord Saville of Newdigate (Chairman), The Hon William Hoyt OC, The Hon John Toohey AC, 'Principal Conclusions and Overall Assessment of the Bloody Sunday Inquiry', 15 June 2010: https://assets.publishing.service.gov.uk/media/5a7580c6e5274a1242c9ed33/0030.pdf

The Watson School of International and Public Affairs, Brown University, 'U.S. Military Aid and Arms Transfers to Israel, October 2023 – September 2025', 7 October 2025: https://costsofwar.watson.brown.edu/paper/AidToIsrael.

Trump, D.J., 'Imposing Sanctions on the International Criminal Court', The White House, 6 February 2025: www.whitehouse.gov/presidential-actions/2025/02/imposing-sanctions-on-the-international-criminal-court/

United Nations Development Programme, 'Clearing most of Gaza's rubble is possible in seven years under right conditions': www.undp.org/stories/clearing-most-rubble-gaza-strip-possible-seven-years-under-right-conditions

United Nations Information System on the Question of Palestine: www.un.org/unispal/

United Nations Security Council Resolutions: https://main.un.org/securitycouncil/en/content/resolutions-0

White House, 'President Delivers State of the Union Address', 29 January 2002: https://georgewbush-whitehouse.archives.gov/news/releases/2002/01/20020129-11.html

White House, 'White House Press Release – President Donald J. Trump's Comprehensive Plan to End the Gaza Conflict', 29 September 2025: www.presidency.ucsb.edu/documents/white-house-press-release-president-donald-j-trumps-comprehensive-plan-end-the-gaza

White House National Archives, 'Peace to Prosperity: A Vision to Improve the Lives of the Palestinian and Israeli People', January 2020: https://trumpwhitehouse.archives.gov/wp-content/uploads/2020/01/Peace-to-Prosperity-0120.pdf

Reports

AOAV, 'The UK Royal Surveillance Flights over the Occupied Palestinian Territory Examined', April 2025

Albanese, F., 'Anatomy of a Genocide', United Nations, 25 March 2024

Albanese, F., 'Report of the Special Rapporteur on the situation of human rights in the Palestinian territories occupied since 1967', United Nations, 20 October 2025

Albanese, F., 'Gaza Genocide a Collective Crime', United Nations, 1 October 2025

Al Haq Advocacy Report, 'Extrajudicial Killing of Unarmed Palestinians in Jenin, Inhuman Acts of Apartheid', 2 December 2025

Amara, A., 'Israel's Perpetual "State of Emergency": Criminalizing Palestinian Civil Society and Political Dissent', Meezan Organisation for Human Rights, March 2016

Araya, D., 'America's Global Dominance is Ending: What Comes Next?', Centre for International Governance Innovation (October 2022)

B'Tselem, 'Welcome to Hell: The Israeli Prison System as a Network of Torture Camps' (July 2024)

B'Tselem, 'Unwilling and Unable: Israel's Whitewashed Investigations of the Great March of Return Protests' (December 2021)

Canadians for Justice and Peace in the Middle East, 'Palestinians and the Right to Resist', Factsheet 236, August 2023

ECCHR, 'Q&A on Arrest Warrants Issued by ICC against Netanyahu and Gallant', April 2025

Hanaeur, L., and Connell, M.P., 'Political Priorities, Poor Intelligence Tradecraft and the Suppression of Dissenting Views: Why Israel Failed to Warn of Hamas's October 7 Attack', Institute for Defense Analyses, September 2024

Human Rights Council, 'Report of Detailed Findings of the International Commission of Inquiry on the Protests in the Occupied Palestinian Territory', March 2019

ICJP, 'Israel bans life-saving international NGOs from operating in Palestine in a catastrophic move to deepen the humanitarian crisis', 5 January 2026

Institute for Middle East Understanding, 'Oslo Accords Timeline: 20 Years of Failed US-Led Peace Talks', 13 September 2013

INSS Insight, 'Beijing Declaration', Tel Aviv University, Insight No: 1886, 1 August 2024

Israel Democracy Institute, 'Two Years since Oct. 7: Majority of Israelis say time has come to end the war', 30 September 2025

Law for Palestine, 'Database of Israeli Incitement to Genocide', 15 January 2024

Ministry of Defense Coordination of Government Activities, 'Food Consumption in the Gaza Strip – Red Lines', January 2008

Montagu, E., 'The Anti-Semitism of the Present Government', 23 August 1917

Office of EU Representative (UNWRA), '2024 Report on Israeli settlements in the occupied West Bank, including East Jerusalem', 14 August 2025

Overton, I., 'Did Britain fly at least 623 spy flights over Gaza? AOAV's data suggests so', AOAV, 22 October 2025

Yesh Din, 'Urgent Appeal to Defense Minister: Immediately Cancel the Order Transferring CA Powers to Political Entities, Which constitutes De Jure Annexation', 8 July 2024

ACKNOWLEDGEMENTS

Thank you to my agent, Louise Dobbin of Repforce Ireland. Louise takes the encouragement and support of writers to a different level. This book is a joint venture, really; it could not have been produced without her.

The earliest reader was Brian Conaghan, an award-winning author with an editorial flair that I could not have done without. Having him in my corner as a friend and adviser made all the difference. Thanks to another friend and skilled man of books, Martin Roper, for his firm guidance and support. Gary Daly for your insights on humanitarian law. Cassia Blondelot, Bríd Ní Chuilinn of Repforce and Edward Horgan, thank you for the various research bounty along the way. Miral Askar, in Egypt, your conscience serves all of us who follow you and your pursuit of truth. Sean Kilbride and John Durnin, thank you both. Terry MacManus, as ever, your assessment was invaluable. Stephen Harrington, friend and tech wizard, thanks for that critical intervention when I thought I'd lost most of the manuscript.

It's a difficult subject matter. There are people who, through their belief and selflessness, make it less so; their determination and dedication to unearthing injustice compels me to do the work. The aforementioned friend Gary Daly, whose concern for the oppressed is singularly inspiring. Nick Maynard and Medical Aid for Palestine, your work is beyond heroic. Thanks to the hundreds of thousands of Irish people who march and protest week in week out, and the smaller number who risked everything by joining the flotilla to Gaza in 2025. And to those politicians in Western countries who campaigned tirelessly for Palestine when most chose to ignore their plight or to feign interest while maintaining the status quo.

The Ireland Palestine Solidarity Campaign, which continues to keep Ireland Palestine-focused. The remarkable courage of some NGOs, especially those in Israel. The work of organisations like B'Tselem, HaMoked, Yesh Din and the Association for Civil Rights in Israel has never been as necessary or as dangerous as now. I am in awe of Physicians for Human Rights in Israel. Some Israeli media, too – *Haaretz*, Israel's outstanding daily newspaper, and *+972* magazine – provide a route to truth in coverage of Israel's excesses.

There are wonderful Palestinian human rights groups, among them Al Haq, Al Mezan and the Palestinian Centre for Human Rights, each of which was targeted by the US in 2025, while, risibly, Al Haq was designated as a 'terrorist organisation' by the government of Israel as far back as 2021. The courage of those at the helm of these organisations is remarkable. Palestine's official media and Gaza's civilian reporters who risk their lives to bring the horror of Nakba II to the world in real time. That so many died doing such essential work, many deliberately targeted by a genocidal regime, is both shocking and humbling for all those who ever worked in journalism.

Thanks to Palestine's Ambassador to Ireland, Jilan Wahba Abdalmajid, for her encouragement and endless work for her country. Thank you too Marwan Yaghi at the UK embassy in London for your support. Thanks are also due to the academics and writers who, for decades, have documented Israel's colonial intent. Their diligence, research, analysis and accounts, particularly those of the extraordinarily brave, Jewish and Israeli among them, will serve generations to come.

My immense gratitude to Merrion Press. Commissioning editor Síne Quinn and publisher Conor Graham again showed courage in backing me with the weight of Merrion's reputation in Irish publishing. Editor Wendy Logue, phenomenal work; I am indebted to you in particular for the insights and attention to detail that made the final copy what I hoped it to be. Thanks also to Ciara Kinsella for the marketing effort and Peter O'Connell for the publicity management. I'm very proud to be published by Merrion Press.

Last, but by no means least, the booksellers. The experience with *Catastrophe: Nakba II* over 2025 taught me that without the commitment of the booksellers in Ireland and the UK, it matters not one whit how much work you've done. All writers are utterly dependent on those who sell our wares. I am grateful to them all for backing me as they did and for making travelling to their shops the great experience that it was.